# Advanced Applications with Microsoft® Word

Microsoft® Office 2003

D1370751

**Susie H. VanHuss, Ph.D.**
*University of South Carolina*

**Connie M. Forde, Ph.D.**
*Mississippi State University*

**Donna L. Woo, Ph.D.**
*Cypress College, California*

**Linda Hefferin, Ed.D.**
*Elgin Community College, Illinois*

THOMSON
SOUTH-WESTERN

Australia · Brazil · Canada · Mexico · Singapore · Spain · United Kingdom · United States

**Advanced Applications with Microsoft® Word**
Susie H. VanHuss, Connie M. Forde, Donna L. Woo, and Linda Hefferin

**VP/Editorial Director**
Jack W. Calhoun

**VP/Editor-in-Chief**
Karen Schmohe

**VP, Director of Marketing**
Carol Volz

**Acquisitions Editor**
Jane Phelan

**Project Manager**
Dave Lafferty

**Consulting Editor**
Mary Todd, Todd Publishing Services

**Marketing Manager**
Valerie A. Lauer

**Production Project Manager**
Colleen A. Farmer

**Manufacturing Coordinator**
Charlene Taylor

**Production House**
GEX Publishing Services

**Printer**
Quebecor World, Dubuque

**Art Director**
Stacy Shirley

**Internal Designer**
Ann Small, a small design studio

**Cover Designer**
Ann Small, a small design studio

**Front Cover Photo Credit**
© Getty Images

For more information about our products, contact us at:

**Thomson Higher Education**
5191 Natorp Boulevard
Mason, Ohio 45040
USA

# [ CONTENTS ]

Key Features . . . . . . . . . . . . . . . . . . . . . . . . . . . . .vi
Welcome to UBI . . . . . . . . . . . . . . . . . . . . . . . . .xi

## PROJECT 1

## UBI Administrative Services

**FOCUS:** *Office Productivity*

**1-1 Learning About Us** . . . . . . . . . . . . . . . . . . .2
Task 1 Mission Statement with Graphics . . . . . . .2
Task 2 Services Report with Styles . . . . . . . . .3
Task 3 Schedule of Fees (Table) . . . . . . . . . . . .5
Task 4 Organizational Chart . . . . . . . . . . . . . . .6
Task 5 Fee Schedule Edits . . . . . . . . . . . . . . . .7
Task 6 Self-Management . . . . . . . . . . . . . . . . .7
Task 7 Software Evaluation . . . . . . . . . . . . . . .7

**1-2 Standardizing Document Formats** . . . . . . .8
Task 1 Letter Format . . . . . . . . . . . . . . . . . . . .8
Task 2 Memo Template . . . . . . . . . . . . . . . . . .10
Task 3 Fax Template . . . . . . . . . . . . . . . . . . . .10
Task 4 Report Format . . . . . . . . . . . . . . . . . . .11
Task 5 Business Plan Outline . . . . . . . . . . . . . .12

**1-3 Updating Directories** . . . . . . . . . . . . . . . .14
Task 1 Employee Directory (Access) . . . . . . . . .14
Task 2 Company Master List . . . . . . . . . . . . . .15
Task 3 Company Directory . . . . . . . . . . . . . . .15
Task 4 Company Policies . . . . . . . . . . . . . . . . .16

**1-4 Managing Files** . . . . . . . . . . . . . . . . . . .18
Task 1 File Management Structure . . . . . . . . . . .18
Task 2 Shared File Management Structure . . . . .19
Task 3 Move Files to New Folders . . . . . . . . . .19

**1-5 Designing Forms** . . . . . . . . . . . . . . . . . .20
Task 1 Application Form . . . . . . . . . . . . . . . . .20
Task 2 Admission Checklist . . . . . . . . . . . . . . .20
Task 3 UBI Services Request . . . . . . . . . . . . . .23

Project 1 Checkpoint . . . . . . . . . . . . . . . . . . . . .24
Communication Skills Training Session 1 . . . . .25

## PROJECT 2

## CMF Communications, Inc.

**FOCUS:** *Communication*

**2-1 Creating the UBI Website** . . . . . . . . . . . .28
Task 1 Website Edits . . . . . . . . . . . . . . . . . . . .28
Task 2 Incubator Companies Web Page . . . . . . .28
Task 3 Organizational Chart Web Page . . . . . . .29
Task 4 About UBI Web Page . . . . . . . . . . . . . .29
Task 5 FAQs Web Page . . . . . . . . . . . . . . . . . .29

**2-2 Setting Up Committees** . . . . . . . . . . . . . .30
Task 1 File Management . . . . . . . . . . . . . . . . . .30
Task 2 Contact List . . . . . . . . . . . . . . . . . . . . .30
Task 3 Confirmation Letter . . . . . . . . . . . . . . .32
Task 4 Agenda . . . . . . . . . . . . . . . . . . . . . . . . .33
Task 5 Minutes . . . . . . . . . . . . . . . . . . . . . . . .35
Task 6 Address Labels . . . . . . . . . . . . . . . . . . .36

**2-3 Preparing the Grand Opening Budget** . . . .37
Task 1 Budget . . . . . . . . . . . . . . . . . . . . . . . . .37
Task 2 Chart . . . . . . . . . . . . . . . . . . . . . . . . . .38
Task 3 Transmittal Letter (Merge) . . . . . . . . . . .38
Task 4 Budget Revision . . . . . . . . . . . . . . . . . .38
Task 5 E-mail with Attachment . . . . . . . . . . . . .39

**2-4 Planning Grand Opening Activities** . . . . . .40
Task 1 Schedule of Events . . . . . . . . . . . . . . . .40
Task 2 E-mail with Attachment . . . . . . . . . . . . .41
Task 3 Website Update . . . . . . . . . . . . . . . . . . .41
Task 4 Final Schedule of Events . . . . . . . . . . . .42
Task 5 E-mail with Attachment . . . . . . . . . . . . .42

**2-5 Preparing a Newsletter** . . . . . . . . . . . . . .43
Task 1 Masthead . . . . . . . . . . . . . . . . . . . . . . .43
Task 2 Newsletter . . . . . . . . . . . . . . . . . . . . . .43

**2-6 Designing Publicity Pieces** . . . . . . . . . . . .45
Task 1 News Release . . . . . . . . . . . . . . . . . . . .45
Task 2 Media Coverage Plan . . . . . . . . . . . . . . .46
Task 3 E-mail with Attachment . . . . . . . . . . . . .49
Task 4 News Release with Merged Comments . .49
Task 5 Invitation . . . . . . . . . . . . . . . . . . . . . . .49
Task 6 Article (Manuscript) . . . . . . . . . . . . . . .50
Task 7 News Release Web Page . . . . . . . . . . . .50
Task 8 Communication Practices . . . . . . . . . . . .50

Project 2 Checkpoint . . . . . . . . . . . . . . . . . . . . .51
Communication Skills Training Session 2 . . . . .52

## PROJECT 3

## UBI Legal Services

**FOCUS:** *Ethics*

**3-1 Preparing Incorporation Documents** . . . . .54
Task 1 Certificate of Incorporation . . . . . . . . . .54
Task 2 Transmittal Letter . . . . . . . . . . . . . . . . .56
Task 3 Corporate Minutes . . . . . . . . . . . . . . . .56
Task 4 Corporation Checklist Form . . . . . . . . . .59
Task 5 Legal Pleading . . . . . . . . . . . . . . . . . . .59
Task 6 Ethics Alive (Manuscript) . . . . . . . . . . .61

**3-2 Preparing Employment Documents** . . . . . .62
Task 1 Non-Competition Contract . . . . . . . . . . .62
Task 2 Employment Letter (Protected Form) . .63

Task 3  Executive Employment Agreement .....66
Task 4  Employee Accident Report ..........67
Task 5  Health Release Form  .............68

**3-3 Preparing Contracts** .................**69**
Task 1  Lease Agreement (Fill-in Form) ......69
Task 2  Independent Contractor Checklist .....70
Task 3  Invoice ..........................71
Task 4  Consulting Agreement .............71
Task 5  Track Changes to Consulting Agreement  72

**3-4 Creating Intellectual Property Agreements 73**
Task 1  Intellectual Property Agreement ......73
Task 2  Legal Forum Flyer ................73
Task 3  License Agreement Outline ..........75
Task 4  Corporate Internet Use Policy ........77
Task 5  Ethical Issues ....................77

**Project 3 Checkpoint** ....................**78**
**Communication Skills Training Session 3** .....**80**

## PROJECT 4

# Champion Sports Venues, Inc.

**FOCUS:** *Time Management*

**4-1 Finalizing Facility Plans** .............**84**
Task 1  Priorities and Time Management .....84
Task 2  E-mail and Meeting Agenda .........86
Task 3  Handout for Meeting ...............87
Task 4  Minutes Using the Agenda Wizard .....88
Task 5  E-mail Using Send to Mail Recipient
         for Review .......................90
Task 6  Revise Document Using Compare
         and Merge .......................91

**4-2 Creating Solicitation Documents** .......**92**
Task 1  Brochure with Graphics .............92
Task 2  Mailing Labels ....................94
Task 3  Merged Letters ...................95
Task 4  Table ...........................96
Task 5  Cost Allocation Pie Chart ...........97

**4-3 Communicating with Stakeholders** ......**98**
Task 1  Stakeholders Update Template .......98
Task 2  Report with Graphics ..............99
Task 3  PowerPoint Presentation ...........102
Task 4  Handout for Meeting ..............105
Task 5  Notice to Be Posted ..............105

**4-4 Soliciting Center Proposals** .........**106**
Task 1  Memo Seeking Approval to Use RFP ..106
Task 2  RFP in Draft Form ...............108
Task 3  E-mail with Draft RFP Attachment ..110
Task 4  FAX Cover Sheet ................110
Task 5  RFP Final Document .............111
Task 6  Transmittal Memo for RFP .........112

**4-5 Determining SportsPlex Inn Feasibility** ..**113**
Task 1  Excel Worksheet for Proforma ......113
Task 2  Memo with Linked Worksheet ......114
Task 3  Microsoft Chart Showing Profit .....115
Task 4  Embedded Chart and Worksheet .....115
Task 5  Invitation Letter (Composition) .....117

**Project 4 Checkpoint** ...................**118**
**Communication Skills Training Session 4** ....**119**

## PROJECT 5

# NetCollege, Inc.

**FOCUS:** *Training*

**5-1 Preparing a Business Plan** ............**122**
Task 1  News Release ...................122
Task 2  Executive Summary with Linked
         Worksheet .....................123

**5-2 Preparing a Training Proposal** ........**127**
Task 1  Training Proposal ...............127
Task 2  Training Proposal (Master
         Document) ....................128
Task 3  Letter of Transmittal ............129
Task 4  Index .........................129
Task 5  Title Page .....................130
Task 6  Table of Contents ..............130
Task 7  Update Training Proposal .........130

**5-3 Creating Training Materials** ..........**131**
Task 1  Training Program Outline .........131
Task 2  Training Worksheet ..............133
Task 3  Instructional Handouts ..........135
Task 4  E-mail with Attachments ..........138

**5-4 Completing Administrative Details** .....**139**
Task 1  Evaluation Form ................139
Task 2  Registration Information (Access) .....141
Task 3  Class Roster (Access Report) ......141
Task 4  Name Badges ..................142
Task 5  Training Program Checklist .........143
Task 6  Certificate of Completion  .......145

**Project 5 Checkpoint** ...................**146**
**Communication Skills Training Session 5** ....**147**

## PROJECT 6

# HealthCare Staff, Inc.

**FOCUS:** *Customer Service*

**6-1 Getting Started** ....................**150**
Task 1  Logo ..........................150
Task 2  Letterhead .....................150
Task 3  Letterhead Macro ...............151
Task 4  Employment Application Form ......151
Task 5  Customize a Toolbar ............154

**6-2 Creating Medical Office Documents** ....**155**
Task 1  SOAP Note Form ...............155
Task 2  SOAP Note ....................157
Task 3  Office Note Form ...............158

Task 4 Office Note . . . . . . . . . . . . . . . . . . . .158
Task 5 Mail Merge . . . . . . . . . . . . . . . . . . .160

**6-3 Preparing Web Pages and
PowerPoint Slides** . . . . . . . . . . .**162**
Task 1 Web Article . . . . . . . . . . . . . . . . . . .162
Task 2 Web Table . . . . . . . . . . . . . . . . . . . .163
Task 3 PowerPoint Slides . . . . . . . . . . . . . .164
Task 4 Memo with Linked Icon . . . . . . . . .166
Task 5 Search Files . . . . . . . . . . . . . . . . . . .166

**6-4 Preparing Medical Reports** . . . . . . .**167**
Task 1 Report with Styles . . . . . . . . . . . . . .167
Task 2 Report Template . . . . . . . . . . . . . . .169
Task 3 Preoperative History and Physical . . . . .170
Task 4 Pathology Report . . . . . . . . . . . . . . .172
Task 5 Saving Files or Web Pages in
Different Formats . . . . . . . . . . . . . .174

**6-5 Designing Medical Forms** . . . . . . . . .**175**
Task 1 Consent for Release of
Information Form . . . . . . . . . . . . . .175
Task 2 Disclosure Statement with Excel Table .176
Task 3 Patient Graphics Sheet . . . . . . . . . . .178
Task 4 Holter Monitor Report . . . . . . . . . .179
Task 5 Holter Report . . . . . . . . . . . . . . . . .179

**Project 6 Checkpoint** . . . . . . . . . . . . . . . .**181**
**Communication Skills Training Session 6** . . . .**183**

PROJECT 7

**Garcia Travel, Inc.**

**Focus:** *International Communication*

**7-1 Evaluating Hotels and Restaurants** . . . . . .**186**
Task 1 Request Letter and Envelopes . . . . . . .186
Task 2 Hotel Evaluation Form . . . . . . . . . . .187
Task 3 Restaurant Evaluation Form . . . . . . . .189

**7-2 Preparing an Itinerary** . . . . . . . . . . . . .**191**
Task 1 Itinerary Planning Sheet . . . . . . . . . .191
Task 2 Itinerary . . . . . . . . . . . . . . . . . . . . .192
Task 3 Peer Review . . . . . . . . . . . . . . . . . . .192
Task 4 E-mail with Attachment . . . . . . . . . .192
Task 5 Productivity Tips and Practices . . . . . .193
Task 6 Software Evaluation . . . . . . . . . . . . .193

**7-3 Finalizing a Budget** . . . . . . . . . . . . . .**194**
Task 1 Budget . . . . . . . . . . . . . . . . . . . . . .194
Task 2 Letter Report . . . . . . . . . . . . . . . . .195

**7-4 Designing Travel Tips** . . . . . . . . . . . . .**197**
Task 1 Research . . . . . . . . . . . . . . . . . . . . .197
Task 2 Memo . . . . . . . . . . . . . . . . . . . . . . .197
Task 3 Travel Information Design . . . . . . . . .198
Task 4 Report on Cultural Etiquette . . . . . . .198
Task 5 Custom Schema to Word Document .199

**Project 7 Checkpoint** . . . . . . . . . . . . . . . .**200**
**Communication Skills Training Session 7** . . . .**201**

PROJECT 8

**Wexford Event Planners, Inc.**

**FOCUS:** *Leadership*

**8-1 Defining Strategic Direction** . . . . . . . . . .**204**
Task 1 Modify Template . . . . . . . . . . . . . . .204
Task 2 Memo . . . . . . . . . . . . . . . . . . . . . . .205
Task 3 Meeting Agenda . . . . . . . . . . . . . . . .206
Task 4 Minutes of Strategic Planning
Meeting . . . . . . . . . . . . . . . . . . . . .206

**8-2 Targeting Services** . . . . . . . . . . . . . . . .**209**
Task 1 WEP Services Overview . . . . . . . . . .209
Task 2 Send Document for Review . . . . . . . .211
Task 3 Compare and Merge Reviewed
Documents . . . . . . . . . . . . . . . . . . .211
Task 4 E-mail with Attachment . . . . . . . . . .212
Task 5 Newsletter with Graphics . . . . . . . . .212

**8-3 Creating Forms and Guides** . . . . . . . . .**214**
Task 1 Preliminary Event Planning Form . . . . .214
Task 2 Fill-in Preliminary Event
Planning Form . . . . . . . . . . . . . . . .214
Task 3 Modify Preliminary Event
Planning Form . . . . . . . . . . . . . . . .216
Task 4 Room Capacity Guide . . . . . . . . . . .217
Task 5 WCC Facilities Guide . . . . . . . . . . .218

**8-4 Estimating Cost and Revenue** . . . . . . .**219**
Task 1 Guest Room Projection . . . . . . . . . . .219
Task 2 Projected Sources of Revenue Chart . . .220
Task 3 Budgeting Checklist . . . . . . . . . . . . .220
Task 4 WCC Strategic Pricing Decisions . . . .222

**8-5 Presenting WEP to UBI** . . . . . . . . . . . .**225**
Task 1 Presentation for UBI Owners . . . . . . .225
Task 2 Revise Presentation . . . . . . . . . . . . . .225
Task 3 Deliver Oral Presentation . . . . . . . . .227

**Project 8 Checkpoint** . . . . . . . . . . . . . . . .**228**

**Keyboarding Skills Training** . . . . . . . . . . . . .**229**
**Technique Rating Sheet** . . . . . . . . . . . . . . . .**236**
**Reference Guide** . . . . . . . . . . . . . . . . . . . .**237**

# KEY FEATURES

*Advanced Applications with Microsoft Word 2E* provides project-based applications that build document processing skills and integrate realistic business practices as well as other key software applications. Projects provide comprehensive coverage of basic and advanced word processing skills, workplace communication skills, along with numerous opportunities for critical thinking.

**Eight projects** focus on various types of businesses, including legal, medical, travel, as well a new special events planning project. Typically, each project is comparable to a two-week assignment. A workplace theme is integrated within each project.

**Tasks** use generic instruction that won't get outdated as new software releases become available. Some tasks apply applications such as *Excel*, *Access*, or *PowerPoint*. Tasks also reinforce key workplace elements and refine work habits. An icon indicates a data file is available on the CD located in the back of this book. Copy to be keyed is identified with a graphic line.

**Business vocabulary** is highlighted to expand understanding of terms and practices.

**Tips** emphasize efficient procedures and provide word processing shortcuts or hints.

**Web activities** link the workplace theme to the project.

**Critical thinking** questions challenge students to think about what they have just done, the content of the document, or procedures that have been applied.

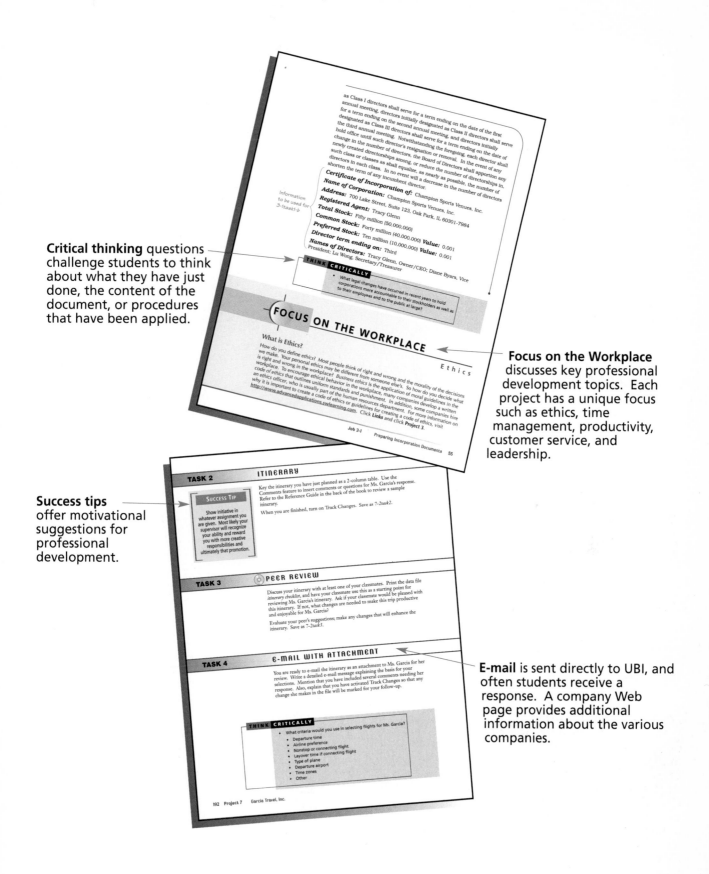

as Class I directors shall serve for a term ending on the date of the first annual meeting. directors initially designated as Class II directors shall serve for a term ending on the second annual meeting. and directors initially designated as Class III directors shall serve for a term ending on the date of the third annual meeting. Notwithstanding the foregoing, each director shall hold office until such director's resignation or removal. In the event of any change in the number of directors, the Board of Directors shall apportion any newly created directorships among, or reduce the number of directorships in, such class or classes as shall equalize, as nearly as possible, the number of directors in each class. In no event will a decrease in the number of directors shorten the term of any incumbent director.

***Certificate of Incorporation of:*** Champion Sports Venues, Inc.
***Name of Corporation:*** Champion Sports Venues, Inc.
***Address:*** 700 Lake Street, Suite 123, Oak Park, IL 60301-7984
***Registered Agent:*** Tracy Glenn
***Total Stock:*** Fifty million (50,000,000)
***Common Stock:*** Forty million (40,000,000) ***Value:*** 0.001
***Preferred Stock:*** Ten million (10,000,000) ***Value:*** 0.001
***Director term ending on:*** Third
***Names of Directors:*** Tracy Glenn, Owner/CEO; Diane Byars, Vice
President; Lu Wong, Secretary/Treasurer

*Information to be used for 3-1task1-b*

**THINK CRITICALLY**
What legal changes have occurred in recent years to hold corporations more accountable to their stockholders as well as to their employees and to the public at large?

## FOCUS ON THE WORKPLACE

*Ethics*

**What is Ethics?**
How do you define *ethics*? Most people think of right and wrong and the morality of the decisions we make. Your personal ethics may be different from someone else's. So how do you decide what is right and wrong in the workplace? *Business ethics* is the application of moral guidelines in the workplace. To encourage ethical behavior in the workplace, many companies develop a written code of ethics that outlines uniform standards and punishment. In addition, some companies hire an ethics officer, who is usually part of the human resources department. For more information on why it is important to create a code of ethics or guidelines for creating a code of ethics, visit http://www.advancedapplications.swlearning.com. Click **Links** and click **Project 3**.

*Job 3-1     Preparing Incorporation Documents     55*

**Focus on the Workplace** discusses key professional development topics. Each project has a unique focus such as ethics, time management, productivity, customer service, and leadership.

**Success tips** offer motivational suggestions for professional development.

**TASK 2          ITINERARY**

Key the itinerary you have just planned as a 2-column table. Use the Comments feature to insert comments or questions for Ms. Garcia's response. Refer to the Reference Guide in the back of the book to review a sample itinerary.

When you are finished, turn on Track Changes. Save as 7-2task2.

**SUCCESS TIP**
Show initiative in whatever assignment you are given. Most likely your supervisor will recognize your ability and reward you with more creative responsibilities and ultimately that promotion.

**TASK 3          PEER REVIEW**

Discuss your itinerary with at least one of your classmates. Print the data file *itinerary checklist*, and have your classmate use this as a starting point for reviewing Ms. Garcia's itinerary. Ask if your classmate would be pleased with this itinerary. If not, what changes are needed to make this trip productive and enjoyable for Ms. Garcia?

Evaluate your peer's suggestions; make any changes that will enhance the itinerary. Save as 7-2task3.

**TASK 4          E-MAIL WITH ATTACHMENT**

You are ready to e-mail the itinerary as an attachment to Ms. Garcia for her review. Write a detailed e-mail message explaining the basis for your selections. Mention that you have included several comments needing her response. Also, explain that you have activated Track Changes so that any change she makes in the file will be marked for your follow-up.

**THINK CRITICALLY**
- What criteria would you use in selecting flights for Ms. Garcia?
  - Departure time
  - Airline preference
  - Nonstop or connecting flight
  - Layover time if connecting flight
  - Type of plane
  - Departure airport
  - Time zones
  - Other

*192   Project 7   Garcia Travel, Inc.*

**E-mail** is sent directly to UBI, and often students receive a response. A company Web page provides additional information about the various companies.

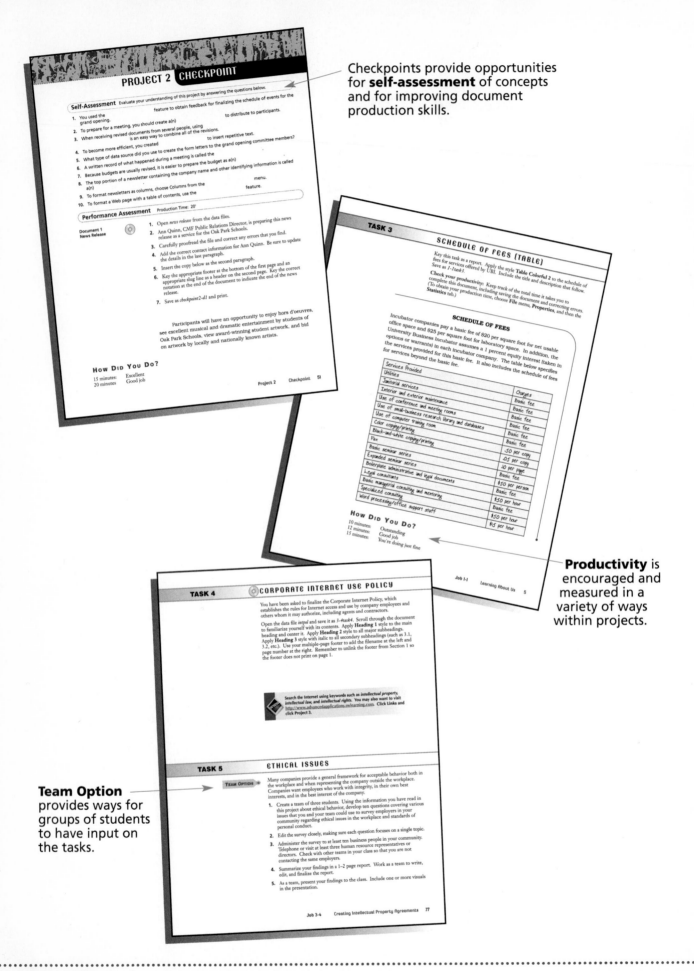

Checkpoints provide opportunities for **self-assessment** of concepts and for improving document production skills.

**Productivity** is encouraged and measured in a variety of ways within projects.

**Team Option** provides ways for groups of students to have input on the tasks.

**Communication Skills Training** encourages strong writing skills.

**Keyboarding Skills Training** includes timed writings and drills.

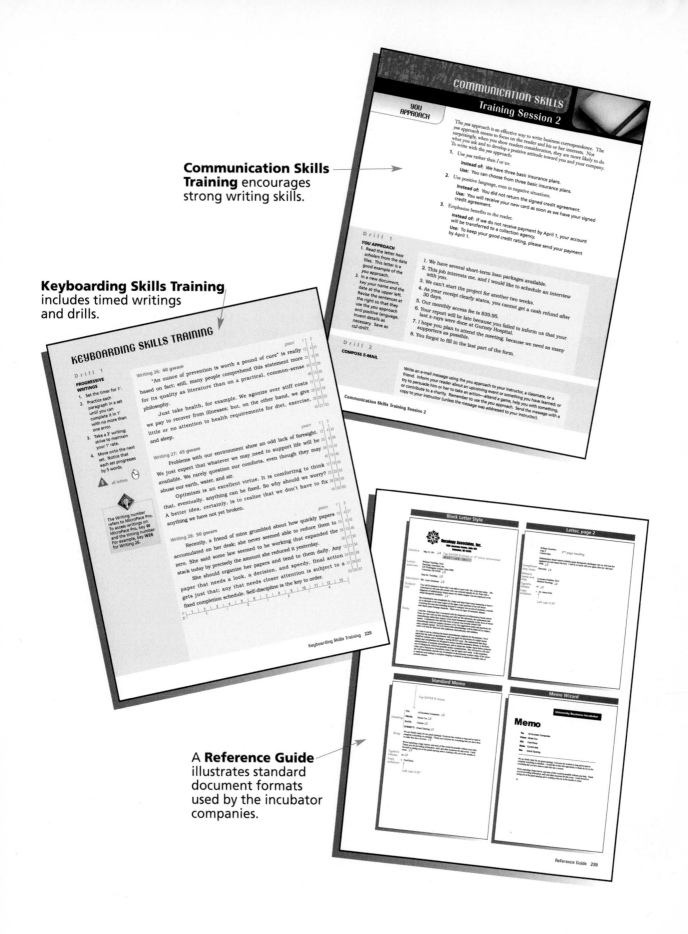

A **Reference Guide** illustrates standard document formats used by the incubator companies.

# Explore Additional Resources

Do you need career enhancement skills or additional practice with the latest technologies? Whether you are looking for comprehensive texts, brief units of instruction, or technology-based applications, Thomson South-Western has the materials to fill all of your needs.

### Integrated Computer Applications 4E VanHuss, Forde, Woo, and Hefferin

0-538-72827-2 Text/CD (Modules 1–8)    0-538-72888-4 Text/CD (Modules 1–11)

Build on essential word-processing skills and reinforce communication, keyboarding, and Internet skills while learning all the tools of *Microsoft® Office*. Coverage includes the basics of *Excel*, *Access*, *Outlook*, and *PowerPoint®* and the integration of these applications with *Word* documents. Organized into distinct modules for custom learning needs.

| | |
|---|---|
| Module 1 | Business Documents with *Word* |
| Module 2 | Presentations with *PowerPoint®* |
| Module 3 | Spreadsheets with *Excel* |
| Module 4 | Desktop Publishing with *Word* |
| Module 5 | Integrated Project (*Word, Excel, PowerPoint®*) |
| Module 6 | Database with *Access* |
| Module 7 | Desktop Information Management with *Outlook* |
| Module 8 | Integrated Project (*Word, Excel, PowerPoint®, Access, Outlook*) |
| Module 9 | Input Technologies |
| Module 10 | Multimedia with *Macromedia® Fireworks®* |
| Module 11 | Web Page Design with *FrontPage®* |

### Communication Skills for the Processing of Words 5E Reiff

0-538-43954-8

Become a more effective communicator and master grammar, punctuation, capitalization, and proofreading skills while formatting business documents. Students become well equipped with the basic communication skills necessary in order to qualify for entry-level jobs and advance in their careers. This text/workbook and accompanying CD are ideal for any word-processing course.

### Human Relations 3E Dalton, Hoyle, and Watts

0-538-43878-9

Explore the human relations issues and challenges of today's workplace. The authors use a unique approach that provides an opportunity to experience and analyze firsthand the contemporary issues of human relations in the twenty-first century. By weaving their varied professional backgrounds and knowledge into every chapter, they provide the insight and awareness that comes only from experience.

# WELCOME
# to University Business Incubator

UBI is very pleased to welcome you as an executive assistant in the President's Office at UBI.  Ms. Nicole Cox, our president, requires that each executive assistant possess a general knowledge of all administrative offices of UBI and of all of our incubator companies. (Incubator?  You will learn what this means in just a moment.)  To acquaint you with our company, you will work in the President's Office and the Legal Services Department at UBI as well as six of the incubator companies that UBI serves.

First, let's acquaint you with UBI and the services we provide.  Then we'll share some standard operating procedures and other information you will need before you begin your first assignment in the President's Office at UBI.

University Business Incubator, or UBI for short, is located at its new facilities at 700 Lake Street, Suite 100, Oak Park, Illinois, a suburb of Chicago. UBI was chartered as a nonprofit organization on March 15, 2000, as a partnership with Foster University and several business organizations. Our goal is to promote economic development in the Oak Park area. We do this by helping young, start-up companies launch their companies successfully. New businesses are most vulnerable and need our assistance.

UBI opened in a research building at Foster University. Initially, we provided space for the UBI staff and four start-up companies or "incubator" companies. Often new businesses need that little extra support or "incubation" to assist them in developing successfully. UBI provides affordable office and laboratory space, links to high-speed data connections, basic office services, and the opportunity to network with faculty and graduate students with similar interests.

As the original start-up companies outgrew the facilities and became a "graduate" of the incubator, the space was quickly filled with new start-up companies. It was not long before UBI outgrew these facilities. Today the new facilities at 700 Lake Street accommodate 12 incubator companies and have space to expand as new companies require its services. In just a few short weeks, UBI, along with its partners, will host a grand opening where the public and friends of UBI will be invited to tour the facilities and to learn about the services UBI provides to the Oak Park area.

As an executive assistant at UBI, you are responsible for working independently. You will use electronic tools to produce your work more efficiently. Use the following standardized procedures to promote corporate identity and to improve productivity.

## Correspondence

A company logo has been created for most of the start-up companies. Insert the appropriate logo for documents such as letters and newsletters that require a letterhead from your data CD-ROM. Insert the current date on all documents for which a date is appropriate; use the block letter format for all companies.

## E-mails

Send e-mail messages to the individual or group at http://www.ubi-sw.com following the guidelines below. You may receive a return message from UBI. **Note:** *If electronic mail is not available, process all e-mails as memos. Use the Professional Memo template.*

Address the e-mail correctly: firstname.lastname@ubi-sw.com. You may check the UBI employee database for all e-mail addresses or check the UBI website. Generally all e-mail addresses are provided in the directions.

If a subject line is provided, you must use the exact subject line shown. If you do, you may receive a message directly from UBI. When appropriate, attach required documents to the e-mail. Print a copy of your e-mail and attachments and submit them to your instructor.

Follow these guidelines when creating e-mail messages:

- Compose a subject line that concisely describes the theme of the e-mail. If a subject line is provided, key it exactly as shown.
- Limit each message to one topic and one screen.
- Use short paragraphs and DS between them.
- Compose messages that are well written and free of errors.
- Do not key in uppercase letters or you will be perceived as shouting.
- Avoid emoticons or e-mail abbreviations; e.g., ;-) for a wink or BTW for "by the way".
- Send e-mails only to those requiring the message.
- Do not forward an e-mail without the sender's permission.

## Time-Saving Tips

- Use AutoText to insert frequently used text. Use automated features to move within documents, to search and replace text, and to verify and clear formatting.
- Insert page numbers on multipage documents unless instructed otherwise.
- Manage orphans and widows on documents effectively.
- Create templates for commonly used documents. By default, templates are saved to the Windows directory, Templates folder. To avoid having another student save on top of a template you have created, you must direct or save your template files to the appropriate Solutions folder.

## File Management

Store documents in a well-defined file management system. Create eight solutions folders and name them *Solutions-Project 1*, *Solutions-Project 2*, etc. Save solutions in the appropriate folder. In Project 1, you will create additional folders for UBI and shared files for the incubator companies. Retain all files so that you may use them again.

## Proofreading and Preparing Documents for Distribution

You are working as a professional, which means your documents must be error free. Establish a mindset that each document contains errors, and you will find them. Consider the effects of these proofreading mishaps.

Welcome letter to new client includes the word *there* for *their*—a common grammar error.

Letter confirming appointment for contract agreement shows *Monday, April 1* when the meeting is *Tuesday, April 1*.

Before submitting documents to your employer (instructor), follow these steps:

1. Proofread all documents to be sure they are error free.

   - Use the Spelling and Grammar function to check each document.
   - Proofread on screen and correct errors not detected by software; use online Thesaurus to enhance text.
   - Check placement and overall appearance in print preview.
   - Check the printed document with the source copy.

2. Print and assemble documents appropriately for final distribution (i.e., place the envelope/s behind the appropriate letter/s, arrange report with preliminary pages and appendices in correct order).

## Data Files

To complete your assignments, you will use data files, which are available from your instructor. Your instructor will install the files for classroom use to *X*:\Advanced Applications (*X* refers to the drive, folder *Advanced Applications*). If you have a data CD-ROM in the back of the book, you may also install it to your personal computer.

## Websites

Go to http://www.ubi-sw.com to access the UBI company website. This company intranet will further acquaint you with UBI and its services and will provide valuable information needed in completing your assignments.

You will also want to check out http://www.advancedapplications.swlearning. com, the website for this text. Here you will find Web links and activities to enrich your experiences at UBI.

## Software Supplement

To aid you in completing the projects, a software supplement is available for your use at http://www.advancedapplications.swlearning.com (click **Student Resources**). The software supplement provides a keywords list to enable you to use the Help feature. In addition, a Function Review lists the steps for many functions of *Microsoft Word 2003*.

## Assessment

Your work at UBI will be evaluated in various ways:

**Assessment Form:** Your instructor will provide you with an Assessment Form. (It is available on the Instructor's Resource CD.) The Assessment Form includes columns for self, peer, and instructor assessment, as well as comments for each task. These forms can be used to track progress and skill development throughout the course.

**Technique Assessment:** Use the Technique Rating Sheet on page 236 periodically to evaluate your keyboarding techniques.

**Checkpoint:** Each project concludes with a Checkpoint for self-assessment. Complete these activities to help you gauge whether you understand the concepts and skills applied within the project.

**Project Test:** Also available on the Instructor's Resource CD is a performance assessment for each project. You will be evaluated on the same criteria as in the project: formatting and document appearance, correctness, following instructions, etc.

## Action Plan for UBI

You are now ready to begin your training program at UBI, starting with the President's Office at UBI. As you rotate to each assignment, you are expanding your knowledge and experience and are becoming a more valuable employee to UBI. Learn everything you can learn from your assignment and refine the skills that you already possess. Good luck with your assignments!

PHOTO: © RYAN MCVAY/PHOTODISC/GETTY IMAGES

# PROJECT 1
# UBI Administrative Services

**1-1**  Learning About Us

**1-2**  Standardizing Document Formats

**1-3**  Updating Directories

**1-4**  Managing Files

**1-5**  Designing Forms

**FOCUS:** *Office Productivity*

You report to the director of Administrative Services. As you learned in the welcome, UBI has provided basic services to four incubator companies. Now that UBI has moved into its new facilities, it offers a wide variety of office services to current companies and is gradually adding eight new incubator companies. In this assignment, you assist in getting the new UBI offices set up for business at the same time that you learn about the new services that UBI offers. Your assignments are varied and include standardizing document formats, designing forms used to make UBI more efficient, and developing manuals and procedures to standardize the new services that UBI offers.

# Learning About Us

Objectives

- Prepare the UBI mission statement
- Prepare a services report with styles
- Prepare a schedule of fees for services
- Prepare an organizational chart for UBI
- Revise the fee schedule

---

## TASK 1  MISSION STATEMENT WITH GRAPHICS

**mission statement:** overall purpose and values of a group or organization

Retain all files; you will need to access them again in later assignments.

The **mission statement** will be posted on the website and will be widely distributed in print version. Therefore, the information should be attractively presented and should contain contact information. One option is to include the logo (*UBI logo*) and the picture of the new facilities (*UBI photo.jpg*), which are included in the data files. You may prefer to create your own design for this page. Key and format the mission statement using a very short line. Use a distinctive, large font or italic for the mission statement. Save the document as *1-1task1* in the Solutions-Project 1 folder.

### Mission

*The mission of the University Business Incubator is to nurture start-up and early-stage businesses to facilitate growth and development during their early years when they are most vulnerable. This mission supports the ultimate goal of fostering economic development in the region. UBI provides entrepreneurs with a unique environment, a wide range of business services, and access to resources designed to enhance each company's long-term success.*

To learn more about business incubators, search the Internet using the keywords *business incubator*. For additional information, visit http://www.advancedapplications.swlearning.com, click **Links**, and then click **Project 1.**

UBI provides a variety of business services as part of the incubator fees as well as many additional fee-based services. The document describing these services has been reviewed, and comments have been added. Key the rough-draft document, applying correct number expression. Use the standard procedures for preparing reports shown in the Reference Guide. Use Widow/Orphan control and be sure that headings remain with the text that follows them. Save as *1-1task2* in the Solutions-Project 1 folder.

# Business Facilities, Services, and Programs   *(WordArt)*

Membership has its privileges! The UBI *sp* offers distinct advantages to promising start-up companies whose managers desire the synergies that result from being in a group of outstanding entrepreneurs with ideas to share. *They also take advantage of significantly reduced overhead expenses shared by incubator members.*

## Facilities   *Level 1 heading*

UBI has a new mortgage-free building at 700 Lake Street in Oak Park, Illinois, in close proximity to the campus of Foster University and seven miles from downtown Chicago. With forty thousand square feet of first-class office space and twenty-five thousand square feet of state-of-the-art laboratory space, it provides an ideal setting to cultivate new businesses. Additional space is available should the incubator outgrow these facilities. The flexible space for each member company is designed to expand as the business grows. Adequate parking is available for employees and visitors. *that is currently being leased out on a short-term basis*

### *Office Suites and Laboratories*   *Level 2 heading*

The size of office suites and the laboratories ranges from five hundred to five thousand square feet of usable space. The space is flexible and contains many movable walls to manage the variable needs of member companies.

### General Service and Support Areas   *Level 3 heading*

Lounges, vending and eating areas, storage space, the loading dock, freight elevator, public elevators, and mechanical and electrical service closets are conveniently located outside the office and laboratory areas. All areas are handicap accessible. *Having these facilities located outside the rented office or laboratory space results in a significant savings of rental costs for each company.*

### Shared Business Service Areas   *Level 3 heading*

A number of business service areas are available to incubator companies:

- The receptionist and reception area are located at the main entrance of the building. Guests are greeted by the receptionist and, depending on the desires of the incubator company, may be sent directly to the appropriate office or laboratory or may wait in the reception area until the member company is ready to receive the guest.

- Three conference rooms are available to members of the incubator for meetings. In addition, a very large conference room and a meeting room are available in the suite occupied by UBI personnel. These rooms may also be used by member companies. *, when available,* *also*

- An extensive small-business research library is available for use by all incubator companies. Access to a number of useful databases is provided.

- Color and black-and-white copying and printing equipment, fax machines, and other basic office services are available at nominal charges.

## *Infrastructure*   Level 2 heading

Utilities (not including telephone services) and janitorial services are included in the basic package. The facility is located in a safe area, and building security is provided. High-speed Internet and data connections are provided.

## Consulting and Office Services   Level 1 heading

UBI staff, consultants, and volunteer mentors provide incubator companies with management assistance, business plan development, resources to evaluate new business opportunities, basic legal documents, and guidance in locating sources of capital. Many of these services are provided free or at a nominal cost. A roster of professionals with expertise in a variety of areas and who have indicated a willingness to work with new business ventures at discounted prices is maintained. Limited word processing and office support are available on a fee basis.

Interaction with faculty, graduate students, and members of the university community perhaps is the most valuable of the resources enjoyed by incubator companies, which frequently employ undergraduate and graduate students on a part-time basis.

## Educational Programs   Level 1 heading

*or at a nominal cost*

Seminars and training programs are offered on a regular basis. Most of these programs are offered free. A computer lab is also available for training purposes. Monthly meetings of company ~~presidents and~~ chief executive officers provide a stimulating forum for the exchange of ideas.

*and may be scheduled by member companies*

**THINK CRITICALLY**

- What are the shared business service areas of the company?
- What is your understanding of infrastructure?

Key this task as a report. Apply the style **Table Colorful 2** to the schedule of fees for services offered by UBI. Include the title and description that follow. Save as *1-1task3*.

**Check your productivity:** Keep track of the total time it takes you to complete this document, including saving the document and correcting errors. (To obtain your production time, choose **File** menu, **Properties**, and then the **Statistics** tab.)

## SCHEDULE OF FEES

Incubator companies pay a basic fee of $20 per square foot for net usable office space and $25 per square foot for laboratory space. In addition, the University Business Incubator assumes a 1 percent equity interest (taken in options or warrants) in each incubator company. The table below specifies the services provided for this basic fee. It also includes the schedule of fees for services beyond the basic fee.

| Services Provided | Charges |
|---|---|
| Utilities | Basic fee |
| Janitorial services | Basic fee |
| Interior and exterior maintenance | Basic fee |
| Use of conference and meeting rooms | Basic fee |
| Use of small-business research library and databases | Basic fee |
| Use of computer training room | Basic fee |
| Color copying/printing | .50 per copy |
| Black-and-white copying/printing | .05 per copy |
| Fax | .10 per page |
| Basic seminar series | Basic fee |
| Expanded seminar series | $50 per person |
| Boilerplate administrative and legal documents | Basic fee |
| Legal consultants | $50 per hour |
| Basic managerial consulting and mentoring | Basic fee |
| Specialized consulting | $50 per hour |
| Word processing/office support staff | $15 per hour |

## HOW DID YOU DO?

| 10 minutes: | Outstanding |
| 12 minutes: | Good job |
| 15 minutes: | You're doing just fine |

# FOCUS ON THE WORKPLACE

## Office Productivity

### Employees Key to Productivity

A productive workforce gives an organization a competitive edge. Productivity in the office is measured by results rather than by quantity produced, and effectiveness is more important than efficiency. The critical elements of effective office systems are employees, processes, and technology.

Productivity is dependent upon utilizing the talents of every employee in a team-oriented environment. Four factors describe productive employees:

- *Competence*—employees must have in-depth company knowledge as well as state-of-the-art job skills and knowledge.
- *Motivation*—the desire to do a job and to do it right the first time.
- *Self-Management*—employees who manage and control their own jobs free their supervisors of unproductive supervisory tasks.
- *Team player*—synergy enhances results. Synergy means that the results of individual efforts can never equal the results of a team working together.

---

## TASK 4     ORGANIZATIONAL CHART

Prepare the following organizational chart in landscape orientation. Use Heading 1 style, centered, for the heading and center the chart vertically and horizontally. Format the AutoShapes using the following RGB Color Model: 214 Red; 158 Green; 0 Blue; and 50% transparency. Use text color 128 Red. Save the document as *1-1task4*.

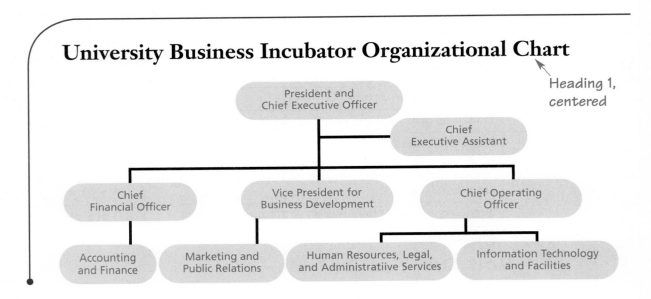

| TASK 5 | FEE SCHEDULE EDITS |
|---|---|

Open file *1-1task3* that you completed earlier and save it as *1-1task5*. Make the following revisions, and then save the file again and print.

1. Change the price of the Expanded seminar series from $50 to **$25** per person.

2. Insert a row below *Interior and exterior maintenance* and add: **Reception room and services** with **Basic fee** charges.

3. Insert a row above *Color copying/printing* and add: **High-speed Internet and data connections** with **Basic fee** charges.

| TASK 6 | SELF-MANAGEMENT |
|---|---|

Use the *Word* Research tool and the Internet to locate information about self-management as it applies to work. Compose at least two paragraphs; use the title **Self-Management**.

1. In the first paragraph, define or describe what self-management means.

2. In the second paragraph, explain why self-management is important in business and particularly to an employee's career development.

3. Edit carefully; use the Thesaurus to enhance word selection. Save as *1-1task6*. This information will be used in a training session.

| TASK 7 | SOFTWARE EVALUATION |
|---|---|

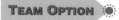

Selecting new application software often involves (1) deciding between competing brands of software, such as *Microsoft Word* or *Corel WordPerfect*; or (2) determining if you should upgrade to a new version of your software, such as upgrading from *Word 2003* to a new version that has just been released.

1. Use the Internet or other resources to compile a checklist of factors that should be considered in making the decision to buy either different software or a new version of the same software. Use the title **Software Evaluation Criteria**. Format using customized bullets (☑). Save as *1-1task7*.

2. Select one of the two topics—changing brands or upgrading to a new version of software—use the criteria on your list to evaluate software and make a recommendation. Team recommendations must be reached by consensus.

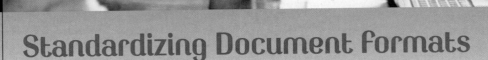

# Standardizing Document Formats

## Objectives

- Key a two-page letter showing placement on letterhead
- Create a memo and a fax template
- Modify report style
- Outline a business plan

## TASK 1 — LETTER FORMAT

UBI has adopted a block letter format with open punctuation and a standard three-line heading for the second page. Read the letter below and then key the document as the company model following the formatting directions contained in it. Save the document as *1-2task1*.

Current date ↓4

Title, First Name, Initial, Last Name
Company Name
Address
City, State, ZIP Code ↓2

Dear Title + Last Name (or appropriate salutation) ↓2

This letter serves as a standard guide for preparing letters. All employees of University Business Incubator must use this style. Incubator companies use their own style. If the letter will be printed on letterhead stationery, position the date at approximately 2.1". If a digitized logo is used, position the date approximately five lines below the letterhead. Use the standard date format of month, day, and year. For templates, select the option to update the date automatically. For individual letters, deselect update automatically so that the original date is displayed whenever you open the file. ↓2

UBI uses block format with open punctuation as its standard letter style. With block format, all lines begin at the left margin. With open punctuation, there is no colon after the salutation and no comma after the complimentary close.

The letter address must always include a personal title (such as Mr., Ms., Mrs.) or a professional title (such as M.D., Ph.D., Esquire, President). Generally, a personal title precedes the name and a professional title follows the name. In some cases, both a personal and a professional title may be used. Note the following examples: Mr. Mason R. Weston, President, or Ms. Jane C. West, Manager. President Mason R. Weston would also be acceptable. A duplicate title such as Dr. Max Zachery, Ph.D., should not be used. Either Max Zachery, Ph.D., or Dr. Max Zachery would be acceptable.

The salutation Dear plus the first name may be used when the writer knows the recipient of the letter very well. In other cases, the writer should use Dear followed by the title and last name of the individual. When a letter is addressed to a company, the salutation should be Ladies and Gentlemen. When the individual is unknown, a salutation addressed to the job title is acceptable (such as Dear Reservation Manager).

The second and subsequent pages of a letter should contain a three-line heading (line 1, name; line 2, page number; and line 3, date). Set this up as a header with a different first page.

Position the closing lines a double space below the last line of the body of the letter. A number of terms are appropriate such as Sincerely, Sincerely yours, and Yours truly. Note that only the first word is capitalized. Position the typed name four lines below the complimentary close to allow room for the signature. Position the job title on the next line. If the title is very short, it may be positioned on the same line as the name with a comma separating the name and title. A comma is not used when the name and title are on separate lines.

Reference initials, enclosures or attachments, and copy notations, if needed, are positioned on separate lines below the signature block. These items may be single-spaced or double-spaced depending on the length of the letter and the placement on the page. ↓2

Complimentary close ↓4

Writer's Name
Title ↓2
xx ↓2
Enclosure:     Name of item enclosed ↓2
c  Title, First Name, Last Name, Job Title

Left tab 0.15"

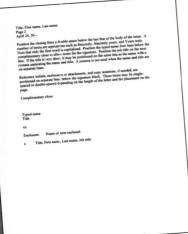

Title, First name, Last name
Page 2
April 24, 20--

Position the closing lines a double space below the last line of the body of the letter. A number of terms are appropriate such as Sincerely, Sincerely yours, and Yours truly. Note that only the first word is capitalized. Position the typed name four lines below the complimentary close to allow room for the signature. Position the job title on the next line. If the title is very short, it may be positioned on the same line as the name with a comma separating the name and title. A comma is not used when the name and title are on separate lines.

Reference initials, enclosures or attachments, and copy notations, if needed, are positioned on separate lines below the signature block. These items may be single-spaced or double-spaced depending on the length of the letter and the placement on the page.

Complimentary close

Typed name
Title

xx

Enclosure:    Name of item enclosed

c       Title, First name, Last name, Job title

# FOCUS ON THE WORKPLACE

## Process Influences Productivity

The way that work is planned, scheduled, organized, and controlled influences productivity dramatically.

- *Plan*—the first step in planning is determining goals. Planning enables employees to work smarter rather than harder.
- *Schedule*—the goals provide the framework for setting the priorities that enable the employee to accomplish the goals.
- *Organize*—work must be standardized and organized to streamline the routine portions and eliminate the unproductive elements.
- *Control*—work must be controlled to ensure its timely completion and its quality.

---

## TASK 2     MEMO TEMPLATE

To save any templates you create to a location other than *Word's* default location, click **Tools, Options, File Locations, User templates, Modify**.

UBI uses a modified version of the Professional memo template as its standard format for memos. Launch the Professional memo template and create a new memo template.

1. Key **University Business Incubator** in the company name box; extend the box so that the name fits on one line.

2. Delete the message head, *How to Use This Memo Template*; change the body text font to Times New Roman 12; and change the alignment to Left. Then change space after to 0 and line spacing to SS.

3. Save the template to Drive A or another appropriate location with the name *UBI memo*.

---

## TASK 3     FAX TEMPLATE

UBI uses a modified version of the Professional fax template as its standard format for fax transmittal forms. Launch the Professional fax template and create a new fax template.

1. Key **University Business Incubator** in the company name box (use two lines); change the alignment in the name box to Right.

2. Key UBI's complete address on the first line of the address box; then key the telephone and fax numbers on the second line of the address box. Delete the text in the Comments section.

3. Save the template to Drive A or another appropriate location with the name *UBI fax*.

# REPORT FORMAT

UBI's standard report format follows the sty~~le~~ ~~used~~ for the UBI Services document except that Title style (same as Heading~~1~~ centered) rather than WordArt is normally used for the title. Open 1-1~~task4 and review the style~~ used. Save the document as 1-2task4.

UBI reports that are bound at the left are printed in duple~~x~~ both sides of the page). Mirror margins are used for these re~~po~~ margins mean the margins on the insides of the pages are the sam~~e~~ and the margins on the outsides of the pages are the same width. T~~he on~~ margins are wider to allow for the binding. Page numbers appear on th~~e~~ outside margins of the pages. Because the first page of the report should n~~o~~ be printed on the back of the title page, a blank page should be left after the title page. The first page and other odd-numbered pages are always right-hand pages. Make the following changes to adapt this report to a bound report. Note that UBI does not include the title page as part of the standard format to allow for creativity.

To set mirror margins, on the File menu, click **Page Setup**; then click the **Margins** tab. Click the down arrow beside Multiple pages and select **Mirror** margins. Set 1.25" inside margins and .75" outside margins.

Remember that you must break the link with the previous section *before* you insert the page numbers in Section 2, the body of the report.

1. Delete the WordArt banner heading and key the heading **Business Facilities, Services, and Programs**; format the title using the Title style.

2. Change the margins to Mirror margins with 1.25" inside margins and .75" outside margins.

3. Insert the Fee Schedule file, *1-1task5*, at the end of the document; change the heading style of *Schedule of Fees* from Title style to Heading 1 style.

4. Change the content in the last paragraph to reflect that the table is on the next page rather than below.

5. Use a Next Page section break at the beginning of the document and create an attractive title page. Use WordArt for the title. Also include the company name and address and the date on the title page. You may use other graphics if desired. Add a blank page after the title page.

6. Edit page numbers beginning with the first page of the body of the report as a header with outside alignment; do not show the page number on the first page of the body. Change the page number of the first page of the report body to begin at 1.

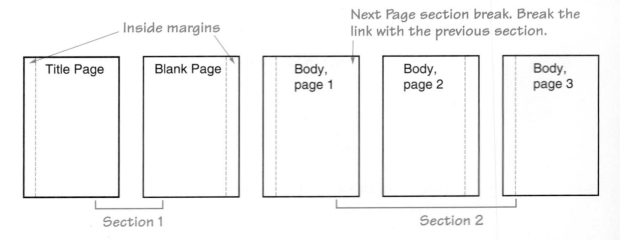

executive summary:
summarizes the key points
the report. Positioned a
first page of the rep

...om
...in a new
...ument,
...witch to Outline
View. Key each
heading, and tap
ENTER. *Word*
applies Heading 1
style to each
heading. To
apply a different
heading style
and level,
click the
Demote 🠖 or
Promote 🠔
buttons on the
Outlining
toolbar.

As part of the application process, each prospective incubator company must prepare a detailed business plan following a specific outline and must submit an executive summary of the plan. Normally, a business plan would be at least 20 to 40 pages long. The executive summary must include all major components of the business plan and should be about three pages long. With start-up companies, more detail might be necessary. If the entire business plan is not submitted, it might be desirable to provide a more detailed executive summary. UBI provides consulting services to help companies complete the business plan and continue refining it after they are admitted to the incubator.

Use the Outline from Scratch feature to key the outline that will be distributed to all companies applying for admission to UBI. Save as *1-2task5*.

# Business Plan for (Company Name)

## Executive Summary

The executive summary must contain the highlights of each key element of the business plan. The summary should be self-contained so that you do not have to refer to the business plan to interpret the contents of the summary.

## Company Overview

This section should give the reader a sense of who owns the company, its mission, and what it seeks to do. Specific sections that are usually included are:

**Company history**

**Mission**

**Structure**

**Products or services**

**Business model**

## Industry and Market Analysis

An overview of the industry and its advantages and disadvantages are used to set the stage for the future development of the business. Both direct and indirect competitors need to be analyzed carefully. Provide information about market share, growth projections, and strategic partners. Specific sections that are usually included are:

**Analysis of industry as a whole**

**Analysis of competitors**

**Current market share and projected growth**

**Strategic relationships**

## Development Strategy

This section should provide information about future products or services and what it will take to develop, produce, distribute, and manage those products or services effectively.  Specific sections that are usually included are:

**Product/service development**

**Facility needs**

**Personnel needs**

**Operational needs**

## Company Management and Organization

This section provides information about who founded the company, the key management team, the board of directors, and investors.  Specific sections that are usually included are:

**Founders**

**Management team**

**Organizational chart**

**Board of Directors**

**Investors**

## Financials

Financial information includes current financial status, projected performance, and anticipated financial needs.  Specific sections that are usually included are:

**Revenue and profit margins**

**Financial projects**

**Capital needs**

## Appendix

Include material that supplements or adds strength to your business plan, but that is not included in the core elements of the plan.

**THINK CRITICALLY**

- Why do incubators require a company to have a business plan as part of the admission process?
- How can information in the business plan be used?

# Updating Directories

## Objectives

- Update UBI employee directory in *Access*
- Update UBI company master list
- Update UBI company directory in *Access*
- Update UBI policies

---

## TASK 1  EMPLOYEE DIRECTORY (ACCESS)

Using a database stored in shared files simplifies access to employee contact information and saves time for all companies.

Since you are a new employee, you need to add your name and appropriate information to the employee directory. Open the *Access* data file *UBI directory* and then open the UBI Employee Directory table. Add the following information to the table by entering the data in table view. Format the datasheet so that the gridlines will be black. Save the database as *UBI directory key*, and print the table.

- Your last name, first name, title (Executive Assistant), and e-mail address in the same style shown for other UBI employees.

- Your office extension 3961, fax 708-555-0176, and office suite 105D.

- Your address: 1837 Lombard Avenue, Cicero, IL 60804-2847 and telephone: 708-555-0199.

- Add your birth date.

- Your hire date was Monday of this week.

---

# FOCUS ON THE WORKPLACE

### Office Productivity

## Technology Impacts Productivity

Technology has a profound effect on both the quantity and quality of work produced in an office. The development of technology usually outpaces its implementation and use.

- *Needs assessment*—employees need to stay abreast of new technology, determine what is needed to be more productive, and communicate those needs effectively.
- *Training*—implementation of technology requires training and the ability of employees to transfer knowledge of current technology to the new technology.
- *Application*—productivity is enhanced when employees utilize the technology available to them.

## TASK 2  COMPANY MASTER LIST

UBI maintains a master list of all incubator companies in the data file *UBI master list*. When an incubator company joins UBI, the master list is updated with the appropriate information. Then the employees of the new company are added to the UBI employee directory.

A new company, PVH-Net, has been approved to join the incubator on the thirtieth of this month. Add the data for the new company; keep the list in alphabetical order. Number pages appropriately. Save the file as *1-3task2 UBI master list*.

PVH-Net, Inc. [PVH]
700 Lake Street, Suite 321
Oak Park, IL 60301-7984
Main Telephone: 708-555-0190
Fax: 708-555-0180
Suites 321-322
Owner/CEO: Paige Hunt

## TASK 3 COMPANY DIRECTORY

The employees of PVH-Net, Inc. [Code: PVH] need to be added to the directory. The information for the CEO and three employees is shown below. Some of the missing information can be retrieved from the UBI master list you just completed. Open the *Access* file *UBI directory key*, and then add the employee information to the UBI Company Directory table. Format the data sheet so that the gridlines will be black. Resave the database (*UBI directory key*), and print the table in Landscape orientation.

| ID | PVH100 | ID | PVH101 |
|---|---|---|---|
| Last Name | Hunt | Last Name | Haley |
| First Name | Paige | First Name | Bryce |
| Extension | 7390 | Extension | 7392 |
| Suite | 321 | Suite | 322A |

| ID | PVH102 | ID | PVH103 |
|---|---|---|---|
| Last Name | Kelly | Last Name | Riley |
| First Name | Sean | First Name | Zoe |
| Extension | 7397 | Extension | 7395 |
| Suite | 322B | Suite | 322C |

UBI has established a new policy on e-mail and Internet use and abuse. UBI uses default margins and a standard heading format for each policy. Key the title at the top of the page in 24-point Arial. Key the subtitle in 13-point Arial and right-align. Insert a graphic line that is consistent with the UBI image below the heading. Pages are numbered at the bottom right. Number this document as page 16; save it as *1-3task4*.

**Check your productivity:** Keep track of the total time it takes you to complete this document, including correcting errors. (To obtain your production time, choose **File** menu, **Properties**, and then the **Statistics** tab.)

# UBI Policies

### E-mail and Internet Use and Abuse

UBI attempts to strike a balance between meeting the needs of employees, protecting the privacy of employees, and protecting the company's interest. However, it is imperative that employees understand that the computer technology provided by UBI is the property of UBI and its contents may be inspected at any time without notice to the employee. It is important to remember that items deleted from the system may be recovered and reviewed. Although UBI has the technology to monitor e-mails, block spam, check for viruses, and limit access to certain sites, it does not routinely monitor the work of employees. However, occasional monitoring of system usage should be expected.

UBI expects ethical and professional behavior of its employees and based on that expectation permits the limited and judicious use of e-mail and access to the Internet for personal use. The following specific guidelines should be followed.

1. Personal telephone calls, e-mails, and Internet surfing must be reasonable and limited so that productivity is not negatively impacted.

2. Employees are responsible for the content of personal e-mails and attachments they receive and send.

3. E-mails that contain solicitations, chain letters, religious, political, racial, or sexual content are unacceptable and will not be tolerated. Legal precedent exists to show that these types of messages may create a hostile work environment.

4. UBI has a zero-tolerance policy for surfing, downloading, or distributing content from sites that contain obscene language or pornographic images, and disciplinary action may be as severe as termination of employment. Remember that many of these sites trace visitors to the site and identify UBI for future contacts. This activity could be damaging to UBI's image.

Check your keyboarding technique using the form on page 236.

5. Confidential company documents should not be distributed over the Internet to protect UBI's intellectual property.

6. UBI employees frequently perform work for incubator companies whose policies may differ from UBI policies. Therefore, employees should assume the most conservative position and avoid using incubator company technology for any personal use whatsoever.

## HOW DID YOU DO?

12 minutes; no errors: Outstanding
15 minutes; no errors: Good job
25 minutes; one minor error: Fair

**TEAM OPTION** This policy provides a good opportunity to discuss key trends in major companies regarding the use and abuse of both e-mail and the Internet. It also provides an opportunity to learn more about software that may be used to monitor employee keystrokes, mouse clicks, and other applications.

1. Form teams of three or four classmates.

2. As a team, review the policy carefully. Assess the fairness of the policy to employees and to UBI. Answer questions such as:

   - What would it be like to work knowing your activities are being monitored? Is this necessary?

   - Why are companies concerned about the content of e-mails and the types of sites being visited on the Internet?

   - How do privacy, values, and ethics enter into the realm of computer and Internet communications in the business world?

3. Brainstorm to come up with additional guidelines that might be appropriate to include in the list.

4. If the group was able to reach a consensus on any new guidelines, add them to the list.

5. Search the Internet to determine if major companies have similar policies and look for information about those policies.

6. Search the Internet to find at least three software products that monitor employee computer activities, block spam, or limit the distribution of confidential documents over the Internet. Look for reviews of the software you found.

7. Give a report (oral, visual, or electronic) on your findings.

# Managing Files

**O b j e c t i v e s**

- Set up a document management system for UBI
- Set up a shared document management system for incubator companies
- Move previously stored files to new folders

## TASK 1

# FILE MANAGEMENT STRUCTURE

Making files available to everyone saves time for those who have access to them, and it is also cost-effective.

UBI needs a file management structure (workgroup files) that makes files available to all its employees. Incubator companies will also have access to these files. Individual departments (Executive, Accounting, Finance, Marketing, Public Relations, Human Resources, Legal, Administrative Services, Information Technology, and Facilities) and their employees will have their own file management structure that is accessible only to them.

Your instructor will tell you which drive on your network should be used for these files. If you are not on a network, set up the files on your A drive. Create folders that reflect the following hierarchy.

University Business Incubator
    About Us
        General
        Services and Fees
        UBI Application
    Document Formats
    Annual Report
    Office Services Center
    Directories
    Legal Document Samples
        Business Structure
        Employment
        Contracts
        Intellectual Property Agreements

```
□─📁 University Business Incubator
    □─📁 About Us
        📁 General
        📁 Services and Fees
        📁 UBI Application
    📁 Annual Report
    📁 Directories
    📁 Document Formats
    □─📁 Legal Document Samples
        📁 Business Structure
        📁 Contracts
        📁 Employment
        📁 Intellectual Property Agreements
    📁 Office Services Center
```

## THINK CRITICALLY

- Why are shared files that are available to all employees more efficient than each employee maintaining all files?

| **TASK 2** | SHARED FILE MANAGEMENT STRUCTURE |
|---|---|

Set up the file management structure for the incubator companies. Any files about specific incubator companies should be placed in these shared files.

Your instructor will tell you which drive on your network should be used for these files. If you are not on a network, set up the files on your A drive. Set up folders that reflect the following hierarchy. Folder names are shown in bold.

**UBI Companies**

**About** + company name (create folders for each incubator company)

**Business Plans** (folder for each incubator company)
**Document Formats** (folder for each company)
**Annual Reports**

| **TASK 3** | MOVE FILES TO NEW FOLDERS |
|---|---|

Dragging a file between two folders on the same drive moves the file. Dragging a file between different drives copies it instead.

Now that you have the UBI file management structure established, move all of the documents that you have prepared in this project to the appropriate folders. Use either My Computer or *Windows Explorer* for this task. Sometimes the quickest way to move and copy information is to drag it from one place to another with the mouse.

Synergy is often described as 1 + 1 = 3. This means if two people work separately, they can each do so much and 1 + 1 = 2. However, if they work together as a team, they can accomplish more; thus 1 + 1 = 3. For more information on synergy, use the *Word* Research tool and also search the Internet using the keywords *synergy + teamwork*. For additional information, visit http://www.advancedapplications.swlearning.com, click Links, and then click Project 1.

# Designing forms

O b j e c t i v e s

- Design an application form
- Create a checklist for entering companies
- Design a services request form

---

## TASK 1  APPLICATION FORM

**Protect Document**
1. Click **Tools**; then **Protect Document**.
2. Check **Editing Restrictions**; select **Filling in forms**.
3. Click **Yes, Start Enforcing Protection**.
4. Key a case-sensitive password and confirm it.

Each company that seeks admission to the University Business Incubator must complete an application form and must provide either a complete business plan or an executive summary of one. In the case of a company that is just an idea and does not yet have a business plan, UBI will work with the potential applicant to prepare one. The Selection Committee will carefully review the data from this form before making a decision on admitting the company to UBI.

Create the application form shown on the next page as a protected form named *UBI application* that can be accessed from the shared files and completed in *Word*. Protect the form with the case-sensitive password ubi. Store the form in the folder UBI Application.

---

## TASK 2  ADMISSION CHECKLIST

Making forms available online saves time in completing the forms and saves printing and distribution costs.

UBI provides a checklist to assist companies in applying for admission to UBI and in completing the admissions process (see page 22). Design a protected form for this purpose. Add the UBI logo from the data files to the top of the form. Use Title style (or Heading 1, centered) for the headings. Add a checkbox at the beginning of each item in this list similar to the first item. Use the password ubi to protect the form. Save the form as *UBI admission checklist* in the appropriate shared folder.

*Add UBI Logo*

To apply for admission to the University Business Incubator, please complete this Application Form.

# UBI Application Form

Company Name: _____

Contact Name: _____

E-mail: _____

Telephone: _____          *Unlimited text fields*

Fax: _____

Address: _____

City: _____

State: _____          *Limit to 2 letters and uppercase*

ZIP Code _____          *Number field*

Company Stage  | Idea |          *Drop-down list fields* →

| Idea |
| New Company |
| Established Company |

Business Type | Corporation | →

| Corporation |
| Partnership |
| Sole Proprietorship |
| Other |

Do you have a business plan? ☐ Yes  ☐ No   *Set Yes as the default.*

How many full-time employees? _____ Part-time employees? _____

Company Profile (describe product/services): _____

Space Requirements:          | <1000 sq. ft. | →

| <1000 sq. ft. |
| 1000-1500 sq. ft. |
| 1501-2500 sq. ft. |
| 2501-3500 |
| >3500 sq. ft. |

# UBI Admission Checklist

## Admission Criteria

☐ Desires an interactive relationship with Foster University students, faculty, and research centers

Is a knowledge-based entrepreneurial business committed to using cutting-edge technology and research

Has adequate financing to sustain at least six months of operation

Desires interaction with other entrepreneurial companies in UBI

Understands and accepts the UBI fee structure

## Prescreening

Completed the UBI application

Has a business plan or is currently developing one

Completed interview with UBI President and Chief Operating Officer

## Final Screening

*PowerPoint* presentation to UBI Selection Committee

Finalized business plan

Finalized office and/or laboratory requirements

## Admission

Completed orientation

Finalized arrangements with facilities staff for move-in

 Most companies provide an orientation program for new employees. An orientation program introduces the employee to the organization and provides information about it. Search the Web for information about "new employee orientation programs." The Human Resource Management Society website is a good place to search for articles on orientation programs.

Many UBI services are available on demand. However, all consulting, mentoring, word processing, office support services, and assistance with research or training must be prearranged. UBI requires written requests one week in advance. Generally, the request is sent to the UBI receptionist (Ana Shelton) by attaching it to an e-mail. The receptionist is responsible for coordinating all service requests.

Design a protected form (use ubi as password) and save it as *request for services* in the appropriate folder. Add the UBI logo from the data files at the top of the form. Use Heading 1 style, centered, for the title: **Request for Services**.

# Request for Services

Person making request:     *Use text form fields*

Company: ☐

Telephone: ☐

Date of request: ☐

Date(s) services needed: ☐

Service category: ☐ Basic (no charge)    ☐ Fee-based    *Use checkbox form fields*

Consulting services: |None| *Use drop-down field—see below*

Consultant preferred: ☐    *Use text form fields*

Description of services needed: ☐

Word processing/office support: |None| *Drop-down field—see below*

Associate preferred: ☐    *Use text form fields*

Description of services needed: ☐

Return this form by attaching it to an e-mail to <u>Ana.Shelton@ubi-sw.com</u> or by printing the form and dropping it off at the reception desk.

*Consulting Services*

| |
| --- |
| None |
| Basic managerial consulting |
| Boilerplate legal assistance |
| Business plan assistance |
| Financial consulting |
| Legal consulting |
| Research |
| Specialized |
| Technical consulting |
| Training |

*Word Processing Services*

| |
| --- |
| None |
| General office work |
| Office 2003 applications |
| PowerPoint presentations |
| Word documents |
| Other |

## Self-Assessment    Evaluate your understanding of this project by answering the questions below.

1. UBI uses the _____ letter style as its standard business letter format.

2. UBI uses a template to standardize the format of documents such as a memo and a(n) _____.

3. Check your file directory. The UBI General folder should contain the files (filename) _____ and _____.

4. Check your file directory. The UBI Document Formats folder should contain the files (filename) _____ and _____.

5. The second-page heading of a two-page UBI letter should include the _____, _____, and the page number.

6. To prevent users from changing a final version of an online form, you must _____ the form.

7. The critical elements of effective systems to improve productivity are _____, processes, and technology.

## Performance Assessment    Production Time: 20'

**Document 1**
**Memo**
1. Use the UBI memo template for this memo from you to All UBI Employees regarding the E-mail and Internet Use and Abuse Policy. Send a copy to your instructor.
2. Save as *checkpoint1-d1*.

A new UBI policy on E-mail and Internet Use and Abuse has been approved, and a copy of the policy is attached. Please add it to your policy manual. The policy has already been incorporated in the online Policy Manual that is available to all UBI employees as well as to the employees of all incubator companies.

President Cox plans to discuss the policy at the staff meeting scheduled for next Friday. She will answer any questions you may have about this new policy. Please review the policy carefully prior to the meeting.

**Document 2**
**Report with Table**
1. Open the data file *managing*.
2. Sort the bulleted items in alphabetical order.
3. Key the table at the appropriate position in the report.
4. Key the copy below the table as the final section of the report.
5. Save as *checkpoint1-d2*.

| Function | Outsourced % | Satisfaction Rating (%) | | |
|---|---|---|---|---|
| | | High | Average | Low |
| compensation and benefits | 48 | 32 | 48 | 20 |
| health and safety | 32 | 25 | 35 | 40 |
| payroll and administration | 70 | 75 | 13 | 12 |
| recruiting and hiring | 30 | 25 | 50 | 25 |
| training | 80 | 60 | 30 | 10 |

**Conclusions and Recommendations**
UBI should consider providing payroll and administration and compensation and benefits to incubator companies. Key factors to consider are staffing costs and the fees that would be required to provide the services. Consulting services should be offered to assist incubator companies with the other functions, but UBI should not provide these services.

## How Did You Do?

15 minutes:    Way to go!
20 minutes:    Good job

## PROOFREADING GUIDES

The final and important step in producing a document is proofreading. Error-free documents send the message that the organization is detail oriented and competent. Apply these procedures when producing any document.

1. Check spelling and grammar using the Spelling and Grammar feature.

2. Proofread the document on the screen. Be alert for words that are spelled correctly but are misused, such as you/your, in/on, of/on, the/then, etc.

3. Check the document for necessary parts for correctness; be sure special features are present if needed—for example, in a letter, check for the enclosure or copy notation. Ensure that the standard style was used.

4. View the document on screen to check placement. Save and print.

These additional steps will make you a better proofreader:

5. Try to allow some time between writing a document and proofreading it.

6. If you are reading a document that has been keyed from a written draft, place the two documents next to each other and use guides to proofread the keyed document line by line against the original.

7. Proofread numbers aloud or with another person.

**Proofreading for consistency** is another important part of preparing documents. Consistency in style or tone, usage, facts, and format conveys an impression of care and attention to detail that reflects well on the writer and his or her organization. In contrast, lack of consistency gives an impression of carelessness and inattention to detail. Lack of consistency also makes documents more difficult to read and understand.

**Proofreading statistical copy** is extremely important. As you proofread, double-check numbers whenever possible. For example, verify dates against a calendar and check computations with a calculator. Remember these tips for proofreading numbers.

- Read numbers in groups. For example, the telephone number 618-555-0123 can be read in three parts: **six-one-eight, five five-five, zero-one-two-three**.

- Read numbers aloud.

- Proofread numbers with a partner.

## Drill 1

### PROOFREADING

1. Open the data file *proof-it* and print it. Use proofreaders' marks to mark corrections. The letter contains ten mistakes: two in formatting, two in capitalization, two in number use, and four in spelling or keying.

2. Revise the letter, format it correctly, and save it as *cs1-drill1*.

# Drill 2

**PROOFREADING AND EDITING**
Key the drill, making all necessary corrections. Save as *cs1-drill2*.

First impressions does count, and you never get a second chance to make a good first impression. This statement applys too both documents and people. The minute you walk in to a room you are judged by you appearance, your facial expressions, and the way you present your self. As soon as a document is opened, it is judged by it's appearance and the way it is presented. First impressions are often lasting impressions therefore you should strive to make a positive first impression for yourself and for the documents you prepare. Learn to manage your image and the image of your documents.

# Drill 3

**PROOFREADING FOR CONSISTENCY**

1. Open the data file *linger*.
2. Proofread the letter for consistency in usage, facts, and format (block letter, mixed punctuation). Verify information against the price list below. Make corrections. Use today's date for the letter and your name for the writer's name. Save the letter as *cs1-drill3*.

| | | |
|---|---|---|
| **Workstation 2010** | **Chimera** | **$1,599** |
| 3.2 GHz processor, 15" display, 512 MB RAM, 60 GB hard drive, CD-RW/DVD combo, 2003 Vibrex Office Suite. | | |
| **Vista XBT** | **Chimera** | **$1,299** |
| 2.8 GHz processor, 15" display, 256 MB RAM, 40 GB hard drive, CD-RW/DVD combo, 2003 Vibrex Office Suite. | | |
| **Amina Optima** | **Finn** | **$1,499** |
| 3.2 GHz processor, 15" display, 512 MB RAM, 40 GB hard drive, CD-RW/DVD combo, docking station, 2003 Capstone Office Suite. | | |
| **Winger Color Laser Printer** | **Primat** | **$1,199** |
| 600dpi, 16ppm, 250-sheet input tray. | | |
| **AZ Color Laser Printer** | **Ventura** | **$1,699** |
| 1200dpi, 26ppm, two 250-sheet input trays. | | |

## PROJECT 2
# CMF Communications, Inc.

**2-1**   Creating the UBI Website

**2-2**   Setting Up Committees

**2-3**   Preparing the Grand Opening Budget

**2-4**   Planning Grand Opening Activities

**2-5**   Preparing a Newsletter

**2-6**   Designing Publicity Pieces

**FOCUS:** *Communication*

You are now assigned to work at CMF Communications, Inc., a company that specializes in public relations, corporate relations, market research, and marketing communications.  UBI has contracted with CMF Communications to plan and coordinate events for the grand opening of UBI's new facilities.  You will communicate with many individuals involved in this event as well as prepare a variety of documents for it.  You will also be involved in revising the UBI website and making sure the appropriate grand opening documents are posted.

**JOB 2-1**

# Creating the UBI Website

Objectives

- Edit the UBI draft website
- Prepare Web documents
- Compose and design About UBI Web document
- Compose and design FAQs Web document

---

## TASK 1  WEBSITE EDITS

A new website is being designed for UBI that will be presented to UBI management for final approval. You are asked to assist in the design. Open the data file *website draft*. Create a new subfolder under the *University Business Incubator* folder named *UBI website*. Save as *2-1task1*. Insert the graphic file *ubi photo* from the data files and size it attractively. Then create a hyperlink for *Contact Us* on the Web page to this e-mail address: Yan.Huang@ubi-sw.com.

---

## TASK 2  INCUBATOR COMPANIES WEB PAGE

To set a bookmark, click **Insert, Bookmark,** and the filename; do not include spaces in the filename.

Open the data file *business incubators*. Save it in the *UBI website* folder as a Web page with the name *2-1task2 companies*, and make the changes that follow. Once you make the changes, create a hyperlink for *Companies* to the file *2-1task2 companies*.

- *Main heading:* Apply **Heading 1** style and center; apply custom font color—Red 214; Green 158; Blue 0.

- *Divider line:* Insert the graphic file *bar* from the data files and center.

- *Name of companies:* Apply **Heading 3** style.

- *Theme:* Apply the theme Afternoon (**Format, Theme, Afternoon**)

- Set a bookmark at the beginning of each company name.

To create a frame, click **Format, Frames,** and then choose **Table of Contents** in Frame.

- Create a frame. Save as *2-1task 2 companies frames*. Check that the hyperlinks work correctly.

---

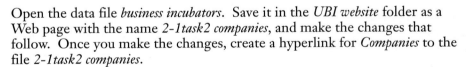

**THINK CRITICALLY**

- How important are hyperlinks in websites and why are they necessary?

---

## TASK 3        ORGANIZATIONAL CHART WEB PAGE

Open the file *1-1task4* you created in Project 1. Save in the UBI Web Site folder as a Web page and name the file *2-1task3 chart*. Make the following edits; then create a hyperlink for *Organization* on the UBI website to the file *2-1task3 chart*.

- *Main heading:* Change to **The UBI Organization**. Apply custom font color—Red 214; Green 158; Blue 0.

- *Position boxes:* Change fill color to light yellow; change line color to brown.

- *Bar:* Insert the data file *bar* below the main heading.

- *Theme:* Apply the theme Afternoon. Adjust shape or font size if necessary so titles fit in shapes.

## TASK 4        ABOUT UBI WEB PAGE

Create a Web page for the About UBI hyperlink. Use the information in the document created in *1-1task2*. Be sure to include the address and phone and fax numbers for UBI. Review some company websites to find ideas for presenting this information attractively and concisely. Apply the theme Afternoon. Save in the UBI Web Site folder as *2-1task4 about UBI*. Then create a hyperlink for *About UBI* to the file *2-1task4 about UBI*.

## TASK 5         FAQS WEB PAGE

**FAQs:** frequently asked questions

Complete the **FAQs** Web page. Use the data file *FAQs* as a start. Complete the page by adding at least five additional questions that are frequently asked by beginning entrepreneurs. Use the Internet to locate these questions. Save the document as a Web page in the UBI Web Site folder as *2-1task5 FAQs*.

Create the Web document that will contain the answers to the FAQs. Visit company websites to find ideas for designing this page. This document should include each question with the concise answer shown below it. Apply the theme Afternoon. Save in the folder UBI Web Site as *2-1task5 FAQ answers*. Apply the **Heading 3** style to each question. Create a new frames page; then create a frame above for the page title. Next, create a table of contents frame. The list of questions is automatically created in the left frame and automatically hyperlinked to the appropriate question.

## JOB 2-2

# Setting Up Committees

Objectives

- Set up appropriate folders for grand opening activities
- Set up contact list
- Send confirmation letter of appointment
- Prepare list of grand opening committee members for distribution on intranet
- Prepare agenda and minutes for first meeting
- Prepare address labels

## TASK 1    FILE MANAGEMENT

For ease in sharing electronic files for the UBI grand opening, create a folder under the *University Business Incubator* folder named *UBI Grand Opening*. Under that folder, create the following subfolders: *Committee Meeting Minutes, Steering, Events Planning,* and *Finance*.

**THINK CRITICALLY**

- What is the value of having electronic files available on a network?
- What problems could this cause?
- How would you address privacy issues?

## TASK 2    CONTACT LIST

For communication purposes, you will need to create a table listing the committee assignments. Save the document as *2-2task2*. The three committees for the UBI Grand Opening are Steering, Events Planning, and Finance. Individuals from UBI, CMF Communications, Inc. and the community make up the committee membership.

Before you key the table, create the following macros with the keyboard shortcuts. Using these macros will save you keying and proofreading time. Be sure to save the macro in the document *2-2task2*.

| University Business Incubator | ALT + U | |
| CMF Communications, Inc. | ALT + C | |
| @ubi-sw.com | ALT + E | |
| 700 Lake Street, Suite 100 (tap ENTER)<br>Oak Park, IL 60301-7984 | ALT + 1 | UBI information |
| 700 Lake Street, Suite 120 (tap ENTER)<br>Oak Park, IL 60301-7984 | ALT + 2 | CMF information |

Here are some instructions to help you create the first macro.

- Open a blank document and save as *2-2task2*.

- Click **Tools, Macro, Record New Macro.** In the Store macro in box, choose **2-2task2**.

- In the Macro name box, key **UBI**. In the Description box, key **University Business Incubator**.

- Click the **Keyboard** button. In the Press new shortcut key box, hold down the ALT key and tap U. Click **Assign**, and click **Close**. Key **University Business Incubator**. (Be sure to proofread carefully.)

- Click the **Stop Recording** button on the floating toolbar. To play the recorded macro, press ALT + U.

Repeat these steps to create the four remaining macros—CMF Communications, Inc., @ubi-sw.com, UBI address, and CMF address.

## Create Membership List

Create a seven-column table in landscape orientation. Column headings are *Title, First Name, Last Name, Organization, Address, E-mail Address,* and *Committee Assignment*. Complete the information for each person.

Use the macros you created to key the organizations and addresses. For the e-mail address, key the first part of the address, e.g., Ann.Quinn. Then key ALT + E to add the remaining part of the e-mail address.

Sort the table by Committee Assignments in ascending order and then by Last name in ascending order. Repeat the column headings on the second page, and ensure that listings are not separated between pages.

## UBI Committee Assignments

Mr. Yan Huang, Steering
Mr. Nathan Schultz, Finance
Mr. Fred Perez, Events Planning

## CMF Communications, Inc. Committee Assignments

Ms. Ann Quinn, Steering
Mr. Scott Burke, Finance
Ms. Janice Herron, Finance
Ms. Carole Guarino, Finance

Ms. Katherine Hiestand, Events Planning
Mr. John Morgan, Events Planning
Ms. Teresa Romaniello, Events Planning

## Other Committee Assignments

Ms. Judith Murphy, Foster University, Marketing Department, 126 Cherry Lane, Oak Park, IL 60301-0126, Judith.Murphy@fsu-sw.edu, Steering

Mr. Glen Yeatman, Oak Park Chamber of Commerce, P.O. Box 323, Oak Park, IL 60301-0323, Glen.Yeatman@opcc-sw.org, Steering

Mr. Brad McGowan, Oak Park Economic Development Council, P.O. Box 35, Oak Park, IL 60301-0035, Brad.McGowan@oped-sw.org, Steering

Ms. Amanda McKell, Oak Park Mayor's Office, P.O. Box 103, Oak Park, IL 60301-0103, Amanda.McKell@opmayor-sw.org, Steering

**THINK CRITICALLY**

- Can you think of other macros to create that will help improve your efficiency?

## TASK 3 CONFIRMATION LETTER

Using the information in the table you prepared in Task 2, prepare the following form letter from Ann Quinn, Public Relations Director at CMF Communications, confirming the appointment of members to the three grand opening committees and informing them of the orientation meeting. Prepare the letter in the block format with open punctuation and the *CMF letterhead* from the data files.

Merge the letters to a new document. Save the main document as *2-2task3 merge*. Save the merged letters as *2-2task3*. In a separate file, generate the envelopes for each letter and print them. Arrange the appropriate envelope behind the appropriate letter. Place flap of envelope toward the front of the letter. Save the main document as *2-2task3 envmerge*. Save the merged envelopes as *2-2task3 envelopes*.

<<AddressBlock>>

<<GreetingLine>>

Thank you for your commitment to assist us in planning the grand opening for the new facilities of the University Business Incubator. Based on the short survey you completed and the nature of your position at <<Organization>>, you have been assigned to the <<Committee_Assignment>> Committee.

The orientation meeting for all committees is scheduled for Monday, January 10, 20--, at 10 a.m. in Conference Room 102 at the University Business Incubator. At this meeting you will hear a brief overview of the UBI grand opening framework, be introduced to all the partners in this important endeavor, and meet briefly with your assigned committee.

Again, we thank you for this commitment of time and energy. With the outstanding people represented here, we are confident the grand opening will be successful. We look forward to celebrating this accomplishment and acquainting the public with the services of the University Business Incubator.

Sincerely

## TASK 4 — AGENDA

You need to prepare the agenda for the orientation meeting of the committees for the UBI grand opening. You have a choice to either format the memo in the simple design shown in the Reference Guide or to use the Agenda Wizard and create an extremely professional-looking document. In either case, fit the agenda on one page and save it as *2-2task4*.

*Agenda Wizard option:* Choose the Boxes template on the Agenda Wizard. Key the date, time, title, and location of the meeting as shown in the box below. When directed to choose options, only select the heading **Special Notes**. Key the topics and the subtopics as agenda topics. Do not include a form for recording minutes. After clicking **Finish**, select the subtopics, set a .25" tab, and then indent the subtopics to the tab.

**Date:** January 10, 20--
**Time:** 10 a.m.–11: 30 a.m.
**Title:** Orientation Meeting of UBI Grand Opening Committees
**Location:** UBI, Conference Room 102

**Agenda Topics**

Welcome, Ann Quinn, CMF Public Relations Director, 10 minutes

Overview of UBI Grand Opening, Yan Huang, UBI Public Relations Director, 30 minutes

Announcement of Partnerships, Nicole Cox, UBI President, 10 minutes

      Oak Park Chamber of Commerce

      Foster University

      Oak Park Economic Development Council

      Oak Park Mayor and City Board of Directors

Committee Assignments, Ann Quinn, CMF Public Relations Director, 5 minutes

      Steering Committee

      Finance Committee

      Events Planning Committee

      Public Relations Committee

Organizational Meeting of Committees, 30 minutes

Adjournment, 5 minutes

**Special notes:**

Committees will meet weekly at a time and date agreed upon by the committee at their brief meeting today.

Each committee is asked to prepare electronic minutes of each committee meeting. Name the file Committee Meeting Date (e.g., Finance Committee Jan 10). Save the file on the shared drive in the subfolder Committee Meeting Minutes that is located in the Grand Opening folder. This procedure will allow the Steering Committee to review all minutes of all committees prior to their weekly meetings.

Wizard: Add subtopics as agenda topics and edit.

Create a two-column table with at least five pointers that you will want to remember when you give a presentation. You will use this chart in Project 4.

Being able to present one-on-one, in small groups, or to large audiences is an important skill. For more information on presenting, visit http://www.advancedapplications.swlearning.com, click **Links**, and then click **Project 2.**

# MINUTES

Insert a nonbreaking space to keep month and date together.

To add the signature lines, set a right tab with underline leader where the first and second lines should end; set a left tab where the second line begins.

Prepare the minutes of the orientation meeting as a two-column table with no borders. Fit on one page. Key the title in 14-point font. Save as *2-2task5* in the Committee Meeting Minutes folder.

**Check your productivity:** Keep track of the total time it takes you to complete this document, including saving the document and correcting errors. (To obtain your production time, choose **File** menu, **Properties**, and then choose **Statistics** tab.)

**ORIENTATION MEETING OF UBI**
**GRAND OPENING COMMITTEES**
**January 10, 20--**

| | |
|---|---|
| Time and Place of Meeting | The orientation meeting of the University Business Incubator grand opening committees was held Monday, January 10, 20--, in Conference Room 102 of the University Business Incubator. The meeting was called to order at 10 a.m. by Ann Quinn, the public relations director of CMF Communications, Inc. |
| Attendance | Fifteen participants attended. |
| Overview of UBI Grand Opening | Yan Huang, public relations director of University Business Incubator, explained the initial plans for the company's grand opening. Three committees have been established to formulate plans for this event. Committees and chairs are: Steering Committee, Yan Huang, Chair; Finance Committee, Nathan Schultz, Chair; and Events Planning Committee, Fred Perez, Chair. The tentative date set for the grand opening is Saturday, March 15. |
| Announcement of Partnerships | Nicole Cox, president of University Business Incubator, thanked all present for their commitment to this important endeavor. She expressed special appreciation to four community partners: Judith Murphy, Foster University, Department of Marketing; Glen Yeatman, Oak Park Chamber of Commerce; Brad McGowan, Oak Park Economic Development Council; and Amanda McKell, Oak Park Mayor. |
| Committee Assignments | Ann Quinn distributed a directory of committee members. (See attachment.) She shared that the directory is also posted on the UBI Web page. |
| Organizational Meeting of Committees | Committee chairs then convened a brief meeting of their respective committees. Their charge was first to set a standing meeting of their committees each week. A recorder is to prepare electronic minutes of each |

meeting and save to the shared drive in the subfolder Committee Meeting Minutes. The file is to be saved with the filename *Name of Committee-Date of Meeting*.

Adjournment          The meeting was adjourned at 11:30 a.m.

_____          _____
Your Name                                              Date

### HOW DID YOU DO?

20 minutes; no errors: Way to go!
25 minutes; no errors: Good job
30 minutes; one minor error: Acceptable

---

**TASK 6**                **ADDRESS LABELS**

You must mail the Steering Committee a packet of materials they will need at their next meeting. Use the table created in Task 2 to prepare Avery 5160 address labels; sort to include only the Steering Committee. Save the main document as *2-2task6 merge*. Save the merged labels as *2-2task6*.

# FOCUS ON THE WORKPLACE

### Communication

## Not Another Staff Meeting!

Do these quotes reflect your views on meetings in the workplace?

"Another boring meeting that doesn't pertain to what I am doing."

"How long will we meet? I have a schedule to keep."

"What is the purpose of this meeting?"

Consider these helpful pointers for planning effective meetings.

- Limit meetings to as few as possible.
- Distribute an agenda in a timely manner that includes date of meeting, time, length of meeting, topics, and reporting parties.
- Lead the meeting to achieve goals and to complete it in a timely manner.
- Prepare minutes immediately after the meeting and distribute to all participants and employees needing the information.

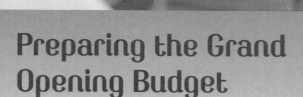

# Preparing the Grand Opening Budget

### Objectives

- Prepare a budget table or *Excel* worksheet
- Create a column chart
- Compose a transmittal letter
- Revise the budget based on comments
- Prepare an e-mail with distribution list and attachment

---

## TASK 1     BUDGET

Since the budget will probably be revised, you may want to set it up as an *Excel* worksheet to make it easier to recalculate.

The Finance Committee drafted a budget for the grand opening. Key the budget as a five-column table or as an *Excel* worksheet. Label the columns as *Activity*, *Number*, *Unit Price*, *Amount*, and *Subtotals*. Insert formulas to calculate the amounts, the subtotals for each category, and the total (the total should be $10,684). Add the title *UBI GRAND OPENING BUDGET* and the subtitle *Prepared by UBI Grand Opening Finance Committee*. Save the document in the Finance subfolder as *2-3task1*.

Printing
    1,000 Invitations @ .25      $250
    500 Newsletters @ .50      $250
    750 Programs @ .10      $75
Postage
    1,000 Invitations @ .34      $340
    50 News releases @ .34      $17
Entertainment
    Band      $1,000
Catering
    500 Lunches @ $5      $2,500
    Decorations      $1,000
    Tent rental      $500
Advertisements
    4 Newspaper ads @ $250 each      $1,000
    3 Television ads @ $250 each      $750
    250 T-shirts with logos @ $7 each      $1,750
Speaker
    Travel      $527
    Hotel and meals      $175
    Honorarium      $500
Total

| TASK 2 | ## CHART |
|---|---|

Prepare a column chart to display the totals of the six categories itemized by the Finance Committee in the budget prepared in Task 1. Decide whether you will use the chart feature of *Word* or *Excel*. If you create the chart in *Word*, choose landscape orientation. If you chose *Excel*, create this as a new chart sheet. Format attractively and add the title *UBI Grand Opening Budget*.

Save the document in the Finance subfolder as *2-3task2*.

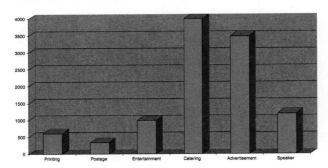

| TASK 3 | ##  TRANSMITTAL LETTER (MERGE) |
|---|---|

Nathan Schultz, chair of the Finance Committee, requests that you send the proposed budget for the UBI grand opening to the Steering Committee for its review. Compose a form letter under Mr. Schultz' signature that:

- States the proposed budget for the UBI grand opening is enclosed.

- Explains the budget represents six budget categories and lists the categories.

- Requests the Steering Committee review the proposed budget by January 20 and e-mail any revisions to Nathan Schultz (provide the e-mail address).

- Ends with a warm closing that commends the work of the Finance Committee in a short ten days and states that Nathan looks forward to the feedback of the Steering Committee so the grand opening plans can continue.

Use *2-2task2* for the data source. Select only those people on the Steering Committee as recipients. Merge the letters to a new document. Save the main document in the Finance subfolder as *2-3task3 merge*. Save the merged letters in the Finance subfolder as *2-3task3*. Print the merged letters.

> **Working in a team-based culture requires special skills. Search the Web for team-building games, activities, treasure or scavenger hunts, and/or exercises. Choose a team and try one of your ideas.**

| TASK 4 | ## BUDGET REVISION |
|---|---|

Nathan Schultz e-mailed you that the Steering Committee recommended revising the budget and chart you prepared in *2-3task1* and *2-3task2*. Their recommendations are shown on the next page. Save the revised budget in the Finance subfolder as *2-3task4a* (total $13,234). Also revise the chart you prepared in *2-3task2* and save it in the Finance subfolder as *2-3task4b*.

| Entertainment | Pianist and soloist for $500 instead of band for $1,000. |
| Catering | Reduce decorations to $300. |
| | Delete tent rental. Chamber of Commerce has agreed to donate a large tent. |
| Advertisements | Add 100 radio ads @ $25 each (insert after television ads). |
| | Add 1 billboard @ $600 per month for 2 months. |
| | Add 6 signs @ $100 each. |

## TASK 5  E-MAIL WITH ATTACHMENT

You need to send the revised budget to all members of the grand opening committees. To save time and to speed up the review process, address the e-mail to the Steering Committee at <u>Opening@ubi-sw.com</u>. **Note:** If you have the capabilities, use the Mail Recipient (for Review) command (**File**, **Send To**, **Mail Recipient for Review**).

Indicate that the revised budget is attached (*2-3task4a*). Request that the members review the attached budget and send any comments to Nathan Schultz by e-mail by January 22.

# FOCUS ON THE WORKPLACE
### Communication

## No One Told Me!

You have most likely heard or even used the excuse that "no one told me" to order signs or invite the press or whatever was not done. The success of any project depends on effective communication with all people involved. The success of UBI's grand opening depends on effective communication of the plans to all groups. Note the steps taken to ensure total understanding.

- Key players at UBI, CMF Communications, Foster University, the mayor's office, the Oak Park Chamber of Commerce, and the Oak Park Economic Development Council were involved in the event planning and implementation.
- The budget was prepared by the Finance Committee, sent to the Steering Committee for their review and input, and then distributed to all committee members for their review.

# Planning Grand Opening Activities

Objectives

- Prepare a schedule of events (table with comments)
- Prepare an e-mail with attachment
- Finalize schedule (merge comments)
- Prepare an e-mail with distribution list and attachment

---

**TASK 1**   SCHEDULE OF EVENTS

Set tabs to indent items within a cell. Press CTRL + TAB to move to the tab within a cell.

The Events Planning Committee is preparing a draft of the schedule of events. Fred Perez, committee chair, has asked you to key the schedule and insert comments requesting feedback from those reviewing this document. Key the schedule as a three-column table with headings *Event*, *Location*, and *Time*.

To receive feedback, insert the following comments at the places indicated.

**Welcome**   Take a look at the order of dignitaries below. Is this appropriate?

**Author**   What is the title of Dr. Thompson's latest book? We will need for the news release.

Save the document in the Events Planning subfolder as *2-4task1*.

## UBI GRAND OPENING SCHEDULE OF EVENTS
### Saturday, March 15, 20--

Dignitaries' Reception, Conference Room 102, 9:00 a.m.
Dedication Ceremony, Cline Auditorium, 10:00 a.m.
  Opening
    Nicole Cox, UBI President
  Welcome
    Amanda McKell, Mayor of Oak Park
    Brad McGowan, Vice President of Oak Park Economic Development Council
    Glen Yeatman, Vice President of Oak Park Chamber of Commerce
    Judith Murphy, Professor of Marketing, Foster University
  Keynote Address
    Dr. William Thompson, Lecturer and Author
Ribbon Cutting, Front entrance, 11:00 a.m.
News Conference, Lobby, 11:15 a.m.
Luncheon, West lawn, 12:00 noon
Tours of UBI, Front entrance, 1:00 p.m.

## TASK 2 E-MAIL WITH ATTACHMENT

E-mail the draft schedule of events for the UBI grand opening to all committees for their review at Opening@ubi-sw.com. Send a copy to Nicole Cox, president of UBI. Compose an e-mail message that:

- States the draft schedule of events for the UBI grand opening is attached.

- Requests the committees review the schedule carefully. Explain that two comments have been inserted for their feedback. Explain that to respond to a comment, they should click in the comment, click Comment on the Insert menu, and then type their response in the new comment balloon.

- Requests that they save the document as *2-4task2lastname* in the Events Planning subfolder by January 23. Tell them that the Events Planning Committee will consider all feedback as they finalize the schedule of events.

**Note:** Use the Mail Recipient (for Review) command if available.

## TASK 3 WEBSITE UPDATE

Prepare the listing of grand opening committees for distribution on the UBI intranet. Open *2-2task2*; key the main heading **University Business Incubator Grand Opening Committees**; apply **Heading 1** style, centered. Select the table and center it horizontally. Apply the theme Afternoon.

Save it as a Web page; change the title to **Grand Opening Committees** and name the file *2-4task3*.

Why is listening, which seems so easy, so difficult? To learn how good listening can benefit you, visit http://www.advancedapplications.swlearning.com, click Links, and then click Project 2. Next, rate your listening skills by completing the listening quizzes found at the websites shown on the Advanced Applications website. Visit http://www.advancedapplications.swlearning.com, click Links, and then click Project 2. Then click the listening skills links shown.

To complete the final schedule of events, you need to review the feedback received from your e-mail request, and then merge all comments into one document. Open *2-4task1* and save as *2-4task4*. Delete your two comments.

Merge the comments from Nicole Cox (*2-4task2b cox*) in the data files into your document. Next merge the comments from Yan Huang (*2-4task2b huang*) and Nathan Schultz *(2-4task2b schultz)*.

Revise the schedule of events *(2-4task4)* using the feedback received.

- Delete *Judith Murphy* and insert *Mark Benoist*, president of Foster University.

- Move *Mark Benoist* to be the first speaker under the Welcome section.

- Add the RSVP notice in parentheses next to Luncheon.

- Key a statement about the title of Dr. Thompson's book in a separate file; save as *2-4task4 notes*. Create a new subfolder under the Grand Opening folder named *Your Name Notes*.

Delete all comments and save the revised schedule in the Events Planning subfolder as *2-4task4*.

> To delete a comment, click the comment and tap DELETE.
>
> To compare and merge documents, click **Tools, Compare and Merge**.

**THINK CRITICALLY**

- Why is it important for Mr. Perez to know the title of Dr. Thompson's latest book?

E-mail the final schedule of events to all members of the grand opening committees at <u>Opening@ubi-sw.com</u>. Request that the members review the attached schedule and e-mail any comments to Fred Perez by January 25.

**Note:** Use the Mail Recipient (for Review) command if available.

> Take advantage of every opportunity to refine your writing skills. Practice, practice, practice.

# Preparing a Newsletter

Objectives

- Design a masthead
- Prepare a newsletter with columns and graphics

---

## TASK 1     MASTHEAD

Create a masthead for the special edition of a newsletter announcing the grand opening. The Events Planning Committee will distribute the newsletter in a mass mailing in February. Use the following as a sample. Use your creativity to develop a unique design. Save the document in the Events Planning subfolder as *2-5task1*.

University Business Incubator

Special Grand Opening Edition

February 20--        Volume 1, Issue 1

---

## TASK 2      NEWSLETTER

Create a special two-column grand opening newsletter dated February 20--. Save the document in the Events Planning subfolder as *2-5task2*.

Number the newsletter Volume 1, Issue 1. Use the masthead you created in Task 1 at the top of page 1. This issue will include the following:

- *UBI Hosts Grand Opening*—an article announcing the grand opening. Insert the data file *Grand Opening*.

- *Grand Opening Events*—a table listing the events, times, and locations.

- *Our History*—an article outlining the history of UBI. Insert the data file *History*.

- *Membership List*—a list of incubator companies with suites, telephone numbers, and owners.

- *Benefits of Membership*—an article listing the benefits of being a member of an incubator company. Insert the data file *Benefits of Membership*.

- *Special Thanks*—a short thank-you to the UBI partners. Insert the data file *Thank You*.

- *Grand Opening Committees*—a list of members of the three grand opening committees.

Use your creativity in formatting the newsletter. Use columns, a picture of the UBI facility, and other appropriate graphics and photos. Consider these tips in your design:

- Use a sans serif font (without cross strokes) for titles and a serif font (with cross strokes) for body text. Use a larger font size (14 point) for titles. Use a smaller font size (11 point) for text.

- Adjust paragraph spacing before and after to fit the copy more precisely.

- Add borders and a pleasant, light-colored shading to emphasize one section of the newsletter on each page, e.g., Membership List and In This Issue.

- Insert graphics and adjust for text wrapping where needed.

- Create a header for the second and third pages that includes the newsletter name and page number.

- On page 1 of the newsletter, add a box showing contact information for you as the newsletter editor and a box for the contents.

**Newsletter Editor**

Student's Name and Title

Telephone:  708-555-0137

E-mail:  Name@ubi-sw.com

**In This Issue**

UBI Hosts Grand Opening........1

Grand Opening Events.............1

Our History..............................2

Membership List ......................2

Benefits of Membership............3

Special Thanks ........................3

Grand Opening Committees .....3

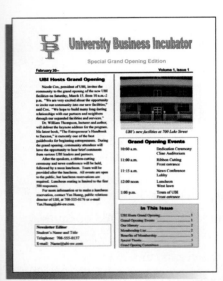

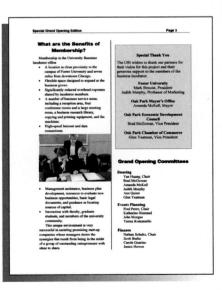

# Designing Publicity Pieces

### Objectives

- Prepare a draft news release
- Create a report on media coverage plan
- Send an e-mail with attachment
- Merge comments in news release
- Design an invitation with special fonts
- Compose and create a feature article

## TASK 1 — NEWS RELEASE

To insert a nonbreaking space or hyphen, choose **Insert, Symbol, Special Characters.**

Key the news release that follows announcing the grand opening to the public. Since you will print this on UBI letterhead, begin the first line at about 2.1" or key it on the UBI letterhead you created in 1-1task1. This release will appear in newspapers, so proofread carefully. Be sure to check dates, times, and spelling of names and businesses. Keep names, dates, and URLs together by inserting a nonbreaking space or a nonbreaking hyphen.

Insert DRAFT as a watermark. Key the footer **-more-** at the bottom of the first page. Key the following slug line as a header on the second page: **UBI grand opening/2**. Be sure to use the Insert Page Number button on the Header/Footer toolbar. Key **###** after the last line of the release to indicate the end. Save the document in the Events Planning subfolder as *2-6task1*.

---

(News Release) — All caps

March 5, 20--

For Immediate Release

Contact Person: Yan Huang
Director of Public Relations
708-555-0176
Yan.Huang@ubi-sw.com

— All caps

University Business Incubator to hold grand opening

(Oak Park,) Ill.- The University Business Incubator will host a grand opening for the community Saturday, March 15, from 10 a.m.-2 p.m. UBI is a nonprofit organization in Oak Park supported by Foster University and a number of local business organizations interested in promoting economic development and entrepreneurship. It has offered a wide variety of office services to four incubator companies and boasts the addition of eight new incubator organizations in the newly expanded facilities.

Dr. William Thompson, lecturer and author, will deliver the keynote address. His latest book, <u>The Entrepreneur's Handbook to Success</u>, is currently one of the best guidebooks for beginning entrepreneurs. During the grand opening, attendees will have the opportunity to hear brief comments from Nicole Cox, president of UBI; Amanda McKell, mayor of Oak Park; Brad McGowan, vice president of the Oak Park Economic Development Council; Glen Yeatman, vice president of the Oak Park Chamber of Commerce; and Judith Murphy, professor of marketing at Foster University.

"We are very excited about the opportunity to invite our community into our new facilities," said Cox. "We're planning to build many long-lasting relationships with our partners and neighbors through our expanded facilities and services."

After the speakers, a ribbon-cutting ceremony and news conference will be held, followed by a noon luncheon. Tours will be provided after the luncheon. All events are open to the public, but luncheon reservations are required. Luncheon seating is limited to the first 500 responses.

For more information or to make a luncheon reservation, contact Yan Huang, public relations director of UBI, at 708-555-0176 or e-mail <u>Yan.Huang@ubi-sw.com</u>. The full schedule of events is also located on the UBI website at <u>http://www.ubi-sw.com</u>.

**THINK CRITICALLY**

- What is the purpose of a news release?
- Why do you think it's important to include a contact person?

## TASK 2      MEDIA COVERAGE PLAN

The Events Planning Committee has developed a plan to secure full media coverage for the UBI grand opening. Key the draft plan that follows. Apply the styles shown. Format the dates with a 1" hanging indent. Format attractively.

Key the following header on the second and subsequent pages. For page numbers, click **Insert AutoText** on the Header and Footer toolbar and click **Page X of Y**.

**Media Coverage Plan**          **Page 2 of 3**

Media Coverage Plan   *Heading 1, centered*

Publicity   *Heading 2, centered*

*Newspaper*   Heading 3

February 15   Send e-mail teaser about grand opening to business editors and reporters.

February 20   Mail invitation to grand opening and news conference information to business editors and reporters.

March 5   Send news release (either mail or e-mail—their preference) to business editors and reporters.

March 7   Send feature article (either mail or e-mail—their preference) to local newspaper for publication the week of the grand opening.

March 10   Call each location where there have been no responses or reservations made, reminding them about the news conference, luncheon, and tours.

*Television*   Heading 3

February 15   Send e-mail teaser about grand opening to business reporters and news directors.

February 20   Mail invitation to grand opening and news conference information to business reporters and news directors.

March 5   Send news release (either mail or e-mail—their preference) to business reporters and news directors.

March 10   Call each location where there have been no responses or reservations made, reminding them about the news conference, luncheon, and tours.

*Radio*   Heading 3

February 15   Send e-mail teaser about grand opening to business reporters and news directors.

February 20   Mail invitation to grand opening and news conference information to business reporters and news directors.

March 5   Send news release (either mail or e-mail—their preference) to business reporters and news directors.

March 10   Call each location where there have been no responses or reservations made, reminding them about the news conference, luncheon, and tours.

Advertising

*Newspaper*

January 15   Reserve upcoming advertising space.

February 1   Develop rough ads for committees to approve.

Format dates with a hanging indent; set tab at 1".

February 15   Send ads to appropriate outlets.

February 25   Check with media outlets to reconfirm ad schedules.

March 1   Begin running ads.

*Television*

January 15   Reserve upcoming advertising space.

February 1   Develop rough ads for committees to approve.

February 15   Send ads to appropriate outlets.

February 25   Check with media outlets to reconfirm ad schedules.

March 1   Begin running ads.

*Radio*

January 15   Reserve upcoming advertising space.

February 1   Develop rough ads for committees to approve.

February 15   Send ads to appropriate outlets.

February 25   Check with media outlets to reconfirm ad schedules.

March 1   Begin running ads.

*Billboards*

January 15   Reserve available space for city billboards.

January 20   Develop design for billboard (if available).

February 1–
March 31   Display grand opening information and general information on billboards.

*Signage*

February 1   Contract with sign designer to produce signs for each entrance to UBI and surrounding roads.

March 1   Put up signs for grand opening.

New Media

*Web Site*

February 1   Update website to include all grand opening information.

*E-mail*

February 10   Send e-mail to all clients of all UBI tenants, inviting them to the grand opening and referring them to the website and other contact information.

March 1   Send follow-up invitation to those not already responding.

## TASK 3    E-MAIL WITH ATTACHMENT

E-mail the news release and the plan to secure media coverage to the Steering, Events Planning, and Finance Committees for their review at Opening@ubi-sw.com. Use the subject **Feedback requested**. Compose an e-mail message that:

- States the news release and the plan to secure media coverage for the UBI grand opening are attached.

- Requests committees review both documents carefully. Also explain that comments have been inserted for their feedback. Tell them to respond to a comment, click in the comment, click Comment on the Insert menu, and then type their response in the new comment balloon.

- Requests them to make any changes to the document. The document has been set up to track changes. Tell them to save the document as *2-6task3 Last Name* in the Events Planning subfolder by January 25. Explain that the Events Planning Committee will incorporate all feedback as they finalize the news release and the media coverage plan.

**Note:** Use Mail Recipient (for Review) if available.

## TASK 4     NEWS RELEASE WITH MERGED COMMENTS

You are ready to finalize the news release. Open *2-6task1*, save it as *2-6task4*, and compare and merge it with the data file *2-6task4 quinn*. Accept all changes. Repeat this process with the data file *2-6task4 morgan*. Accept all changes; delete the comment made by Morgan.

Remove the watermark. Save the revised news release in the Events Planning subfolder as *2-6task4*.

## TASK 5     INVITATION

You are now ready to design the invitation to the UBI grand opening. Use your creativity in the design. Include the UBI logo and the following UBI grand opening details. (The vertical lines indicate what should be keyed on each line.) Save the document in the Events Planning subfolder as *2-6task5*.

---

**Grand Opening**

**University Business Incubator**

You are cordially invited to attend | the grand opening celebration of | University Business Incubator | 700 Lake Street, Suite 100 | Saturday, March 15, 20-- | ten o'clock | Dedication Ceremony | Ribbon Cutting | News Conference | Luncheon | Tours of New Facilities | RSVP 708-555-0192

## TASK 6 — ARTICLE (MANUSCRIPT)

Prepare a feature article in manuscript format about tips for the beginning entrepreneur that will be published in the local newspaper the week of the grand opening. The length of the article should be approximately two DS pages. Include a quote from Nicole Cox, president of UBI.

Use the Internet to locate information you need to compose the article. Be sure to use either a footnote or textual citation to document sources if you have a direct quote longer than three lines. End the article with this statement: **For more information, contact Yan Huang, public relations director of UBI, at 708-555-0176**.

Also, refer to the UBI open house for the public on Saturday, March 15, beginning at 10 a.m. with dedication and ribbon-cutting ceremony, luncheon, and tours of UBI. Save the document in the Events Planning subfolder as *2-6task6*.

## TASK 7 — NEWS RELEASE WEB PAGE

Create a hyperlink for *What's New* on the UBI website. Open the website file *2-1task1* you created earlier. Open the news release *2-6task4* and save in the UBI Web Site folder as a Web page; name the file *2-6task7 news release*.

Make the following edits.

- *Contact information:* Delete at top of news release.
- *Spell check:* Right-click and choose *Ignore All* to remove red wavy lines under words not in dictionary.
- *Theme:* Apply the theme Afternoon. (Delete several spaces in front of the address, if necessary, so the address and phone number fit on one line again.)

On the UBI Web page, select **What's New** and create a hyperlink to the *2-6task7 news release* file.

## TASK 8 — COMMUNICATION PRACTICES

With a teammate, make a list of the practices the grand opening Steering Committee has followed in Project 2 that build good communication skills. Save as *2-6task8*. Compare your list with another team's list. Write a short memo to your instructor indicating how you can apply at least one of these practices in your relationships at school.

# PROJECT 2 **CHECKPOINT**

## Self-Assessment  Evaluate your understanding of this project by answering the questions below.

1. You used the _____ feature to obtain feedback for finalizing the schedule of events for the grand opening.

2. To prepare for a meeting, you should create a(n) _____ to distribute to participants.

3. When receiving revised documents from several people, using _____ _____ is an easy way to combine all of the revisions.

4. To become more efficient, you created _____ to insert repetitive text.

5. What type of data source did you use to create the form letters to the grand opening committee members?

6. A written record of what happened during a meeting is called the _____.

7. Because budgets are usually revised, it is easier to prepare the budget as a(n) _____.

8. The top portion of a newsletter containing the company name and other identifying information is called a(n) _____ .

9. To format newsletters as columns, choose Columns from the _____ menu.

10. To format a Web page with a table of contents, use the _____ feature.

## Performance Assessment  Production Time: 20'

**Document 1**
**News Release**

1. Open *news release* from the data files.

2. Ann Quinn, CMF Public Relations Director, is preparing this news release as a service for the Oak Park Schools.

3. Carefully proofread the file and correct any errors that you find.

4. Add the correct contact information for Ann Quinn. Be sure to update the details in the last paragraph.

5. Insert the copy below as the second paragraph.

6. Key the appropriate footer at the bottom of the first page and an appropriate slug line as a header on the second page. Key the correct notation at the end of the document to indicate the end of the news release.

7. Save as *checkpoint2-d1* and print.

Participants will have an opportunity to enjoy hors d'oeuvres, see excellent musical and dramatic entertainment by students of Oak Park Schools, view award-winning student artwork, and bid on artwork by locally and nationally known artists.

## HOW DID YOU DO?

15 minutes:  Excellent
20 minutes  Good job

## YOU APPROACH

The *you* approach is an effective way to write business correspondence. The *you* approach means to focus on the reader and his or her interests. Not surprisingly, when you show readers consideration, they are more likely to do what you ask and to develop a positive attitude toward you and your company. To write with the *you* approach:

1. Use *you* rather than *I* or *we*.

   **Instead of:** We have three basic insurance plans.

   **Use:** You can choose from three basic insurance plans.

2. Use positive language, even in negative situations.

   **Instead of:** You did not return the signed credit agreement.

   **Use:** You will receive your new card as soon as we have your signed credit agreement.

3. Emphasize benefits to the reader.

   **Instead of:** If we do not receive payment by April 1, your account will be transferred to a collection agency.

   **Use:** To keep your good credit rating, please send your payment by April 1.

## Drill 1

### YOU APPROACH

1. Read the letter *hess scholars* from the data files. This letter is a good example of the *you* approach.
2. In a new document, key your name and the date at the upper left. Revise the sentences at the right so that they use the *you* approach and positive language. Invent details as necessary. Save as *cs2-drill1*.

1. We have several short-term loan packages available.
2. This job interests me, and I would like to schedule an interview with you.
3. We can't start the project for another two weeks.
4. As your receipt clearly states, you cannot get a cash refund after 30 days.
5. Our monthly access fee is $39.95.
6. Your report will be late because you failed to inform us that your last x-rays were done at Gurney Hospital.
7. I hope you plan to attend the meeting, because we need as many supporters as possible.
8. You forgot to fill in the last part of the form.

## Drill 2

### COMPOSE E-MAIL

Write an e-mail message using the you approach to your instructor, a classmate, or a friend. Inform your reader about an upcoming event or something you have learned; or try to persuade him or her to take an action—attend a game, help you with something, or contribute to a charity. Remember to use the *you* approach. Send the message with a copy to your instructor (unless the message was addressed to your instructor).

# PROJECT 3
# UBI Legal Services

**3-1**  Preparing Incorporation Documents

**3-2**  Preparing Employment Documents

**3-3**  Preparing Contracts

**3-4**  Creating Intellectual Property
Agreements

**FOCUS:** *Ethics*

You will provide administrative support in the Legal Services Department. One of the UBI legal assistants is out on leave for a month, and your knowledge of computer applications made you a natural choice to replace him. You will report to the director of Legal Services. The rules for the preparation of legal documents vary from venue to venue, state to state, and country to country; but in this project you will work with real legal documents that are typical in many companies. While working with these documents, you will be introduced to a variety of legal terms and reinforce your computer software skills.

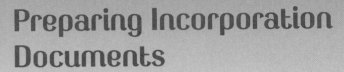

# Preparing Incorporation Documents

O b j e c t i v e s

- Prepare a certificate of incorporation
- Prepare a letter of transmittal
- Prepare corporate minutes
- Create a corporation checklist form

---

**TASK 1**  **CERTIFICATE OF INCORPORATION**

Filing the **Articles of Incorporation** registers a new corporation with the state.

These legal forms are included for instructional purposes only and should not be used without consulting an attorney.

We have been asked to prepare the **Articles of Incorporation** for Champion Sports Venue. The Certificate of Incorporation consists of articles for the certificate of incorporation for each state and a transmittal letter addressed to the appropriate state filing agency.

Open the protected form *cert-inc* from the data files. The password is UBI. Scroll through the document to familiarize yourself with its contents. Save as *3-1task1a*.

Unprotect the form. A style named Center Title has been applied to the centered headings. Modify the style to change all the centered headings to 14 point. With the Styles Task Pane still visible, select and bold the text **5.1 Authorized Capital Stock**. Click the **New Style** button in the Styles Task Pane, and key the new style name **Sidehead**. Click **OK**.

Select each of the two-digit side headings and apply the sidehead style throughout the rest of the document. In Article 5.2, indent the text 0.5" beginning with (i) through (xi). Add a header with the company name at the left and the form name at the right. Suppress the header on page 1.

Create a macro that adds a footer with the filename at the left and the page number at the right. Suppress the footer on page 1. This is the standard footer for all of our multiple-page legal documents, so make sure it can be used in all documents.

Add the following copy as paragraph 6.3. Be sure the paragraphs that follow it are numbered correctly. Protect the document and resave the file. Complete the form by adding the information provided on the next page to the fields. Save the revised file as *3-1task1b*.

Classes. The directors shall be divided into three classes, designated Class I, Class II, and Class III. Each class shall consist, as nearly as may be possible, of one-third of the total number of directors constituting the entire Board of Directors. Each director shall serve for a term ending on the date of the <Term> annual meeting of stockholders following the annual meeting at which such director was elected, provided that directors initially designated as Class I directors shall serve for a term ending on the date of the first annual meeting, directors initially designated as Class II directors shall serve for a term ending on the second annual meeting, and directors initially designated as Class III directors shall serve for a term ending on the date of the third annual meeting. Notwithstanding the foregoing, each director shall hold office until such director's resignation or removal. In the event of any change in the number of directors, the Board of Directors shall apportion any newly created directorships among, or reduce the number of directorships in, such class or classes as shall equalize, as nearly as possible, the number of directors in each class. In no event will a decrease in the number of directors shorten the term of any incumbent director.

*Information to be used for 3-1task1-b*

***Certificate of Incorporation of:*** Champion Sports Venues, Inc.

***Name of Corporation:*** Champion Sports Venues, Inc.

***Address:*** 700 Lake Street, Suite 123, Oak Park, IL 60301-7984

***Registered Agent:*** Tracy Glenn

***Total Stock:*** Fifty million (50,000,000)

***Common Stock:*** Forty million (40,000,000) ***Value:*** 0.001

***Preferred Stock:*** Ten million (10,000,000) ***Value:*** 0.001

***Director term ending on:*** Third

***Names of Directors:*** Tracy Glenn, Owner/CEO; Diane Byars, Vice President; Lu Wong, Secretary/Treasurer

**THINK CRITICALLY**

- What legal changes have occurred in recent years to hold corporations more accountable to their stockholders as well as to their employees and to the public at large?

# FOCUS ON THE WORKPLACE

### Ethics

## What is Ethics?

How do you define *ethics*? Most people think of right and wrong and the morality of the decisions we make. Your personal ethics may be different from someone else's. So how do you decide what is right and wrong in the workplace? *Business ethics* is the application of moral guidelines in the workplace. To encourage ethical behavior in the workplace, many companies develop a written *code of ethics* that outlines uniform standards and punishment. In addition, some companies hire an *ethics officer*, who is usually part of the human resources department. For more information on why it is important to create a code of ethics or guidelines for creating a code of ethics, visit **http://www.advancedapplications.swlearning.com**. Click **Links** and click **Project 3**.

To file the Articles of Incorporation for Champion Sports Venues, Inc. in Springfield, you must prepare a letter to the Illinois Secretary of State. This letter will be used to create the new corporation. Use the company letterhead (*CSV letterhead*) from the data files. UBI Legal also uses the block letter format with open punctuation. Check the Internet for the current Secretary of State's name; supply the salutation and the formal complimentary closing, *Very truly yours*. Send the letter from Mr. Tracy Glenn. Remember to include the appropriate enclosure notations. Add a footer with the filename at the left; save the file as *3-1task2*.

*Supply name*
Illinois Secretary of State
Corporation Division
2345 Randolph Street
Springfield, IL 62703

RE: Articles of Incorporation—Champion Sports Venues, Inc.

The original and duplicate original of the Articles of Incorporation for Champion Sports Venues, Inc. are enclosed together with our check for $150 to cover the filing fee.

Please return the duplicate original to the undersigned. If you have any questions regarding this matter, please feel free to contact me.

> **SUCCESS TIP**　Become familiar with a company's code of ethics *before* accepting a job. If possible, talk with employees to see how well the company follows its own code of ethics.

**minutes:** the official record of what took place at a meeting

Regardless of its size, by law a corporation must meet a minimum of once annually and record its organizational meeting transactions. Before you begin this task, read through the minutes to familiarize yourself with the contents of corporate minutes. Prepare the final version of the **minutes** of the Organizational Meeting of Drake Biotech Ventures, Inc. Review and use the standard format of legal documents on page 238 in the Reference Guide. DS the body.

Correct any errors you find, replace *Chairman* with *Chairperson*, and insert the following endnote using a lowercase alphabetic reference where indicated on the next page: **Lisa Bryant was absent from this meeting**.

Begin the first page at approximately 2.1", and add a footer beginning on the second page with the filename at the left and the page number at the right. Use Widow/Orphan control and Keep with next to ensure no headings are separated from the text that follows. Save the file as *3-1task3*.

# MINUTES OF ORGANIZATIONAL MEETING OF
# INCORPORATORS

The organization meeting of the incorporators of Drake Biotech Ventures, Inc. was held on the third day of December, 20--, at 7:00 p.m., pursuant to a written waiver of notice, signed by all the incorporators fixing said time and place.

The following incorporators were present in person: Kayla Frye, Paul Leski, Paula price, Edward Martin, Xian Wang, Bruce Lamar, and Gerald Odom, being all of the incorporators of the corporation. Kayla Frye acted as Chairman and Paul Leski was appointed Secretary of the meeting. *insert endnote*

The Chairman announced that a Certificate of Incorporation had been issued to this corporation by the State of Illinois and that a certified copy of the Certificate has been forwarded for recording in the Office of the Recorder of Deeds and instructed the Secretary to cause a copy of the Certificate of Incorporation to be prefixed to the minutes.

Upon motion, duly made, seconded, and carried, it was

**RESOLVED**, That the Certificate of Incorporation of the corporation be and it hereby is accepted and that this corporation proceed to do buisness thereunder.

The Secretary presented a form of Corporate Bylaws for the regulation of the affairs of the corporation, which were read article by article. Upon motion, duly made, seconded, and carried, said Bylaws were unanimously adopted and the Secretary was instructed to cause the same to be inserted in the minute book immediately following the copy of the Certificate of Incorporation.

The Chairman stated that the next business before the meeting was the election of a Board of Directors. Paula Price, Edward Martin, Xian Wang, Lisa Bryant, and Gerald Odom were nominated for directors of the corporation; to hold office for the ensuing year and until others are chosen and qualified in their stead. No other nominations having been made, the vote was taken and the aforesaid nominees declared duly elected.

Upon motion, duly made, seconded, and carried, it was

**RESOLVED**, That the Board of Directors be and they are hereby authorized to issue the capital stock of this corporation to the full amount or number of shares authorized by the Certificate of Incorporation, in such amounts and proportions as from time to time shall be determined by the Board, and to accept in full or in part payment thereof such property as the Board may determine shall be good and sufficient consideration and necessary for the business of the corporation.

Upon motion, duly made, seconded, and carried, it was

**RESOLVED**, That the proper officers of the corporation be and they hereby are authorised and directed on behalf of the corporation, and under its corporate seal, to make and file such certificate, report, or other intsrument as may be required by law to be filed in any state, territory, or dependency of the United States, or in any foreign country, in which said officers shall find it necessary or expedient to file the same to authorize the corporation to trasact business in such state, territory, dependency or foreign country.

Upon motion, duly made, seconded, and carried, it was

**RESOLVED**, That the Treasurer be and hereby is authorized to pay all fees and expenses incident to and necessary for the organization of the corporation.

Upon motion, duly made, seconded, and carried, the meeting thereupon adjourned.

_____

Paul Leski, Secretary

# FOCUS ON THE WORKPLACE

Ethics

## Legal or Ethical: What is the Difference?

Some actions that are legal are not very ethical. How is that possible? What is the difference between *legal* and *ethical*? The term *legal* refers to laws or rules established by the government. *Ethical* refers to values, beliefs, or attitudes of behavior. Acting ethically in the workplace is more than just obeying the law—it involves acting responsibly. Possibly, some actions that individuals consider ethical are illegal. Can you think of some workplace examples?

## TASK 4  CORPORATION CHECKLIST FORM

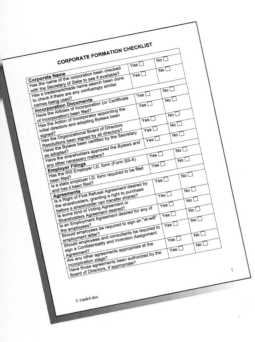

When working with new companies, UBI Legal Services uses a simple checklist to help them keep track of various legal tasks that need to be completed when forming a new company. You decide to create a form from an existing document to automate the process.

**Check your productivity:** Keep track of the time it takes you to complete this activity using the Total editing time feature on the Statistics tab of Properties. (Click **File Properties**.)

Open the data file *corpcheck* and save it as *3-1task4*. Select the text below the title and convert it to a one-column table, separating the text at paragraphs. Add two columns to the right and increase the width of the first column to approximately 3.75". Adjust the width of columns 2 and 3 to approximately 1". Change the title to 14 point, all caps.

Merge the cells in each row that contains a heading and create a style named *Row Head* with 13 point, Arial, bold. Apply the style to each row heading.

Insert the following comment at the end of the title line: **This form must be used for all new UBI companies. Simply check the appropriate box for each question.**

In column 2, key **Yes** followed by a space; then add a checkbox form field. In column 3, key **No** followed by a space and add another checkbox form field. Copy and paste these items into the remaining question rows.

Run your multiple-page footer macro to insert the filename and page number in a footer. The footer should not appear on the first page. Protect the form and save the file.

Print and close the file.

### HOW DID YOU DO?

Record the number of minutes it took you to complete this task. _____

Now that you have completed the task, take some time to scroll through the document to familiarize yourself with its contents.

## TASK 5  LEGAL PLEADING

Use the Pleading Wizard to create a legal pleading. Once you access the templates, click the **Legal Pleadings** tab; then double-click **Pleading Wizard**. Select **Create a new pleading template for another court**, and then click **Next**. Type the name of the court as follows: **SUPERIOR COURT OF THE STATE OF WASHINGTON**.

Leave the court name aligned at the left and click **Next**. The page settings for most courts should remain as Courier font, double-spaced, 25 lines per page, 8.5" x 11" paper, and 1" margins all around; so click **Next**.

The default is for line numbers to appear starting at 1 and incrementing by 1. Click **Next**.

Leave the border at double on the left and single on the right, again as this is what most courts require. Click **Next**.

The caption box should be in Style 1. Click **Next**.

Information at the beginning of the pleading should be **Attorney and Firm Names**. Information in the footer should be **Summary of pleading title** and **Page Numbers**. Click **Next**.

The next screen asks you if you want a signature block. Choose **Yes**, but select sign with **Plain** and put the firm name and address below the attorney's name. Make sure the **Include <date> before signature** box is checked. Click **Next**.

Save the template as *3-1task5* and click **Next**. Click **Finish** to create your legal pleading. Now the pleading template is ready to use. Use the information below to complete the legal pleading.

SUPERIOR COURT OF THE STATE OF WASHINGTON

**Plaintiff:** Judith R. Robinson, et al

**Attorney for the Plaintiff:**     Brick Vandersnick Law Firm
3829 Spring Street
Chicago, IL 60630-2849

**Defendant:** Steven Johnson, et al

*This information does not appear on the document.*

**Attorney for the Defendant:** Wilson, Leavy, and Garcia

**Case No.:** 01-37-97-36

Key the pleading text. Spell-check and proofread the document. At the end of the copy, insert the datafile *plead-insert*.

Save the file as *3-1task5*. Print and close the file.

**Pleading Text:**

Defendants operate a company website that contains a database listing employee names, addresses, telephone numbers, social security numbers, and other personal information.

Plaintiffs assert that publication of this personal information invades their privacy interests and is causing them undue exposure to identity theft since the site is susceptible to intrusion by unauthorized users.

**The Issue for this Court.** No challenge is raised at this time to the legality of defendants' access to plaintiffs' private information. The only question presented in this Motion is whether plaintiffs can, by asserting a right to privacy, stop the dissemination of any or all personal information that has come into the defendants' hands.

**Washington State Law Addresses Only the Question of Access to Information.** In the State of Washington there is a Constitutional provision that appears to address privacy. Article 1, Section 7, which was adopted in 1889, states simply, "No person shall be disturbed in his private affairs, or his home invaded, without authority of law." This Constitutional provision has been interpreted as relating solely to possible governmental intrusion into private affairs. See, e.g., State v. Myrick, 102 Wn.2d 506 (1984). It therefore provides no assistance in resolving this dispute.

## TASK 6      ETHICS ALIVE (MANUSCRIPT)

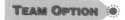 **TEAM OPTION**

Ethics are an important part of every business.

1. Form teams of three or four classmates.

2. Develop a code of ethics. Include such topics as:

   • Lying or cheating.

   • Taking credit or responsibility only for your own actions or work.

   • Using company or school property for personal needs (include computers, the Internet, e-mail, supplies, copiers, etc.).

   • Keeping information confidential.

3. Search the Internet for information on ethics. See if you can locate company codes of ethics.

4. Encourage each team to share its ideas with the other teams to determine whether you agree on what should be included in a code of ethics.

5. Key the code of ethics in manuscript format (double-spaced report) and distribute it to the class. Have one or two students present the findings orally.

# Preparing Employment Documents

### Objectives

- Create a non-competition contract
- Compose an employment letter
- Prepare an executive employee agreement
- Prepare an employee accident form

## TASK 1 — non-competition contract

Adjust the right-aligned tab in the footer to the side margins in this file.

UBI companies request a non-competition (non-compete) agreement stating that the seller of a business agrees that for a certain period of time, he/she will not, directly or indirectly, compete with that business in a designated area.

1. Open the data file *noncomp*, and save it as *3-2task1 form*. Scroll through the document to familiarize yourself with its contents. Change all underlines in the body of the contract (except the sections and signature lines at the end) to text form fields. Leave one space before and after each field. In Section 7, insert the six text form fields, and then underline each one.

2. Justify all text, change the title to 14 point and center. Modify Heading 3 style to add Keep with Next (if it is not already selected) and increase the spacing after to 6 points. Apply this style to each section title. Add the standard footer to all pages except the first.

3. In Section 1, add this new subsection 1.2 and renumber the next section:

   "Retained Business" means the business and assets of Seller being retained by it.

4. In Section 2, delete subsection 2.2. Renumber the remaining sections. Move to Section 13, and add the following sentence at the end:

   Notwithstanding the foregoing, this Agreement is additional to and not in lieu of the rights and obligations of the parties under the Consulting Agreement between the parties.

5. Run your multiple-page footer macro to insert the filename and page number in a footer. Protect the form and save it again. Then fill in the form with the following information and save it as *3-2task1*.

---

Date:  Sixth day of November 20--; **Purchaser**:  Joshua Foster; **Seller**: Rhonda Pokoj; **Territory**:  One hundred (100) mile radius of Chicago city limits; **Period of Non-Compete**:  Five (5) years

| **Seller** | Rhonda Pokoj | **Purchaser** | Joshua Foster |
| --- | --- | --- | --- |
| **Address** | 189 Lakeshore Drive | **Address** | 700 Lake Street, Suite 300 |
| | Chicago, IL 60611-6312 | | Oak Park, IL 60301-7984 |

# FOCUS ON THE WORKPLACE

## Maintaining Confidentiality at Work

Confidentiality is crucial for many businesses because it allows them to be competitive. Think about what might happen to a fast-food restaurant if its secret recipe became public information. If you reveal a company's confidential information, you are violating ethical standards. In addition, you might be held legally responsible for any losses the company suffers. Companies guard their confidential information by making employees sign confidentiality agreements. Typical examples of confidential company information include the following:

Manufacturing processes     Recipes
Computer codes     Product information
Customer lists     Business strategies
Marketing plans     Technical drawings
Financial trade secrets

---

**TASK 2**      **EMPLOYMENT LETTER (PROTECTED FORM)**

This letter will serve as the standard legal employment agreement for many of UBI's clients. Scroll through the document to familiarize yourself with its contents. Key the letter replacing bold text in brackets with text form fields. Run your multiple-page footer macro to insert the filename and page number. Add two lines at the end of the letter at the left margin for the employee to sign and date the agreement. Adjust the spacing between letter parts or the side margins so that the signature lines are on the second page. Protect the form and save it as *3-2task2*. Print and close the form.

[Date]

[Address block]

Dear [Salutation]

[Company] (the "Company") is pleased to offer you a position as [Position], at a salary, payable twice per month, which is equivalent to a yearly salary of [Salary]. In addition, you will be eligible for an annual bonus up to [Bonus], solely at the discretion of the Board of Directors. The Company will also compensate you for reasonable out-of-pocket expenses incurred for the relocation of your family and your belongings.

You will also be entitled to the benefits that the Company customarily makes available to employees in positions comparable to yours, and it will be recommended to the Board of Directors that you be granted an option for the purchase of [Share amount] shares of the Company's Common Stock. The option will be granted under the Company's Stock Option Plan and, assuming you remain an employee, will vest with respect to 25 percent of the shares subject to the option one year after the commencement of your employment and, at the end of each month thereafter, with respect to an additional 1/48 of the shares subject to the option; provided, however, that if your employment is terminated by the Company other than for "Cause" during your first year of employment, the option will vest, at the end of each month, with respect to 1/48 of the shares subject to the option.

vesting: giving an employee a right to share in a pension fund in the event of termination of employment

No other acceleration of vesting will occur in connection with any termination of your employment or any acquisition of the Company. Per federal legislation, at least half of the shares underlying the stock option must be purchased for cash at the option exercise price, as soon as possible after the grant is approved. These shares will be subject to a repurchase option in favor of the Company to the extent they are "Unvested."

If your employment is terminated by the Company other than for "Cause" at any time during your employment, you will continue to receive salary compensation for an additional six months and, if at the end of such period you remain unemployed, you will be eligible for additional salary compensation for the lesser of (i) six months, or (ii) until you find other employment.

The Company asks that you complete the enclosed "Employee Confidential Information and Inventions Agreement" prior to commencing employment. In part, this Agreement requests that a departing employee refrain from using or disclosing said Company's Confidential Information (as defined in the Agreement) in any manner which might be detrimental to or conflict with the business interests of said Company or its employees. This Agreement does not prevent a former employee from using his or her general knowledge and experience no matter when or how gained in any new field or position.

Under federal immigration laws, the Company is required to verify each new employee's identity and legal authority to work in the United States. Accordingly, please be prepared to furnish appropriate documents satisfying those requirements; this offer of employment is conditioned on submission of satisfactory documentation.

| SUCCESS TIP | Keep business information confidential. Revealing confidential information is a violation of ethics, and you could be held liable for any losses the business suffers as a result. |

The Patent and Trademark Office website provides a wealth of information on trademarks, including a database of registered trademarks as well as pending trademark applications. The European Patent Office website provides information on foreign patents and includes the European Patent Office's mission statement. To learn more about these sites, visit http://www.advancedapplications.swlearning.com. Click Links and click **Project 3.**

We hope that you and the Company will find mutual satisfaction with your employment. All of us are very excited about your joining our team and look forward to a beneficial and fruitful relationship. Nevertheless, employees have the right to terminate their employment at any time with or without cause or notice, and the Company reserves for itself an equal right. We both agree that any dispute arising with respect to your employment, the termination of that employment, or a breach of any covenant of good faith and fair dealing related to your employment shall be conclusively settled by final and binding arbitration in accordance with the Voluntary Labor Arbitration Rules of the American Arbitration Association (AAA) at the AAA office in Springfield.

This letter and the "Employee Confidential Information and Inventions Agreement" contain the entire agreement with respect to your employment. The terms of this offer may only be changed by written agreement, although the Company may from time to time, in its sole discretion, adjust the salaries and benefits paid to you and its other employees. Should you have any questions with regard to any of the items indicated above, please call me. Kindly indicate your consent to this employment agreement by signing and returning a copy of this letter and the completed "Employee Confidential Information and Inventions Agreement" to me by the close of business on **[Date]**, **[Year]**. Upon your signature below, this will become our binding agreement with respect to your employment and its terms merging and superseding in their entirety all other or prior agreements and communications by you as to the specific subjects of this letter.

Very truly yours

**[Executive]**

_____
Employee's Name

_____
Date

THINK **CRITICALLY**

- Who do you think is better protected by this agreement—the employer or the employee—and why?

The Executive Employment Agreement contains the terms of employment and states compensation and benefits to be earned by the prospective employee during the employee's service to the company.

This lengthy document has been saved as five individual files to make editing easier. You will need to compile the subdocuments into a master document and create a table of contents. Styles have been applied to all but one document.

Open the data file *comp*. Modify Heading 1 style to Arial 13 point with 12 points before and 6 points after. Apply **Heading 1** to the following side headings: *Employment*, *Performance of Duties*, and *Compensation*. Save the file as *3-2task3*.

Change to Outline View and insert the following data files as subdocuments at the end of the file. If you are prompted to rename a style, answer **Yes to All**, and then save the file.

*benefits*

*termination*

*confidential*

*witness*

Once the subdocuments are inserted in the master document, return to Normal View and generate a table of contents at the beginning of the document using the defaults. Insert a Next Page Section Break between the table of contents and the first page of the document text.

Create a footer in Section 1 (the table of contents) to insert the page number as a lowercase Roman numeral aligned at the right margin. Edit the footer in Section 2 to remove the link to Section 1. Add the filename at the left margin and start the page number with Arabic 1 at the right margin. Suppress the footer on the first page.

Update the table of contents. Resave the file. Print only the table of contents and the first page of the file. Close the file.

> Use Insert Subdocument on the Outlining toolbar to insert the files.

---

**THINK CRITICALLY**

- What does indemnification mean?
- What employee benefits would you like to have?

# FOCUS ON THE WORKPLACE

## Blowing the Whistle

A *whistle-blower* is an employee who reveals the illegal or unethical actions of his or her company or another employee. When your company is involved in harmful or illegal practices, the effect on all concerned parties should outweigh your company loyalty. Though blowing the whistle is the ethical thing to do, some risks are involved.

---

**TASK 4**　　　　　　EMPLOYEE ACCIDENT REPORT

Use Draw Table to create rows of varying length.

Whenever an employee has an accident, this Employee Accident Report is completed to record it. Create this form as a table with a row height of 0.5" and a border style of your choice. Create a footer macro that will be used on one-page documents to insert the filename as a footer at the left margin. Depending on the document length, you will use one of the two footer macros on each document you create. Center the page vertically. Save the file as *3-2task4*. Print and close the file.

### EMPLOYEE ACCIDENT REPORT

| Name | | Date |
|---|---|---|
| Address | | |
| Social Security No. | Home Phone | |
| Job Title | | |
| Describe Accident | | |
| Date and Time of Accident | Signature of Employee | |

---

**THINK CRITICALLY**

- Why is it important for a company to keep accurate records of employee accidents?
- Identify some situations when an employer should be held financially responsible for employee injuries. Identify some situations when employees should be held accountable for their injuries.

Open *health form* from the data files and save it as *3-2task5*.

The completed form should look similar to the figure below. The form was created in a table. It needs to have text form fields added after each request for information.

Insert checkbox form fields where indicated on the form. Use your macro to insert the filename at the left margin. Protect the form, and then save and print it. Close the file.

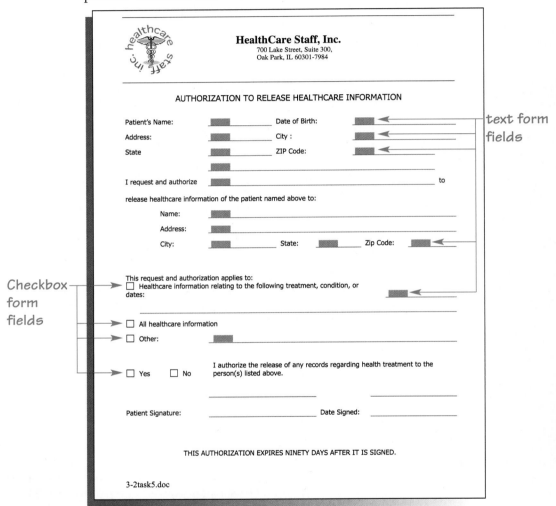

The Health Insurance Portability and Accountability Act (HIPA) legislation requires any business that uses a health-care provider to protect individuals' personal health information. It gives patients increased access to their medical records. Conduct research on the Internet to see how business owners of all types and sizes are affected by this legislation.

## THINK CRITICALLY

- How can a small-business owner manage to stay up to date with all the changes in legislation while at the same time successfully running the business?

# JOB 3-3

# Preparing Contracts

### Objectives

- Prepare a lease agreement form
- Prepare an independent contractor checklist
- Prepare an invoice with *Excel*
- Compare consulting agreements
- Track changes to a consulting agreement

## TASK 1     LEASE AGREEMENT (FILL-IN FORM)

**lease:** a contract by which one conveys equipment, real estate, or facilities for a specified term and a specified amount

We use a standard lease agreement for tenants who rent office space in our building. Create the lease as a form with fields replacing the copy in brackets.

Change the title to 14 point and add the signature lines as shown in the illustration. Set the paragraph indent to 1", use the macro to add the standard footer for a one-page document, protect the form, and save it as *3-3task1-lease*.

Complete the lease for a new tenant using the information provided on the next page. Save the completed lease as *3-3task1*.

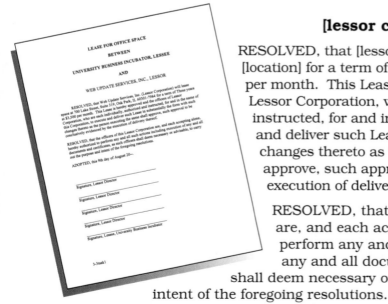

### LEASE FOR OFFICE SPACE BETWEEN

### UNIVERSITY BUSINESS INCUBATOR, LESSEE

### AND

### [lessor company name], LESSOR

RESOLVED, that [lessor] (Lessor Corporation) will lease space at [location] for a term of [years of lease] years at $[price per month] per month. This Lease is hereby approved and the officers of the Lessor Corporation, who are each individually, authorized and instructed, for and in the name of this Corporation, to execute and deliver such Lease in substantially the form with such changes thereto as the person executing the same shall approve, such approval to be conclusively evidenced by the execution of delivery thereof.

RESOLVED, that the officers of this Lessor Corporation are, and each accepting alone, hereby authorized to perform any and all such actions including execution of any and all documents and certificates, as such officers shall deem necessary or advisable, to carry out the purpose and intent of the foregoing resolutions.

ADOPTED, this [date] day of [month] [year].

_____

Signature, Lessor Director

*Repeat 3 more times*

Signature, Lessee, University Business Incubator

**Lessor:** Web Update Service, Inc.

**Location:** 700 Lake Street, Suite 319, Oak Park, IL 60301-7984

**Years of Lease:** Three

**Price per Month:** $3,500

**Date:** 9th of August, 20--

## TASK 2  INDEPENDENT CONTRACTOR CHECKLIST

You can select multiple headings at once using the CTRL key.

This Independent Contractor Checklist contains sample questions for a prospective consultant or independent contractor. It needs some additional formatting. Open the data file *indcon* and save it as *3-3task2*.

Apply **Heading 3** for the main heading. Modify Heading 3 so that it applies horizontal center alignment. With all heading categories selected, remove all underlining, apply a top and bottom 1/2-point paragraph border, and add 12-point paragraph spacing before and 6-point paragraph spacing after. Bullet all items under each category.

Use the macro to insert the standard footer for multiple-page documents. Suppress the footer on the first page. Save, print, and close the file.

# FOCUS ON THE WORKPLACE

### Ethics

## Ethics Around the Globe

Ethics becomes an even more confusing concept when we consider the vastly different beliefs and attitudes of people from around the world. For example, it is ethical to show up for work on time in the United States, but it is not considered a priority in some other countries. It is unethical and illegal to offer bribes in the United States, yet certain countries consider it an accepted practice.

In addition to ethical differences, there are also legal differences that need to be considered when conducting business around the world. You will find that not all countries have strict laws regarding copyrights and patents or child labor. It is important to be aware of legal and ethical requirements when conducting business around the globe.

UBI uses a standard invoice to bill for its legal services. Prepare an invoice for work completed for HealthCare Staff, Inc. during the month of April.

**Check your productivity:** Keep track of the time it takes you to complete this activity using the Statistics tab of Properties.

Open the *Excel* data file *invoice* and save it as *3-3task3*; then make the following changes:

| | |
|---|---|
| Cell A8: | insert **April** |
| Cell A10 | address the invoice to **Alyssa Wang** |
| Cell A11 | key the company name: **HealthCare Staff, Inc.** |
| Cell A12 | key the address: **700 Lake Street, Suite 305** |
| Cell A13 | key the city: **Oak Park, IL 60301-7984** |

Add the services performed that follow. Then insert a formula in cell E16 and copy it to cells E17, E18, and E19. Insert a formula to total the invoice in cell E20. Format cell E20 as Currency with no digits after the decimal. Add a footer with the filename at the left. Save, print, and close the file.

| | Description of Work Performed | Hours | Rate |
|---|---|---|---|
| *April 4* | *Prepare Corporate Bylaws* | *1* | *50* |
| *April 10* | *Prepare Tax Forms* | *6* | *50* |
| *April 18* | *Specialized Consulting* | *2* | *50* |
| *April 30* | *Monthly Word Processing Charges* | *10* | *15* |

## HOW DID YOU DO?

Record the number of minutes it took you to complete this task. _____

**consulting agreement:** a contract between a company and an individual or other organization hired to assist the company with certain tasks for a limited period of time

You have been asked to make changes to a **consulting agreement**. To facilitate proofreading by the client, you need to indicate where changes were made. Use Compare and Merge to show the revisions.

Open the data file *conagree*, and save it as *3-3task4*. Change the title to 14 point and center it. Apply **Heading 3** style to headings in all caps. Delete Section 1.2 and add Section 4.3 as follows:

> 4.3 The Consultant shall also be entitled to such additional increments and bonuses as shall be determined from time to time by the Board of Directors of the Company.

Move Section 7.3 before Section 7.2 and renumber each section as necessary. Use the multiple-page footer macro to add the filename at the left and the page number at the right. Suppress the footer on page 1. Resave the file. Compare *3-3task4* with *conagree*. Merge the changes and save the merged document as *3-3task4 compare*. Print and close the file.

The Consulting Agreement needs to be revised again. This time, use Track Changes to show changes you make to the file.

Open the data file *conagree*, and save it as *3-3task5*. Turn on Track Changes. Delete Section 1.2 and add Section 4.3 as follows:

4.3 The Consultant shall also be entitled to such additional increments and bonuses as shall be determined from time to time by the Board of Directors of the Company.

Move Section 7.3 before Section 7.2 and renumber the sections as necessary. Use the multiple-page footer macro to add the filename at the left and the page number at the right. Suppress the footer on page 1.

Add the following sections in the correct position and be sure the remaining sections are numbered correctly. Save, print, and close the file.

9. PARTICIPATION IN EMPLOYEE BENEFIT PLANS To the extent permitted by the terms of such plans and of any insurance policies purchased under such plans, the Consultant and any beneficiary of the Consultant shall be accorded the right to participate in and receive benefits under and in accordance with the provisions of any insurance, medical and dental insurance, or reimbursement program of the Company.

10. KEY-PERSON INSURANCE The Company presently owns a life insurance policy on the Consultant's life in the face amount of Five Million Dollars. The Company shall remain the owner and beneficiary thereof and shall pay the annual premium of such policy during the term hereof. Upon the termination of the Consulting Period, for any reason whatsoever, the policy shall be assigned to Consultant.

11. INJUNCTIVE RELIEF The Consultant acknowledges and agrees that, in the event any of the restrictions of Articles 3 and 7 herein are violated, the Company will be without adequate remedy at law and will therefore be entitled to enforce such restrictions by temporary or permanent injunctive or mandatory relief obtained in an action or may have at law or in equity, and the Consultant hereby consents to the jurisdiction of such Court for such purpose, provided that reasonable notice of any proceeding is given, it being understood that such injunction shall be in addition to any remedy which the Company may have at law or otherwise.

Search the Internet using keywords such as *employee theft* and *computer crime*. See if you can locate recent news stories involving misuse of the Internet or other computer crimes.

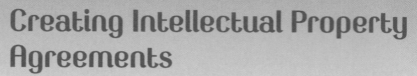

# JOB 3-4

## Creating Intellectual Property Agreements

**Objectives**

- Prepare intellectual property agreement
- Create flyer for legal forum
- Create license agreement outline
- Prepare corporate Internet use policy

---

## TASK 1  INTELLECTUAL PROPERTY AGREEMENT

**intellectual property:** names, images, likenesses, voices, signatures, or other elements of persona and identity

UBI's **Intellectual Property** Agreement is being revised. You have been asked to make revisions while keeping all versions of the file so they can be reviewed. Oftentimes, you will want to go back to a previous version of a file, and versioning helps you keep track of multiple copies of a file in one place.

Open the data file *intprop*. Set the file to automatically save a version on close. Save the file as *3-4task1checked*. Spell-check the file and make necessary corrections. Go to Versions, click **Save Now**, and add the following versions comment: **spell-checked version**. Resave the file.

To save a version of a file, choose **File** menu, **Versions**.

Create a paragraph style named *my number* that uses Arabic numbers with 6-point spacing after each number. Apply the style beginning with the paragraph that starts *The Company's Acknowledgment of Licensor's Rights* through the remainder of the document. Save this version of the file as *3-4task1numbered* and add the following versions comment: **numbered version**. Delete Section 4 and then save the file as *3-4task1deleted*. Save this version and add the following versions comment: **Section 4 deleted**.

Use your multiple-page footer macro to add a footer that includes the filename at the left and page number at the right. Save this version as *3-4task1footer*. Add the following versions comment: **footer version**. Click the **File** menu and select **Versions** to view the various versions of this file. Print the Numbered version. Close the file. If prompted to save the file, click **Yes**.

---

## TASK 2 LEGAL FORUM FLYER

UBI Legal Services is planning to host a legal forum entitled *Legal Issues in the Workplace*. You have been asked to prepare a flyer that can be mailed to all business clients.

Create a flyer for the forum from the information on the next page. Use landscape orientation, a two-column format, and clip art of your choice. Use a large font size for the heading and center it above the columns at the top of the flyer. Italicize the name of each workshop session. Use a different font face to set off the registration information from the rest of the text. Add an appropriate page border. Use your footer macro to add the filename at the left. Save as *3-4task2*.

You are invited to attend

Legal Issues in the Workplace

Sponsored by University Business Incubator Legal Services

**Keynote Session**
8:00 a.m. to 9:00 a.m.
Violence in the Workplace—
Are You Protected?
Nicole Cox, UBI President/CEO
Lafayette Ballroom

**Are Your Workers Flying High?**
Drug Testing in the Workplace
9:15 a.m. to 10:30 a.m.
Room 100

**When Is Hands-on Training
Sexual Harassment?**
10:45 a.m. to Noon
Room 102

**Lunch Noon to 1**
Lafayette Ballroom

**Protection of Trade Secrets**
1:15 p.m. to 2:45 p.m.
Room 104

**Risk Management Issues**
3:00 p.m. to 4:15 p.m.
Room 204

**If Employees Fall Down
the Elevator Shaft,
Who Pays the Freight?**
4:30 p.m. to 5:45 p.m.
Room 200

**Networking Reception**
6:00 p.m. to 8:00 p.m.

*Registration Information*

November 28, 20--
Chicago Sheraton Civic Center
1440 Michigan Avenue
Chicago, IL 60610

Register today!

Phone 708-555-0176
Fax 708-555-0137
$100 per person

---

**You are invited to attend**
**Legal Issues in the Workplace**
**Sponsored by University Business Incubator Legal Services**

Keynote Session
8:00 a.m. to 9:00 a.m.
Violence in the WorkplaceÑAre You Protected?
Nicole Cox, UBI President/CEO
Lafayette Ballroom

Are Your Workers Flying High?
Drug Testing in the Workplace
9:15 a.m. to 10:30 a.m.
Room 100

When Is Hands-on Training Sexual Harassment?
10:45 a.m. to Noon
Room 102

Lunch Noon to 1
Lafayette Ballroom

Protection of Trade Secrets
1:15 p.m. to 2:45 p.m.
Room 104

Risk Management Issues
3:00 p.m. to 4:15 p.m.
Room 204

3-4task2.doc

If Employees Fall Down the Elevator Shaft,
Who Pays the Freight?
4:30 p.m. to 5:45 p.m.
Room 200

Networking Reception
6:00 p.m. to 8 p.m.

**November 28, 20--**
**Chicago Sheraton Civic Center**
**1440 Michigan Avenue**
**Chicago, IL 60610**

**Register today!**

**Phone 708-555-0176**
**Fax 708-555-0137**
**$100 per person**

# FOCUS ON THE WORKPLACE

## An Employee's Ethical Responsibilities Regarding the Internet

The use of e-mail and the Internet in the workplace has grown at an astounding rate. Employees have a responsibility to apply ethical and legal standards when using these communications. Some issues to be aware of include the following:

- *Confidential e-mail*. E-mail can be broadcast around the world. When you are sending or responding to a confidential e-mail message, be sure you send it only to authorized people.
- *Copyrighted material*. Much of the information on the Web is protected by copyright laws. To avoid violation of copyright, always give credit to the originator of the information. For example, if you are creating a company brochure that provides information collected from websites, give credit to the source of the information.
- *Copyrighted music*. Employees who download and play music at work are using company time for personal business, which is unethical. This may also cause the network to slow down. In addition, downloading copyrighted music without the artist's permission may be illegal.

---

## TASK 3 — LICENSE AGREEMENT OUTLINE

### SUCCESS TIP

Do not use your computer at work for personal business.

This outline contains information regarding a license agreement. Use the second list style under Bullets and Numbering (1. for level 1; 1.1 for level 2; and 1.1.1 for level 3). Add the title **Software License Agreement** at the top of the outline as Body Text. Do not tap ENTER. Insert a Continuous Section Break after the title. Use a top margin of 2" for Section 1, and a top margin of 1" for Section 2. Use your multiple-page footer macro to add the filename at the left and page number at the right. Verify that the footer did not automatically link to Section 1 and repeat on the first page of the document. If it did, adjust the footer so that it only prints on page 2. Save the file as *3-4task3* and print.

Definitions
   Confidential Information
   Disclosing Party
   Receiving Party
   Proprietary
Licenses
   Development and Documentation License
   Distribution License
   Compatibility and Trademark License
   Right to Sublicense
   Inspection Rights
   Limitation on Scope of Agreement
   End-User Licensing
Delivery and Sourcing
   Delivery of Licensed Materials
   Third-Party Sourcing

Royalty, Fees, and Reports
    Royalties
    Maintenance and Support Fees
    Reports
Payment Terms
    Payment
    Royalty-Free Products
    Taxes
Update Responsibilities and Enhancements
Support
    Development Support
    Customer Support
    Technical Support Levels
        First-Level Support
        Second-Level Support
        Third-Level Support
    Support Timing
    Direct Customer Support
Marketing and Publicity
    Marketing
    Publicity
    Branding
    Nonsolicitation
Proprietary Rights
    Title
    Proprietary Rights Notices
    U.S. Government Restricted Rights Legend
Indemnification
    Remedies
    Other Indemnity
Confidentiality
Limits of Liability
Export Regulations
Term and Termination
    Right to Terminate
    Effect of Termination
    Survival
Miscellaneous
    Notices
    Amendments
    Severability
    Governing Law
    Choice of Forum
    Injunctive Relief
    Attorneys' Fees

## THINK CRITICALLY

- What is proprietary information?
- Look up the definition of indemnity and provide examples.

You have been asked to finalize the Corporate Internet Policy, which establishes the rules for Internet access and use by company employees and others whom it may authorize, including agents and contractors.

Open the data file *intpol* and save it as *3-4task4*. Scroll through the document to familiarize yourself with its contents. Apply **Heading 1** style to the main heading and center it. Apply **Heading 2** style to all major subheadings. Apply **Heading 3** style with italic to all secondary subheadings (such as 3.1, 3.2, etc.). Use your multiple-page footer to add the filename at the left and page number at the right. Remember to unlink the footer from Section 1 so the footer does not print on page 1.

Search the Internet using keywords such as *intellectual property, intellectual law,* and *intellectual rights*. You may also want to visit http://www.advancedapplications.swlearning.com. Click **Links** and click **Project 3**.

# TASK 5

# ETHICAL ISSUES

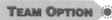

Many companies provide a general framework for acceptable behavior both in the workplace and when representing the company outside the workplace. Companies want employees who work with integrity, in their own best interests, and in the best interest of the company.

1. Create a team of three students. Using the information you have read in this project about ethical behavior, develop ten questions covering various issues that you and your team could use to survey employers in your community regarding ethical issues in the workplace and standards of personal conduct.

2. Edit the survey closely, making sure each question focuses on a single topic.

3. Administer the survey to at least ten business people in your community. Telephone or visit at least three human resource representatives or directors. Check with other teams in your class so that you are not contacting the same employers.

4. Summarize your findings in a 1–2 page report. Work as a team to write, edit, and finalize the report.

5. As a team, present your findings to the class. Include one or more visuals in the presentation.

# PROJECT 3 CHECKPOINT

## Self-Assessment
Evaluate your understanding of this project by answering the questions below. Key your answers, if necessary.

1. What feature in *Word* inserts information such as the filename or a page number at the top or bottom of each page of a document? What additional feature of *Word* can you use when you are repetitively inserting the same types of information at the top or bottom of your documents?

2. Explain the purpose of Widow/Orphan control.

3. Explain the purpose of text form fields in a document.

4. _____ are the application of moral guidelines in the workplace.

5. Name the benefits of using the master document feature of *Word*.

6. The official record of what took place at a meeting is referred to as _____.

7. List two examples of confidential company information.

8. A(n) _____ is an employee who reveals the illegal or unethical actions of his or her company or of another employee.

9. Explain why ethics becomes even more confusing when companies are engaged in global business.

10. _____ _____ includes names, images, likenesses, voices, signatures, or other elements of persona and identity.

## Performance Assessment
Production Time: 25' (maximum)

**Document 1**
**Monthly Invoice**
Check the number of minutes it took you to complete Task 3, page 71. Try to improve your time on this activity.

## How Did You Do?

Record the number of minutes it took you to complete this task. _____
Compare this time with that of Task 3, page 71. Indicate whether your time improved or not and by how much.
_____

1. Open the data file *invoice*, save it as *checkpoint3-d1*, and prepare the October invoice for Champion Sports Venues.

2. Insert the following information:
   A8: October
   A10: Mr. Tracy Glenn
   A11: Champion Sports Venues, Inc.
   A12: 700 Lake Street, Suite 123
   A13: Oak Park, IL 60301-7984

3. Complete the invoice using the following information:

| Date | Service | Hours | Rate |
|---|---|---|---|
| October 4 | Legal consulting | 3 | 50 |
| October 10 | Fax | 9 | .10 |
| October 22 | Photocopying | 215 | .05 |
| October 31 | Monthly word processing | 12 | 15 |

4. Insert a formula in cell E16 that multiplies Amount times Rate. Copy the formula to cells E17, E18, and E19. In cell A20, insert the formula to total the invoice.

5. Format the *Total* column as Currency, and include a dollar sign in the final total. Add a footer with the filename at the left. Save and print the invoice.

# PROJECT 3 CHECKPOINT

**Document 2**
**Table of Intellectual**
**Property Terminology**

## HOW DID YOU DO?

Record the number of minutes it took you to complete this task. _____

Compare this time with that of Task 4, page 59. Indicate whether your time improved or not and by how much.

_____

Check the number of minutes it took you to complete Task 4, page 59. Try to improve your time on this activity.

1. Open the data file *intprop-terms*. Save it as *checkpoint3-d2*.

2. Scroll through the document to familiarize yourself with its contents.

3. Select the text, and convert it to a table with two columns, separating the text at tabs.

4. Change the side margins to 1" and the top and bottom margins to .75".

5. Reduce the width of the first column to fit the text attractively on one page.

6. Insert a row at the top of the table and merge the cells. Key the following title in the new row in 14 point bold and center it: **Intellectual Property Terminology**.

7. Apply the **Table Classic 2** AutoFormat, and deselect the Last row checkbox.

8. Use your footer macro to insert the filename at the left.

9. Save the table again as *checkpoint3-d2* and print.

**CAPITALIZATION GUIDES**

## Capitalize:

1. **First word of a sentence and of a direct quotation.**

   > We were tolerating instead of managing diversity.
   > The speaker said, "We must value diversity, not merely recognize it."

2. **Proper nouns**—specific persons, places, or things.

   > *Common nouns:* continent, river, car, street
   > *Proper nouns:* Asia, Mississippi, Buick, State St.
   > *Exception:* Capitalize a title of high distinction even when it does not refer to a specific person (e.g., President of the United States).

3. **Derivatives** of proper nouns and **geographical** names.

   > *Derivatives:* American history, German food, English accent, Ohio Valley
   > *Proper nouns:* Tampa, Florida, Mount Rushmore

4. **A personal or professional title** when it precedes the name; capitalize a title of high distinction without a name.

   > *Title:* Lieutenant Kahn, Mayor Walsh, Doctor Welby
   > *High distinction:* the President of the United States

5. **Days of the week, months of the year, holidays, periods of history, and historic events.**

   > Monday, June 8, Labor Day, Renaissance

6. **Specific parts of the country** but not compass points that show direction.

   > Midwest       the South       northwest of town
   > the Middle East

7. **Family relationships** when used with a person's name.

   > Aunt Carol       my mother       Uncle Mark

8. **A noun preceding a figure** except for common nouns such as line, page, and sentence.

   > Unit 1       Section 2       page 2       verse 7       line 2

9. **First and main words of side headings, titles of books, and works of art.**
   Do not capitalize words of four or fewer letters that are conjunctions, prepositions, or articles.

   > *Computers in the News*       *Raiders of the Lost Ark*

10. **Names of organizations and specific departments** within the writer's organization.

    > Girl Scouts       our Sales Department

11. **The salutation of a letter and the first word of the complimentary closing.**

    > Dear Mr. Bush       Ladies and Gentlemen:       Sincerely yours,
    > Very cordially yours,

## D r i l l  1

**CAPITALIZATION**
Review the rules and examples on the previous page. Then key the sentences, correcting all capitalization errors. Number each item and DS between items. Save as *capitalize-drill1*.

1. according to one study, the largest ethnic minority group online is hispanics.
2. the american author mark twain said, "always do right; this will gratify some people and astonish the rest."
3. the grand canyon was formed by the colorado river cutting into the high-plateau region of northwestern arizona.
4. the president of russia is elected by popular vote.
5. the hubble space telescope is a cooperative project of the european space agency and the national aeronautics and space administration.
6. the train left north station at 6:45 this morning.
7. the trademark cyberprivacy prevention act would make it illegal for individuals to purchase domains solely for resale and profit.
8. consumers spent $7 billion online between november 1 and december 31, 2000, compared to $3.1 billion for the same period in 1999.
9. new students should attend an orientation session on wednesday, august 15, at 8 a.m. in room 252 of the perry building.
10. the summer book list includes *where the red fern grows* and *the mystery of the missing baseball.*

## D r i l l  2

**CAPITALIZATION**

1. Open the file *capitalize2* from the data files and save it as *capitalize-drill2*.
2. Follow the specific directions provided in the data file. Remember to use the correct proofreaders' marks:

≡ Capitalize    sincerely
*lc* Lowercase    My Dear Sir

3. Resave and print. Submit the rough draft and final copy to your instructor.

## D r i l l  3

**CAPITALIZATION OF LETTER PARTS**
Key the letter parts using correct capitalization. Number each item and DS between each. Save as *capitalize-drill3*.

1. dear mr. petroilli
2. ladies and gentlemen
3. dear senator kuknais
4. very sincerely yours
5. dear reverend Schmidt
6. very truly yours
7. cordially yours
8. dear mr fong and miss landow
9. respectfully yours
10. sincerely
11. dear mr. and mrs. Green
12. dear service manager

## D r i l l  4

**CAPITALIZATION**

1. Open the file *capitalize4* from the data files. Save it as *capitalize-drill4*.
2. This file includes a field for selecting the correct answer. You will simply select the correct answer. Follow the specific directions provided in the data file.
3. Resave and print.

# PROJECT 4
# Champion Sports Venues, Inc.

4-1    Finalizing Facility Plans

4-2    Creating Solicitation Documents

4-3    Communicating with Stakeholders

4-4    Soliciting Center Proposals

4-5    Determining SportsPlex Inn
       Feasibility

**FOCUS:** *Time Management*

You report to Tracy Glenn, the president and owner of Champion Sports Venues, Inc. (CSV), a company that has been in the incubator since June 30, 2004. Diane Byars, the former chief executive assistant of CSV, chose not to move from downtown Chicago to the suburban Oak Park location. CSV has hired a new chief executive assistant, Crystal Jordan, who will begin her position in several weeks. Champion Sports Venues contracted with UBI for you to serve as its chief executive assistant until Crystal arrives. CSV is partnering with Oak Park Developers and Foster University to develop and manage an Olympic-type sports venue. You will be involved in planning this exciting new venture.

# finalizing facility Plans

## Objectives

- Determine priorities for completing work
- Arrange a meeting and prepare an agenda
- Prepare conceptual plan as a handout
- Prepare minutes of meeting with follow-up action items
- Send conceptual plan for review
- Merge comments and revisions to conceptual plan

---

**TASK 1**  **PRIORITIES AND TIME MANAGEMENT**

When you reported to Champion Sports Venues (CSV) this morning, you found the following note attached to a folder in your in-basket.

Welcome to CSV!

I am at a meeting, but will be back in a couple of hours. Before Diane Byars left, she said she put notes about the urgent things that need to be done in this folder. Will you organize these notes and determine the priority in which the items described need to be done? We can talk about the various projects as soon as I get back.

Tracy Glenn

Much of the material consists of small sheets of paper with handwritten notes about things that need to be done. Some notes contain references to files and location of materials to complete the tasks. Since you must organize and prioritize the information before Tracy (he prefers to be on a first-name basis with all employees) gets back, prepare a summary of the various notes that you found in the folder. Use a list format so that you can analyze all of the material and sort it by priority. Once the priorities have been ranked, write a brief justification for your rankings and begin to organize the work so that you can be more productive.

Use two-digit numbers for all items (01, 02, 03, 04, 10, etc.) so that the numbers will sort properly.

1. Open *task list* from the data files. Review all of the tasks and then determine the priority in which each task needs to be done. Rank all tasks from 1 to 12 by keying the number in the space provided under the heading *Priority*. (Priority 1 is the highest and 12 is the lowest.)

2. Sort the list in ascending order, save the document as *4-1task1a*, and print.

3. Create a new document using the same format as *4-1task1a* with two headings: *(1) Priority* and *(2) Justification and Notes about the Task*.

4. List the tasks in order of your final priority ranking. Write a sentence or two explaining why you gave the task the priority you assigned. Add a note about things you did to make the task more efficient while waiting for Tracy. (An example might be to note the phone number for individuals you have to call. Use the UBI and Company directories databases for the information.)

5. Save the document as *4-1task1b*, and print.

6. Some of the tasks were hard to rank in sequence because the items had approximately the same priority; therefore, you decide to try a different ranking system that would put tasks in categories. Open the data file, *task list*, and save it as *4-1task1c*.

7. Use *4-1task1b* as a reference but change the ranking system to: **A** for the most urgent tasks, **B** for the second level of urgency, **C** for the third level of urgency, and **D** for items that are not urgent at this time. Several tasks may have the same priority, and not all categories have to be used.

8. Sort the items in ascending order; resave (*4-1task1c*) and print the document

**TEAM OPTION** Team decisions generally are better than individual decisions. Select three or four classmates to work with as a team.

1. Compare the rankings that each of you made for *4-1task1b*. Note the items that are ranked differently. Discuss why they were ranked differently. Reach a consensus (group decision) on the best ranking for this task. Do not vote; discuss the tasks until you can all reach agreement.

2. Repeat Step 1 for *4-1task1c*.

**SUCCESS TIP** The ability to set priorities, organize materials, and manage time effectively is critical in every job.

Use the UBI Employee Directory database for e-mail addresses.

### SUCCESS TIP

Be resourceful; locate information without having to ask for it.

Tracy indicated that participants preferred to meet at 10 o'clock on Wednesday mornings. Send an e-mail to Ana Shelton, the UBI receptionist who handles all reservations, and request Conference Room 117A from 9:45 to 12:00 for Wednesday of next week. (**Note:** 9:45 allows time for room setup.) Also request that 10 parking spaces be reserved for visitors.

1. Prepare an agenda for the meeting. According to the file, CSV uses the Agenda Wizard, Modern style to prepare agendas and minutes. Include the form for minutes. (*Option:* Use the format in the Reference Guide.) Save the document as *4-1task2* and print.

2. E-mail the document as an attachment to the distribution list (facilities@ubi-sw.com) for review and ask for an immediate reply if any changes need to be made.

---

Date:     *Insert date for Wednesday of next week*
Time:     10:00 a.m.
Title:     Oak Park SportsPlex Facility Task Force
Location:     UBI Conference Room 117A
Meeting called by:     Tracy Glenn
Type of meeting:     Final approval of plans for Phase 1
Facilitator:     Nicholas Madison
Attendees:

| | |
|---|---|
| Trevor Allen | Alexia Quinn |
| Danielle Cole | Jessica Rivers |
| Tracy Glenn | Megan Suggs |
| Blake Logan | Dylan Taylor |
| David Marks | Lu Wong |
| Kayla Parks | Student's Name |

Please bring: Plans and budget distributed at last meeting
Agenda topics

| | | |
|---|---|---|
| Overview of meeting | Tracy Glenn | 10 |
| Approval of minutes | Student's Name | 05 |
| Resolution of last meeting's issues | Danielle Cole | 10 |
| Phase 1 components review | Blake Logan | 15 |
| Budget | Lu Wong | 20 |
| Timeline | Blake Logan | 15 |
| Action plan | Tracy Glenn | 30 |

---

**THINK CRITICALLY**

- Why should you print the minutes form and the Agenda at the same time?
- What are the advantages and disadvantages of including the time for each item on the Agenda?

# FOCUS ON THE WORKPLACE

## Healthy Attitudes

Successful people share a common trait—they use their time effectively. They also respect the time of others. Using time effectively requires both a composite of many skills and a healthy attitude about time.

The critical skills needed to manage your time effectively are the ability to assess what is really important, to be able to judge how much time something is worth, and to give the important things priority over less important things. Effective use of time requires focus on the top priority of the moment and the ability to avoid distractions even when they are interesting and enticing.

---

## TASK 3  HANDOUT FOR MEETING

**conceptual plan:** a plan that contains general concepts or ideas rather than specific, final plans

Either AutoText or AutoCorrect can be used. With AutoCorrect, the change is made as soon as the lowercase letters are keyed.

Tracy Glenn decides that for the overview of the meeting he wants to add additional information to the draft **conceptual plan** for the Oak Park SportsPlex. The Facilities Task Force is already familiar with all of the concepts, but this would give the group an opportunity to provide input on the document that contains the background information for the efforts to raise investment money for the project.

Tracy uses shortcuts in his drafts but prefers the names to be written out in full. Use AutoCorrect and add the following options:

| | |
|---|---|
| opsp | Oak Park SportsPlex |
| csv | Champion Sports Venues |
| csvi | Champion Sports Venues, Inc. |
| fsu | Foster University |
| opd | Oak Park Developers |

1. Open *conceptual plan* from the data files; save as *4-1task3*.

2. Insert the paragraphs shown on the next page at the beginning of the document.

3. Apply **Heading 1** style to all side headings shown in bold and **Heading 2** to all headings shown in regular font.

4. Insert the data file *project feasibility* at the end of the document. Ensure that document formatting is consistent. Add footnote 2 at the end of the last paragraph: **See Phase 1 plans for information about the specific components to be included in Phase 1**.

5. Insert page numbers as right-aligned headers; do not show the number on the first page.

opsp, an Olympic-type sports venue, is a joint venture project being developed by: csvi, opd, and fsu. The fsu Athletics Department sponsors 20 athletics teams and has excellent facilities for its highly rated athletics program. However, it needs additional practice facilities. fsu does not have adequate recreational and intramural facilities for its regular student body. fsu owns 80 acres of land adjoining its athletics facilities that are available to develop recreational facilities that can be used by its student body.

opd owns 600 acres of land adjoining the 80 acres of land owned by fsu. This land is being used to develop a research park, a residential housing development, and two golf courses. csv develops and manages sports venues. csv brought the three organizations together for this development so that they could benefit from the synergies of a joint project at much lower costs than they could develop independently.

## THINK CRITICALLY

- What is the value of adding words to AutoCorrect or AutoText? How do you determine what entries are worth adding?
- Why would you send out a conceptual plan rather than a finalized plan?

## TASK 4 — MINUTES USING THE AGENDA WIZARD

During the meeting, you made handwritten notes to use in preparing the minutes on the form that was generated with the Agenda Wizard. Key the minutes on the Agenda form; however, use complete sentences. Include the agenda with the minutes so it will be a part of the records. Substitute the actual date for the meeting date and the deadline starting with tomorrow's date. Use 00/00/00 format.

1. Open *4-1task2* that you prepared and save it as *4-1task4*; then key the minutes. Delete any rows in the table that remain blank.

2. Resave and print the minutes.

**SUCCESS TIP**    Be on time and adhere to the time allotted for agenda items.

| 10 | Overview of meeting | Tracy Glenn | |
|---|---|---|---|

Discussion: Reviewed handout. Critical to approve phase 1 plans today to stay on target.

Conclusions: Agreed to make decision at today's meeting.

| Action items: | Person responsible: | Deadline: |
|---|---|---|
| Send out conceptual paper to group for review today. Return promptly. | Student's name | 3 days |

| 05 | Approval of minutes | Student's Name |
|---|---|---|

Discussion: None

Conclusions: Approved as submitted.

| 10 | Resolution of issues raised at last meeting | Danielle Cole |
|---|---|---|

Discussion: Two issues raised were: (1) inclusion of football stadium in project and finalize legal agreement. Foster University prefers not to include stadium because of concerts and other stadium uses. (2) Recommendations of attorneys were reviewed.

Conclusions: Accept legal recommendations. Stadium not included.

| Action items: | Person responsible: | Deadline: |
|---|---|---|
| Follow-up with attorneys | Danielle Cole | Today |

| 15 | Phase 1 components review | Blake Logan |
|---|---|---|

Discussion: Plans for each component that were tentatively agreed on at the last meeting were reviewed.

Conclusions: One change was made—a small fitness center was combined in the same building as the volleyball and basketball practice facility and will be part of Phase 1. The large fitness center was moved to Phase 2. Phase 1 outdoor facilities will include: championship-size soccer field, 4 multipurpose practice fields, walking/running trails, track, 8 tennis courts, basketball practice areas, outdoor swimming and diving pools, and one golf course.

| Action items: | Person responsible: | Deadline: |
|---|---|---|
| Review changes with architect. | Blake Logan | 1 week |

| 20 | Budget | Lu Wong | |
|---|---|---|---|
| Discussion: Reviewed budget to determine if it must be adjusted because of changes in fitness center plans. | | | |
| Conclusions: The budget was adjusted to include only the estimated costs for the small fitness center and move large center to Phase 2. | | | |
| Action items: None | | Person responsible: | Deadline: |

| 15 | Timeline | Blake Logan | |
|---|---|---|---|
| Discussion: Goal: Phase 1 completed within two years. | | | |
| Conclusions: Timeline needs to be adjusted to move large fitness center to separate facility and add small fitness center. | | | |
| Action items: Revise timeline as indicated. | | Person responsible: Blake Logan | Deadline: 2 days |

| 30 | Action plan | Tracy Glenn | |
|---|---|---|---|
| Discussion: Reviewed plans in depth. | | | |
| Conclusions: Approved Phase 1 plans. | | | |
| Action items: Proceed with plans as scheduled. | | Person responsible: All | Deadline: |

## TASK 5

# E-MAIL USING SEND TO MAIL RECIPIENT FOR REVIEW

Send the Conceptual Plan presented as a handout at the meeting for final review by the Facilities Task Force. Use the Send to Mail Recipient for Review function and send it to the distribution list (facilities@ubi-sw.com) as you did in Task 2.

# REVISE DOCUMENT USING COMPARE AND MERGE

Click **Tools; Compare and Merge**; key the name in the File name box; then click **Merge into Current Document**.

Cole, Logan, and Wong have returned the Plan you sent each of them to review with their comments. Their files are contained in the data files named after them. Merge their changes into the original document and determine which changes to accept. Open *4-1task3* and save it as *4-1task6*.

1. Use Compare and Merge to merge the following files into the current document, in this order: *plan-cole*, *plan-logan*, *plan-wong*.

2. Review each insertion and deletion and accept each change individually except for one change made by Lu Wong in the last paragraph of the Project Feasibility Section. Reject the insertion *at least five miles of.* The five-mile length is proposed; the exact length of the trails has yet to be determined.

3. Resave and print the document.

For more information on making meetings efficient, use the Research tool and also search the Internet using keywords such as *efficient meetings* or *productive meetings.* You may also visit http://www.advancedapplications. swlearning.com, click **Links**, and then click **Project 4**.

# FOCUS ON THE WORKPLACE

## Time Management

The critical attitudes needed are an understanding of and an appreciation for the value of time and the desire to use it for the greatest advantage. Respecting the time of others is a part of that attitude. If you cannot meet a deadline, notifying the individual ahead of time enables him or her to take action to mitigate the negative consequences of your inability to perform as expected. Being proactive and informing people before a deadline takes far less time than being reactive and trying to explain why you did not do what was expected.

# Creating Solicitation Documents

### Objectives

- Design information brochure for potential investors
- Prepare brochure mailing labels
- Key follow-up letter and merge with list
- Format a table with Phase 1 costs
- Create a cost allocation pie chart

---

## TASK 1     BROCHURE WITH GRAPHICS

Your first task is to design a brochure inviting potential investors to participate in an informational seminar. The brochure will be two pages—printed front and back and folded in half. Page 1 will consist of a mailing panel at the left and the cover at the right. Page 2 will consist of clip art and text at the left and text at the right. This brochure is designed to get attention, not to provide very much information. Comprehensive information will be provided at the meeting.

**1.** Use landscape orientation and margins of .75" for top, bottom, and sides.

**2.** Format the document in two equal columns with .5" space between columns.

**3.** Format the return address in a text box and change the text direction to vertical as shown in the illustration. Position the text box approximately .5" from the gutter.

Oak Park SportsPlex
Champion Sports Venues, Inc.
700 Lake Street, Suite 123
Oak Park, IL 60301-7984

**4.** Use WordArt for the title, *Oak Park SportsPlex*.

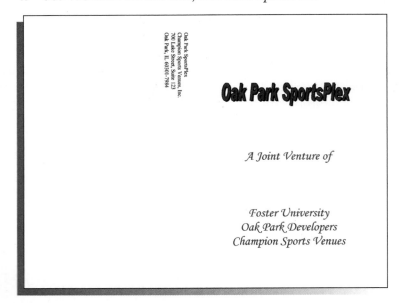

To Group the clips, press CTRL and click each clip. Then click **Draw** on the Drawing toolbar and select **Group**.

5. Use ZapfChancery, 28-point font for the remaining centered text on both pages. If this font is not available, choose another that is similar.

   A Joint Venture of
   Foster University
   Oak Park Developers
   Champion Sports Venues

6. Format the first column of the second page with clip art and text. Select four images representing some of the sports offered at the SportsPlex. Adjust the size so that two images will fit horizontally in the column. Position the images as shown in the illustration and group them. Key the following text above and below the grouping of clip art:

   **Above:** Be a part of Oak Park's most exciting sports and leisure activities venue

   **Below:** A few of the many sports and leisure activities soon to be available in the Oak Park SportsPlex

7. Key the following text in the right column:

   You are invited to learn more about a unique opportunity to become an investor in a lucrative new venture

   Call Champion Sports Venues 708-555-0167

   To participate in an informational seminar offered only to a few qualified investors

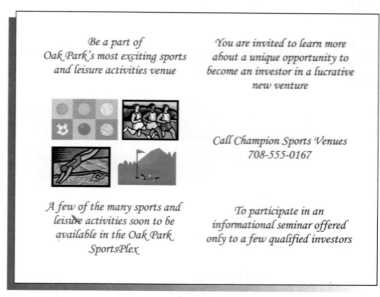

8. Print the document and save it as *4-2task-1*.

**THINK CRITICALLY**

- Why is it preferable to present limited information in the brochure and present more detailed information at the meeting?

- Why indicate that the seminar is offered only to a few qualified investors?

Click **Tables** in the Objects column and then double-click **Brochure List** to add the names and addresses. Click **Reports** in the Objects column and then double-click **Labels Brochure List** to display and print the labels.

The Facilities Task Force provided many mailing labels to mail the brochure you prepared. However, you have additional names and addresses and must prepare labels for these individuals. You must also add these names and addresses to the *SportsPlex* database.

1. Open the *Access* database, *sportsplex*, from the data files; save as *4-2task2*.

2. Add the 12 names and addresses shown below to the Brochure List table.

3. The Label Wizard was used to set up a report named *Labels Brochure List* to print labels using Avery Standard 2162 labels and sorted in alphabetical order by the last name. Print this report and check the accuracy of each entry.

4. Save (*4-2task2*) and close the database.

Mr. Roger Geddings
2047 N. Humphrey Avenue
Oak Park, IL 60302-1023

Julie Parker, M.D.
145 Frank Lloyd Wright Lane
Oak Park, IL 60302-1067

Ms. Jill McEntire
141 N. Marion Street
Oak Park, IL 60302-1089

Mr. Eric Pinckney
596 Madison Street
Oak Park, IL 60302-1263

Mr. Brian Edwards
2654 S. Laramie Avenue
Cicero, IL 60804-3827

Ms. Amanda Johnson
5802 W. Ogden Avenue
Cicero, IL 60804-4179

Ms. Sharon Goldstein
9573 Cermak Road
Berwyn, IL 60402-4837

Mr. Luiz Rodriguez
3259 W. Roosevelt Road
Berwyn, IL 60402-5240

Mr. Daniel Spurlock
8537 Grand Avenue
River Grove, IL 60171-8356

Ms. Danielle Blackmond
3893 River Road
River Grove, IL 60171-5248

Ms. Kimberly Bennett
3528 N. Neva Avenue
Elmwood Park, IL 60707-2465

Mr. Jason Meekins
6973 W. Grand Avenue
Elmwood Park, IL 60707-4619

# MERGED LETTERS

Use the Mail Merge Wizard for this task.

**Note:** Champion Sports Venues uses block style with open punctuation as its standard letter format. Always use the current date, your reference initials, and appropriate notations.

A form was distributed at the seminar giving participants an opportunity to request that members of the Sponsorship Team meet with the potential investor. All members on the brochure list signed the form requesting the individual meeting. Prepare the follow-up letter using the *CSV letterhead* from the data files and merge the letter with the Brochure List (*4-2task2*) you prepared. Generate envelopes.

1. Use Mail Merge and prepare the following letters.

2. Review the letters; save as *4-2task3*.

3. Generate an envelope for each letter and print them.

4. Arrange the letters and envelopes for signing.

Thank you for attending the informational seminar featuring the new Oak Park SportsPlex. We appreciate your interest in this exciting venture that we believe will be a major economic development catalyst for this region.

At the meeting you checked on the information form that you would like an individual visit from members of our Sponsorship Team to talk with you more specifically about investment opportunities. Blake Logan and I plan to visit with you within the next two or three weeks. My assistant will call you for an appointment.

A copy of the conceptual plan for the Oak Park SportsPlex is enclosed. We will be prepared to review the financial analysis of Phase 1 with you at the meeting.

We are delighted that you wish to consider becoming an investor in Oak Park SportsPlex and look forward to working with you.

Sincerely / Tracy Glenn / Chief Executive Officer / c Blake Logan

Left tab 0.15"

## THINK CRITICALLY

- Why is it better to create labels from a database than to key each label individually?
- What difference does sending a personalized letter to everybody who requested follow-up information from the seminar make?

The Facilities Task Force has completed its first estimate of the cost of Phase 1 of the project.

**SUCCESS TIP**

Format and style should contribute to readability as well as appearance.

1. Format a two-column table using Table AutoFormat style Table 3D Effects 2.

2. Title the table **Estimated Cost of Phase 1**.

3. Center and bold column heads—Column 1, **Components**; Column 2, **Development/Construction Costs**.

4. Save as *4-2task4* and print.

5. After you view the table, you decide that the style does not help the readability of the table. Therefore, modify the format by applying the table style Table Contemporary to make the table easier to read.

6. Center the table vertically. Resave.

| Basketball/volleyball practice and fitness facility | $8,250,000 |
| Golf course | $4,500,000 |
| Running/walking trails | $650,000 |
| Soccer and multipurpose practice fields | $1,000,000 |
| Swimming and diving pools with locker rooms | $1,125,000 |
| Tennis courts | $825,000 |
| Track | $650,000 |
| Total estimated cost | sum column |

**THINK CRITICALLY**

- What factors should be considered in selecting a style for tables?
- What makes the Table Contemporary style easier to read than the Table 3D Effects 2 style?

**cost allocation:** the way costs are divided among the various project components

If you need help with this task, use keywords *create chart using Microsoft Chart* to search Help.

It is important to show how the costs for Phase 1 are allocated. Use *Microsoft Chart* to create a pie chart using data from Task 4 to show the percentages of the total cost for each component of Phase 1.

1. Create a 3D pie chart.

2. Use the following abbreviated labels for the legend: **BB/VB**, **Golf**, **Trails**, **Fields**, **Pools**, **Tennis**, and **Track**; show the legend at the bottom.

3. Use the title **Phase 1 Cost Allocation**.

4. Show percentages and leader lines.

5. Select the individual pie slices and change the color of those that are very close in color to distinguish the various slices from each other.

6. Adjust the chart by making it larger.

7. Save the document as *4-2task5* and print.

**Phase I Cost Allocation**

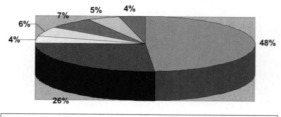

BB/VB   Golf   Trails   Fields   Pools   Tennis   Track

### THINK CRITICALLY

- Why is a pie chart effective in showing how costs are allocated?

- Why is it important to show the data both in the table and in the pie chart rather than just selecting either the table or the pie chart?

# FOCUS ON THE WORKPLACE

### Time Management

## Improve Productivity to Save Time

At the end of each day, leave tomorrow's project on your desk and clear your desk of all other papers. If possible, spend a few minutes filing any materials to which you no longer need immediate access.

At the end of each week, clean your entire workspace, leaving out only what you will need for the next week.

# Communicating with Stakeholders

### Objectives

- Design a standard banner heading for stakeholder updates
- Prepare an update for stakeholders
- Prepare a *PowerPoint* presentation for potential investors
- Remove the restriction and post update on website

---

## TASK 1 · STAKEHOLDERS UPDATE TEMPLATE

**stakeholder:** anyone who has a vested interest in an organization such as partners, employees, investors, students, and clients

Champion Sports Venues believes that it is very important to communicate frequently and effectively with all current and potential **stakeholders** of the SportsPlex. You have been asked to design a banner heading that will be used for a series of updates sent to stakeholders periodically. After you design the document, save it as a template named *update template*.

> **SUCCESS TIP**
>
> Make repetitive tasks efficient to allow more time for creative tasks.

*[Screenshot: Update Template – Microsoft Word showing banner]*

**Oak Park SportsPlex**

**Update No. 1**

April 13, 20--

1. Open a new document and change the left and right margins to .75"; apply to the whole document.

2. Use WordArt to create a banner; select the Column B, Row 4 style from the WordArt Gallery. Change the Fill Effects on the Gradient Tab to Preset and select Rainbow.

3. Key **Update No. 1** using Title heading style (centered, Arial Font, Size 16, bold). On the next line, insert the date field and check update automatically. (Use Title heading style or Heading 1 style centered.)

4. Change to Normal style and position the insertion point at 2"; format two equal-sized columns (3.25") with .5" spacing. Apply from this point forward.

5. Save as a document template named *update template*.

> To balance columns, insert a continuous break at the end of the copy.

Some documents contain confidential information and are restricted. Other documents may be posted on the website as general information. Timing sometimes determines whether information is proprietary or general. A document containing draft information that is subject to change may be restricted. Once the information is finalized, the document may become general information with no restrictions.

**Check your productivity:** Keep track of the minutes it takes you to complete this task. Assume that you are being paid $15 hour. What was the cost of this report? minutes _____ time in hours (minutes/60) _____ cost (hours x $15) $ _____

1. Use the Update template you just created in Task 1 to prepare the first Update. Save as a *Word* document named *4-3task2*.

2. Use a horizontal line to separate the footer from the text. Add the following footer to all pages to restrict the document distribution:

   This report contains confidential and proprietary information that is provided only to investors and potential investors of the Oak Park SportsPlex. Do not copy, distribute, or share the information contained in this report.

3. Key the following information below the banner head, the update number, and date. Use the two-column format set up in the template. Bold all headings. Leave a blank line before and after the headings. Balance the columns so that both will end at approximately the same position.

4. When you complete the document, resave it as *4-3task2*.

Oak Park SportsPlex Approved!

Champion Sports Venues, Foster University, and Oak Park Developers finalized the agreement to develop Oak Park SportsPlex as a joint venture. The project is a win-win situation not only for the three joint venture partners but also for the surrounding communities. This exciting venue is expected to have a major economic impact on the region.

Three-Tiered Venue Designed

The SportsPlex project is unique in that its facilities are designed to appeal to three very distinct groups—students and the general public, competitive and even Olympic-caliber athletes, and luxury corporate and individual users. Upscale recreational facilities are critical to the success of Oak Park's new residential development and research park. Championship-caliber facilities are critical to the success of Foster University's athletic program. At the same time, the needs of the general student body and the community must be met.

The three-tier approach enables the joint venture partners to leverage the facilities they would have to build to make their own operations successful. Maximum utilization of facilities, in turn, makes the entire project financially feasible.

Student and General Public

This population desires a wide range of activities that are affordable. Some activities are available to the public at no charge, such as the track and the walking and running trails. The public can also pay a reasonable general membership fee that provides access to the facilities that are available to students. Student activity fees entitle students to use many of the facilities—designated tennis courts, practice fields, the swimming pool, and basketball courts. Certain facilities, such as one of the golf courses and the fitness center, require additional fees.

Championship-Caliber Athletes

Competitive athletes have the use of Foster University varsity athletic facilities. They also have access to facilities such as the golf course, the swimming and diving pools, and the fitness centers. The Athletics Department pays for usage of facilities for student-athletes at a cost that is lower than it would cost them to build facilities exclusively for their student-athletes. During the summer months when student-athletes are not on campus, these facilities plus some of the new facilities will be marketed as an Olympic-type residential training facility. One dormitory and a new inn will be used for housing these athletes who will train at the SportsPlex.

Corporate and Individual Users

This group expects the most upscale facilities. They also expect exclusivity for the initiation and monthly fees they pay. This group will have membership in a private club with amenities solely for their use. The championship golf course, a separate club house, separate racquetball and handball courts, a section of indoor tennis courts, and a fitness center will be limited to use by this group.

Facility Development Plan

The facilities will be developed in three phases. The joint venture partners have invested funds to cover the costs of Phase 1. All components of Phase 1 are expected to be completed within two years. The use of existing athletic and recreational facilities of Foster University will be phased in during this two-year period. The estimated costs for Phase 1 and the allocation of those costs are shown below.

*Change the column format for the next section to one column and insert the Estimated Cost of Phase 1 table you prepared (4-2task4) as an object created from the file 4-2task4 centered below the columns.*

SUCCESS TIP  Frequent communication enhances customer satisfaction.

*Insert the Phase 1 Cost Allocation pie chart you prepared (4-2task5) as an object created from the file 4-2task5 centered below the table.*

*Change the format from this point forward in the document to two equal-sized columns and balance the columns.*

Golf Course Design

Investors and potential investors will receive a special invitation to preview the golf course design. The golf course to be developed in Phase 1 is the course that will be open to the public. The basic layout is shown in this report. Note that this course is a compact course designed to minimize land usage.

*Insert golf course design from the data files. Size the picture to fit it in the left column (3.5"). Picture may extend into gutter space if necessary.*

The preliminary design of the championship course, which will be used by private club members, the varsity golf team, and competitive athletes, will also be previewed at the meeting with the course designers. The championship course will have a more linear design. As you would expect, a linear design requires much more land than the course shown in this report. The walking and running trails will be located around the perimeter of the championship course.

Other Components of Phase 1

Our architect has been commissioned to develop a model of the site plan showing all components of Phase 1. The model will be on display as soon as the architect completes it.

Investment Opportunities

Qualified investors are being offered the opportunity to invest in Oak Park SportsPlex. These funds will be used for the development and construction of Phases 2 and 3. Cost estimates for Phases 2 and 3 have not been finalized. Land costs are not included as Foster University and Oak Park Developers already own all of the land needed for this project.

Investment Structure

Investment opportunities are structured into three categories:

1. Minimum investment of $250,000 but less than $500,000.
2. Investments larger than $500,000 but less than $1,000,000.
3. Investments of $1,000,000 or more.

In addition to the return on the investment, all categories of investment include club membership benefits.

THINK **CRITICALLY**

- What are the advantages of using the standard template for the update to stakeholders?
- Does the confidentiality footer have any value other than keeping the material from becoming public information?

qualified investor: a person who meets a minimum financial criterion such as having a net worth of at least $1 million

You will prepare a *PowerPoint* presentation that will be used to present information to additional potential donors. Most of the information will come from the Oak Park SportsPlex Update No. 1. Use this document for reference. After you create each slide, add the notes to be used during the presentation.

Display the task pane (**View, Task Pane**) and then select **Design Templates** and **Layers**. Apply to all slides.

Display the slide master (**View, Master, Slide Master**). Then click in the number area, and insert number (**Insert, Slide Number, check Footer** and **Slide Number; Apply to All**).

1. Open a new presentation and save it as *4-3task3*.

2. Apply the **Layers Design** template to all slides. Add a footer containing the slide number to the master slide; do not show the number on the title slide.

3. Create the following slides:

**Slide 1:** Oak Park SportsPlex
(use the WordArt banner from the Update template for the main title). In the subtitle placeholder, list the three joint venture partners.

**Notes:** Opportunities for investment by qualified investors will be explained during this presentation.

**Slide 2:** Phase 1 Components

Use two-column bulleted text format:

Basketball/volleyball practice facility and fitness center
Championship-sized soccer field
Diving pool
Golf course
Multipurpose practice fields (4)
Running/walking trails (5 miles)
Swimming pool
Tennis courts (8)
Track

**Notes:** Use of existing Foster University athletic facilities will be phased in during this portion of the project.

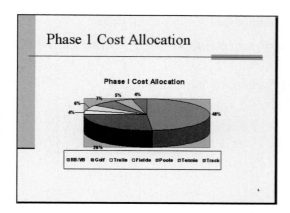

### Slide 3:  Estimated Cost of Phase 1

Use slide layout with title and one contents area.  Import the table you created in *4-2task4*.  (Select the contents area; then use **Insert, Object, Create from File**, and select **4-2task4**.)  If necessary, adjust the size and position of the table by selecting it and dragging the corners.

**Notes:**  Some of the components have been combined in the cost estimates.

### Slide 4:  Phase 1 Cost Allocation

Use the same layout as Slide 3.  Import the pie chart you created in *4-2task5*.  Use the same procedures that you used with the previous slide.  (Select the diagram.  When the Diagram toolbar displays, select **Layout**; then **Scale diagram**.  Drag the box to widen it.)

**Notes:**  The chart shows the percentage of the total cost for each of the combined components of Phase 1.

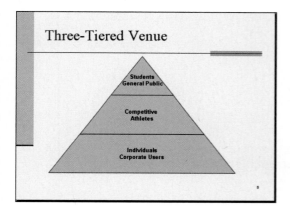

### Slide 5:  Three-Tiered Venue

Use the same layout as Slide 3.  Insert a Pyramid diagram.
Key in the bottom tier:  **Individuals; Corporate Users**.
Key in the middle tier:  **Competitive Athletes**.
Key in the top tier:  **Students; General Public**.
Enlarge the font to 16 point and bold it.  Scale the diagram to widen it so the text will fit in the tiers.

**Notes:**  The tier structure is based on revenue-generating potential, with the individual and corporate users expected to produce more revenue than the other two tiers.

### Slide 6:  Investment Categories

Use title and one-column bulleted layout.

**Notes:**  Present proformas and discuss projected ROI (return on investment) as well as the other benefits associated with the project.

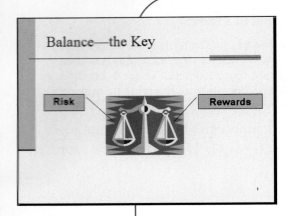

**Slide 7:** Balance—the Key

Use title and one contents area layout. Locate a clip art of scales or some other symbol representing the concept of balance. Use callouts to indicate the concepts of Risk and Rewards. (Callouts are located in AutoShapes on the Drawing toolbar.) Adjust the size of the image. Bold and expand the font size of text in the callouts.

**Notes:** Emphasize that this project is not risk free. The opportunity for rewards is significant; however, the risk involved in the project is also significant.

4. Add slide transition Right Cover Down, medium speed; apply to all slides.

5. Animate the slides using the Wipe animation scheme; apply to all slides.

6. Preview and print slides using grayscale if you do not have a color printer.

7. Print handouts three per page and print notes pages.

8. Resave the presentation (*4-3task3*).

**SUCCESS TIP**  Vary slide layout to make presentations interesting.

**THINK CRITICALLY**

- Why would you want to limit investments to qualified investors if others who do not meet the criteria can come up with the money?
- Why is it important to stress the risks as well as the rewards when you are trying to convince people to invest in a project?

AOT-12

...sked to make an oral presentation using the *PowerPoint* slides ... Task 3 and the report in Task 2 for additional information. ...he notes pages, and the report to prepare your presentation. ...rt you prepared in *2-2task4* for presentation pointers.

TEAM

...team members to make the presentation. The first presenter ..., introduce other presenters, and give an overview of what ...t. The second presenter can cover slides 2–5. The third presenter can cover slides 6–7. Ask for questions at the end of the presentation.

**TASK 5**          **NOTICE TO BE POSTED**

Prepare the following notice for employees at Champion Sports Venue.

1. Format using Landscape orientation; .5" margins on all sides; Verdana font, 48 point for heading and 24 point for text.

---

# Notice

The 10,000-square-foot property pictured below adjoins the SportsPlex site. It has been listed for sale at $1.5 million and would be a great buy for an entertainment center. Join us for a preview of the property at 3:00 today. Meet in the UBI Reception Area.

---

2. Open *front view* from the data files with *Microsoft Office Picture Manager*. Increase Contrast setting to 10 and Brightness setting to 15; save in your solutions folder as *revised front view*. Insert picture on left; crop top .25". Size to about 4.5".

3. Open *back view* with *Microsoft Office Picture Manager* and use AutoCorrect to enhance the image. Save in your solutions folder as *revised back view*. Insert picture on right; crop top .25". Size to about 4.5".

4. Key the following information and save as *4-3task.5*.

Notice

The 10,000-square-foot property pictured below adjoins the SportsPlex site. It has been listed for sale at $1.5 million and would be a great buy for an entertainment center. Join us for a preview of the property at 3:00 today. Meet in the UBI Reception Area.

# Soliciting Center Proposals

## Objectives

- Seek approval to use Request for Proposal (RFP)
- Prepare a draft RFP
- Send the draft RFP as an e-mail attachment to be reviewed
- Prepare a fax cover to send the RFP to a reviewer who is traveling
- Review comments and finalize the RFP
- Prepare a transmittal memo for the RFP

## TASK 1

### MEMO SEEKING APPROVAL TO USE RFP

**RFP (request for proposal):** an invitation to submit a plan with costs and details for completing a job or project

As a joint venture partner in the Oak Park SportsPlex, Champion Sports Venues has the contract to provide overall management for all facilities. Tracy Glenn wishes to partner with a builder on the residential training center. A Phase 3 Development Team has been designated to oversee the project. Tracy asked you to prepare a memo to the team to explain his recommendation to use an **RFP** rather than a bidding process for the construction of the center and to ask for their approval to do so.

**Check your productivity:** Tracy has to leave in 15 minutes. He would like to sign the memo before he leaves. Can you finish it in time?

Check your keyboarding technique using the evaluation form on page 236.

1. Use the Memo Wizard to prepare the memo on the next page to the Phase 3 Development Team from Tracy Glenn.

2. Select Contemporary style and change the title to **Champion Sports Venues, Inc.**

3. Change the memo font to 12 point. Save as *4-4task1* and print.

4. Send an e-mail to Bert Odom with a copy of this memo as an attachment from you indicating Tracy asked you to send the memo to him. His e-mail address is Bert.Odom@ubi-sw.com.

## HOW DID YOU DO?

Record the number of minutes it took you to prepare the memo for Tracy's signature. Remember, this means it must be error free. _____

As you are aware, Champion Sports Venues has the contract to manage all facilities including the Oak Park SportsPlex Inn. At the last meeting, the Phase 3 Development Team agreed that the construction and the management of the Inn must be closely coordinated and should preferably be designed as a team effort if the project is to be successful. You asked me to think about the best way to accomplish this objective and to recommend a plan of action to the Phase 3 Development Team.

My recommendation is to have our team identify at least three builders with experience building inns or hotels, and Champion Sports Venues will send each a Request for Proposal (RFP) for the building of the Oak Park SportsPlex Inn. Our team will review and approve the RFP before it is sent to the builders.

The advantage of using an RFP rather than a bidding process is that general information is provided in the RFP, and it is up to the builder to supply all of the specific information and the costs involved. With the bidding process, we would have to supply all of the specific information, and the builder would give us a quotation on how much it would cost to build the inn according to the specifications provided. By reviewing the RFP from several builders, many ideas can be gained from each proposal and incorporated in the final plans for the inn. We would reserve the right to negotiate with any builder to finalize the agreement.

If you agree with this approach, I will begin drafting the RFP.

**THINK CRITICALLY**

- Why do you think Tracy Glenn recommended the RFP rather than a bidding process?
- How does selecting and limiting the number of builders to which the proposal is being sent rather than sending it to all builders in the area impact time management?

Use the following information to prepare a draft of the Request for Proposal that will be sent to three developers selected by the Phase 3 Development Team.

**Use the Format Painter.**

1. Open *RFP* from the data files and save it as *4-4task2*.

2. Add a printed watermark, **DRAFT**, to this document.

3. Add the following heading using Title (or Heading 1, centered) style:

   Request for Proposal for SportsPlex Inn

4. Use single-space report format and Heading Styles 1 and 2 for headings as noted.

5. Make the changes that follow in the RFP.  Also, correct any unmarked errors you find in the data file.

6. Verify that all formatting changes have been made and the format is consistent, and resave the document (*4-4task2*).

*The Oak Park SportsPlex Phase 3 Development Team*

~~Champion Sports Venues, Inc.~~ requests proposals for a turnkey project including the development, ~~and~~ construction ⋏*and furnishing* of an Inn located on the Oak Park SportsPlex property adjacent to Foster University.  This request is being sent to a small group of selected and qualified developers.  A copy of the survey of the property delineating the ~~property~~ *four-acre tract* designated for the Inn *SportsPlex* ⋏ is being sent to you directly from the engineering firm that completed the survey work.

Use of *the* ⋏ SportsPlex Inn     (Heading 1)

*The SportsPlex Inn must be designed to serve two different clientele groups.  (1) Demand cu The SportsPlex Inn must be designed to serve two different clientele groups.* (1) Demand currently exists for basic rooms to be used by prospective students, guests of current students, athletic recruits of Foster University, and general travelers who plan to stay for one or two nights.  (2) Demand also exists for upscale rooms for business travelers who are doing business with the companies located in the Oak Park Research Park, with the executives participating in management training programs at Foster University, and for guests of residents in the upscale residential developments of Oak Park.

## Basic Rooms     (Heading 2)

The basic rooms are designed to meet the demand for the first group described above.  This group look for rooms that are nice, very functional, and moderately priced.  The room size and furnishings should be comparable to the mid-level national chains.  The initial room price is expected to be $805 per night.

## Upscale Rooms     (Heading 2)

The upscale rooms are designed to meet the demand for the ~~more~~ affluent *second* group described above.  This group looks for rooms that are large, comfortable, and ~~and~~ more luxurious than the basic rooms.  Many of them requests suites, and many request concierge-level service.  The initial room price for the upscale rooms is expected to be $105-$125, and the suite price is expected to be $1125-$150 per night.

*Insert <u>inn requirements</u> from the data files here.*

*Add to end of list of Exterior Requirements:*

* *Landscaping comparable to the surrounding area must be included in the design and construction.*

* *Patios and garden-type sitting areas outdoors are highly desirable.*

*Add to end of list of Interior Requirements:*

* *A gift shop is desirable but not required.*

* *All of the appropriate service areas (laundry, storage, catering kitchen, etc.) required for efficient operation of the facility must be included in the design.*

* *As a minimum, ice and vending areas must be provided on every other floor.*

* *Appropriate office space must be included for the staff and management of the facility.*

## TASK 3     E-MAIL WITH DRAFT RFP ATTACHMENT

Send the following e-mail message with the Draft RFP attached from you to these three individuals who have been designated to review the draft:

Bert.Odom@ubi-sw.com

Marianne.Marks@ubi-sw.com

Leslie.Rumph@ubi-sw.com

*Please review the draft RFP that is attached. As soon as I receive your changes, I will incorporate them and send the RFP to the developers selected by the Phase 3 Development Team.*

## TASK 4     FAX COVER SHEET

The fourth individual, Dylan Kennedy, who was designated to review the Draft RFP is currently traveling and requested that you fax the document to him at 803-555-0179. Prepare a fax cover to send the document, including on it the same message that you used for the e-mails you sent; copy Tracy Glenn. Use the Contemporary fax template. Add the Champion Sports Venues name and address to the fax. Save as *4-4task4*.

# FOCUS ON THE WORKPLACE

### Time Management

### Good Organization Saves Time

Organize both your work and your workplace to be more effective. Use the following techniques to improve your organization:

- Use an online calendar, task list (in priority order), and reminder list.
- Keep active projects separate from inactive or older projects.
- Keep active projects in easily accessible areas.
- Put files and materials away as soon as you finish using them.
- Minimize personal items on your work area.
- Prepare projects for the next day at the end of each workday.

Bert Odom, Marianne Marks, and Leslie Rumph returned the draft document with comments. These documents were saved in the data files by their last names. Dylan Kennedy called and left the following message concerning his review of the faxed document:

*I think it's fine. Add a title page and send it out.*

Finalize the RFP by completing the following steps:

Use a Next Page Break to provide a blank page for the Table of Contents and start page numbers on the body of the report at 1. Break the link between Section 1 for the preliminary pages and Section 2 for the body before changing the numbering style.

1. Open *4-4task2* and save it as *4-4task5*.

2. Open each of the data files for Odom, Marks, and Rumph and merge them into the existing document.

3. Delete the comment added by Odom. Review the changes suggested by the three reviewers and accept them.

4. Remove the DRAFT watermark.

5. Design a title page for the report, being as creative as you can. Use the title **Request for Proposal for SportsPlex Inn**. Add a page border on all pages and use any other graphics desired to enhance the style of the title page. Include Requested by: **The Oak Park SportsPlex Phase 3 Development Team** and the current date.

6. Prepare a Table of Contents showing all headings. Number the contents page ii.

7. Number other pages at the top right. Do not show the number on the first page.

8. Preview and resave the document (*4-4task5*).

Use the Memo Wizard to prepare a memo to Selected Developers from Tracy Glenn. Select Contemporary style, which Champion Sports Venues uses for all of its memos. Change font size to 12 point for all text.

Change the title to **Champion Sports Venues, Inc.** and copy the memo to the Oak Park SportsPlex Phase 3 Development Team.

Use the subject Request for Proposal.

Do not include the footer with confidential and the page number. If it appears, delete it. Then key the text. Save as *4-4task6a*.

Open *4-4task5* and save it as *4-4task6b*. Insert a page break after the title page to create a blank page for the transmittal memo.

Copy the memo (*4-4task6a*) to this blank page, and update the fields on the Table of Contents using the Update page numbers only feature.

Resave and print the document (*4-4task6b*).

*You are invited to submit a proposal for the development, construction, and furnishing of the Oak Park SportsPlex Inn. Information required for the proposal is contained in this document. This document is being sent to three builders/developers who have experience in constructing hotels and motels.*

*We would appreciate your letting us know within a week if you plan to submit a proposal for this project. If you need further information about the project, please let me know. You can reach me at 708-555-0144.*

*We look forward to hearing from you.*

**THINK CRITICALLY**

- Why is it preferable to retain the right to accept, reject, or negotiate any proposal that is submitted rather than simply accepting the proposal with the lowest cost?
- What would your reaction be if you were a builder and received an RFP with this provision included?

# Determining SportsPlex Inn feasibility

Objectives
- Complete the summary proforma on the SportsPlex Inn
- Prepare a cover memo for the proforma
- Create a 3-D column chart showing profit
- Prepare an update for investors
- Compose a letter to invite developer to meeting

---

## TASK 1  EXCEL WORKSHEET FOR PROFORMA

**proforma:** an analysis
showing expected profit
under specified conditions

The Phase 3 Development Team asked Tracy to prepare a conservative
**proforma** projecting profits for the SportsPlex Inn based on a range of
projected occupancy rates. Tracy provided the basic data for the proforma in a
worksheet and asked you to complete it. Follow these instructions to do so.

1. Open *inn proforma* from the data files and save it as *4-5task1*.

2. On row 9, complete the Total Income information for each column by
   summing the data in rows 5–8.

3. On row 16, complete the Total Allocated Expenses information for each
   column by summing the data in rows 12–14.

4. On row 24, complete the Total Unallocated Expenses information for
   each column by summing the data in rows 19–22.

5. Compute the Profit for each column by using the following formula:
   Total Income minus the sum of the Total Allocated Expenses plus the
   total Unallocated Expenses. For example, the formula for column B
   would be =B9-(B16+B24) and the formula for column C would be
   =C9-(C16+C24).

6. Center and bold the title and bold the column heads in row 3, place
   double underlines below the profit figures in row 26, resave the document
   (*4-5task1*), preview, and print.

---

**THINK CRITICALLY**

- Why do you think Tracy used an average room rate of $85
  when 20 or 25 percent of the rooms may be rented at a
  higher rate?

- Why do you think he selected occupancy rates of 70, 75, and
  80 percent when the range could be from 0 to 100 percent?

Tracy plans to bring the proforma to the next meeting of the Oak Park SportsPlex Phase 3 Development Team. To ensure that everyone understands and agrees with the assumptions used in developing it, he decides to summarize them in a memo with the proforma attached.

To link the worksheet, use **Insert, Object, Create** from File tab; then browse to find *4-5task1* and click **Link**.

1. Prepare the memo using the usual style to Oak Park SportsPlex Phase 3 Development Team from Tracy Glenn with copies to Foster University and Oak Park Developers. Use *Proforma for SportsPlex Inn* as the reference. Increase the memo font to 11 point.

2. Insert a page break at the end of the memo and link to the worksheet containing the proforma (*4-5task1*). Save as *4-5task 2*.

Based on very conservative proforma assumptions, the SportsPlex Inn will be very profitable at occupancy rates of 70 percent or higher. The proforma is shown on the last page of this memo.

The conservative assumptions on which the proforma was based are listed below.

1. The Phase 3 Development Team agreed that the initial room rate for basic rooms would be $85 per day. Although some rooms are likely to be rented at higher rates, the percentage of rooms at the higher rate is hard to estimate, and a conservative approach was selected.

2. Foster University has committed to using the SportsPlex Inn for participants in its Executive Education programs and for recruits who are being considered for athletic scholarships and who make official visits to Foster University. Oak Park Developers will encourage the businesses located in its research park to use the SportsPlex Inn for business associates needing hotel accommodations. Competitive athletes using the training facilities other than during the summer when lower-cost dormitory space is available are likely to use the SportsPlex Inn. Based on usage by these groups as well as by other travelers, the lowest average occupancy rate of 70 percent is believed to be very conservative.

3. The income and expense estimates are based on the experience of six similar hotel properties for the past three years.

4. The allocated expenses include the total debt service for development, construction, and furnishing the SportsPlex Inn. The land already owned by the joint venture group represents the only investment required for this project.

I think we will all agree that a minimum projected profit of approximately $1.2 million is better than we had anticipated in our preliminary discussions.

# TASK 3 · MICROSOFT CHART SHOWING PROFIT

Tracy has asked you to create a *Microsoft Chart* to illustrate the relationship between the occupancy rate and the expected profit. Two separate projections were used for the 80% Occupancy column—one based on a room rate of $80 (columns F and G) and the other based on a room rate of $85 (columns H and I). Use the data based on the $85 room rate.

1. Open a new document and save it as *4-5task3*.

2. Create a 3D column chart showing the profit at 70%, 75%, and 80% occupancy based on the $85 per day rate. Expand the size of the chart if necessary.

3. Format the three columns in distinctly different colors of your choice and add the title:

   Projected Annual Profit
   Based on $85 Room Rate

4. Resave the document (*4-5task3*) and print.

**THINK CRITICALLY**

- Why is it important to use the $85 room rate for the 80% Occupancy column of the chart?
- Why not include both columns?

# TASK 4 · EMBEDDED CHART AND WORKSHEET

The Phase 3 Development Team approved the SportsPlex Inn based on the information presented at the meeting. Tracy was asked to prepare an update for investors and potential investors. Five updates have already been prepared by various individuals. Follow these instructions to prepare Update No. 6.

1. Create a new document from the Update template you prepared. Save it as *4-5task4*.

2. Change the Update No. to 6.

3. Include the footer on each page containing the confidentiality notation that you used in Update No. 1 (*4-3task2*).

4. Key the text on the next page; bold the headings; then balance the columns.

5. Change the format to one column and import the Microsoft chart you completed in *4-5task3* and embed it at the approximate center below the balanced columns.

To embed an Object, use **Insert**, **Object**, **Create** from File, browse to locate the file, deselect **Link** if it is checked, and click **OK**.

6. Insert a page break and then import the proforma you completed in *4-5task1* and embed it on the second page.

7. Preview the document and make any adjustments needed.

8. Resave the document and print it.

Overall Progress on Oak Park SportsPlex

Work is currently underway on the various components of Phase 1 of the SportsPlex. If you have not had an opportunity to see the progress, we encourage you to drive by the site at your convenience.

Phase 2 and Phase 3 Development Teams

To speed up the planning process for the remainder of the Oak Park SportsPlex, two separate teams were formed to work on the development of each phase. This approach has proved to be very successful in expediting the work. Update 5 contained a report from the Phase 2 Development Team on the progress made on the plans for the fitness center. In this update, the Phase 3 Development Team makes a major announcement about its progress.

SportsPlex Inn Approved

On the basis of a very conservative proforma, the Phase 3 Development Team approved the plans for the SportsPlex Inn. The Inn is projected to be very profitable. The chart on this page shows the projected profits at three occupancy rate levels and is based on the initial $85 room rate that was approved for the basic rooms. No allowance was made for the additional income projected from the upscale rooms and suites. The proforma shown on the next page provides additional details. Please note that the only investment required for this project is the land that is already owned by the joint venture. The proforma includes debt service for development, construction, and furnishing the SportsPlex Inn.

**THINK CRITICALLY**

- Why is it important to include the confidentiality notation on this document?

# INVITATION LETTER (COMPOSITION)

Use the *CSV letterhead* from the data files, the standardized format (block style; open punctuation), and your title, chief executive assistant.

The Phase 3 Development Team reviewed four proposals from developers who responded to the RFP on the SportsPlex Inn. The Team agreed that Kyle Morgan's of MWRC Developers was the best one and asked you to compose a letter inviting Mr. Morgan and his team to meet with the Phase 3 Development Team. Use the following information to compose the letter.

1.  The address for MWRC Developers is 197 Madison Street, Oak Park, IL 60302-5486.

2.  You may use the following unorganized, rough notes made during the meeting in drafting the letter. Do not disclose that Mr. Morgan's quotation was the second lowest of the four proposals or that the lowest quotation was only $40,000 lower and did not include some of the desirable features included in the MWRC proposal.

    • Team liked proposed design very much—would suggest a few changes.

    • Team impressed with the experience firm had in developing similar projects.

    • Team would like to talk about price which was somewhat higher than expected and about possible value engineering.

    • MWRC is only developer being invited to meet with the Team at this time to consider negotiating a contract.

    • The Team already has meeting scheduled one week from today at 9:30 a.m. in UBI Conference Room 117A. If this date is not acceptable, ask Mr. Morgan to propose several alternate dates.

3.  Copy the Oak Park SportsPlex Phase 3 Development Team.

4.  Edit your letter carefully.

5.  Save the document as *4-5task5* and print it. Sign your name.

---

**SUCCESS TIP** | Editing is an important part of writing letters.

## Self-Assessment
Evaluate your understanding of this project by answering the questions below.

1. A printed _____ can be used to add DRAFT across all pages.

2. To combine comments from multiple reviewers into one document, use the _____ feature.

3. Use the _____ feature to keep multiple clips together and to be able to move them as one unit.

4. _____ or Insert Object can be used to embed a chart.

5. A(n) _____ chart should be used to show percentages of a whole.

6. A(n) _____ was used to standardize the banner heading for updates sent to stakeholders.

7. A message printed at the bottom of every page of a document is called a(n) _____.

8. To balance columns so they all end at approximately the same position on the page, insert a(n) _____.

9. Use the _____ to add the slide number, date, and footer on all *PowerPoint* slides.

10. To control the way each slide displays, use the _____ feature.

## Performance Assessment
Production Time: 30'

**Document 1**
**Two-Column Update**

1. Create Update No. 12; use today's day and the *update template* you created earlier. Save as *checkpoint4-d1*.

2. Use bullets for listing field events and numbers for project phases; apply **Heading 3** style to headings.

3. Open *ck4-1* and *ck4-2* from the data files with *Microsoft Office Picture Manager*; use AutoCorrect to enhance the image on both photos. Save the revised files in your solutions folder and then insert the photos in appropriate places in the file. Fit the update on one page.

4. Save your changes, preview, and print.

### HOW DID YOU DO?

| | |
|---|---|
| 20 minutes: | Outstanding |
| 24 minutes: | Good job |
| 30 minutes: | Satisfactory |

Previous updates have kept you abreast of the progress of the new track and field facility. The decision to modify the original plans for a running track to include field events delayed the project approximately six weeks, but the outstanding response to these changes in the facility made the delay worthwhile.

Field Events Added

Facilities for the following field events have been incorporated into the project: long jump/triple jump runway and pit, high jump pad, pole vault runway and landing area, and discus and hammer throwing pad and landing area.

The Oak Park SportsPlex track and field facility will now meet the regulations to host track and field events at any level.

Track and Field Five-Phase Project

Site analysis and preparation, design and engineering, construction and installation, accurate finishing and marking, and Grand Opening.

Phase 4 has been completed. The all-weather eight-lane track is a polyurethane, full-pour, impermeable system used for world-class competition. This environmentally friendly track that meets the highest certification standards will serve the needs of Foster University and the community for many years to come. Even though the track and field facility has not officially opened, many athletes and community members are already trying it out.

Grand Opening

Plans for the grand opening are being finalized. The next Update will contain your invitation to this exciting event in the development of the Oak Park SportsPlex.

**SUBJECT/VERB AGREEMENT**

## Use a singular verb

1.  With a **singular subject**. (The singular forms of *to be* include: am, is, was. Common errors with *to be* are: you was, we was, they was.)

    She monitors employee morale.
    You are a very energetic worker.
    A split keyboard is in great demand.

2.  With most **indefinite pronouns**: *another, anybody, anything, everything, each, either, neither, one, everyone, anyone, nobody.*

    Each of the candidates has raised a considerable amount of money.
    Everyone is eager to read the author's newest novel.
    Neither of the boys is able to attend.

3.  With singular subjects joined by *or/nor, either/or, neither/nor.*

    Neither your grammar nor punctuation is correct.
    Either Jody or Jan has your favorite CD.
    John or Connie has volunteered to chaperone the field trip.

4.  With a **collective noun** (*family, choir, herd, faculty, jury, committee*) that acts as one unit.

    The jury has reached a decision.
    The council is in an emergency session.
    But:
    The faculty have their assignments. (Each has his/her own assignments.)

5.  With words or phrases that express **periods of time, weights, measurements**, or **amounts of money**.

    Fifteen dollars is what he earned.
    Two-thirds of the money has been submitted to the treasurer.
    One hundred pounds is too much.

## Use a plural verb

6.  With a **plural subject**.

    The students sell computer supplies for their annual fundraiser.
    They are among the top-ranked teams in the nation.

7.  With **compound (two or more) subjects** joined by *and*.

    Headaches and backaches are common worker complaints.
    Hard work and determination were two qualities listed by the references.

8.  With *some, all, most, none, several, few, both, many*, and *any* when they refer to more than one of the items.

    All of my friends have seen the movie.
    Some of the teams have won two or more games.

## Drill 1

**SUBJECT-VERB AGREEMENT**

1. Review the rules and examples on the previous page.
2. Open *subjectverb1* from the data files. Save it as *subjectverb-drill1*.
3. Follow the specific directions provided in the data file.
4. Save again and print.

## Drill 2

**SUBJECT-VERB AGREEMENT**

1. Open *subjectverb2* from the data files. Save it as *subjectverb-drill2*.
2. Follow the specific directions provided in the data file.
3. Save and print.

## Drill 3

**SUBJECT/VERB AND CAPITALIZATION**

1. Key the ten sentences at the right, choosing the correct verb and applying correct capitalization.
2. Save as *subjectverb-drill3* and print.

1. both of the curies (was/were) nobel prize winners.
2. each of the directors in the sales department (has/have) given us approval.
3. mr. and mrs. thomas funderburk, jr. (was/were) married on november 23, 1936.
4. my sister and her college roommates (plan/plans) to tour london and paris this summer.
5. our new information manager (suggest/suggests) the following salutation when using an attention line: ladies and gentlemen.
6. the body language expert (place/places) his hand on his cheek as he says, "touch your hand to your chin."
7. the japanese child (enjoy/enjoys) the american food her hosts (serve/serves) her.
8. all of the candidates (was/were) invited to the debate at boston college.
9. the final exam (cover/covers) chapters 1-5.
10. turn south onto interstate 20; then take exit 56 to bossier city.

## Drill 4

**EDITING SKILLS**
Key the paragraph. Correct all errors in grammar and capitalization. Save as *editing-drill4*.

This past week I visited the facilities of the magnolia conference center in isle of palms, south carolina, as you requested. bob bremmerton, group manager, was my host for the visit.

magnolia offers many advantages for our leadership training conference. The prices are reasonable; the facilities is excellent; the location is suitable. In addition to the beachfront location, tennis and golf packages are part of the group price.

# PROJECT 5
# NetCollege, Inc.

**5-1** Preparing a Business Plan

**5-2** Preparing a Training Proposal

**5-3** Creating Training Materials

**5-4** Completing Administrative Details

**FOCUS:** *Training*

You are now working for NetCollege, Inc., a training company that provides high-level technology training to managers, engineers, and other business professionals. NetCollege is currently applying to enter the UBI as an incubator company, and Jose Martinez, owner and CEO, has assigned you to assist with the preparation of the company's business plan and the news release announcing UBI's newest incubator company. The remainder of your assignment will be developing the training proposal, instructional materials, and other details required to implement a new technology training program.

# Preparing a Business Plan

Objectives

- Prepare executive summary of business plan
- Prepare news release

## TASK 1  NEWS RELEASE

To change the header on the second page, click the **Page Setup** button on the Header and Footer toolbar and select **Different odd and even.**

NetCollege is joining the UBI as an incubator client. You are to prepare the news release on NetCollege letterhead (data file *NC letterhead*), so begin the first line at about 2". Add the footer **-more-** to the bottom center of the first page; add the slug line **NetCollege joins UBI/(page number)** as a left-aligned header on the second page; and key **###** (centered) after the last line of the release to indicate the end. Save the release as *5-1task1* in the Solutions-Project 5 folder.

---

**NEWS RELEASE**                                        **Contact Person:** Linda Boyd
March 12, 20--                              VP of Corporate Business Development
**For Immediate Release**                                  708-555-0166
                                                    Linda.Boyd@ubi-sw.com

NetCollege joins UBI as newest incubator client

OAK PARK, Ill.—NetCollege Inc., a Chicago-based technology training company, has joined University Business Incubator as its latest client. NetCollege provides various levels of information technology training to managers, engineers, and other business leaders. With this latest addition, UBI now has 13 clients, including a biotech research firm, a travel agency, a communications firm, computer services providers, and several other diverse organizations.

"We're very excited about the opportunity to affiliate with UBI," said Jose Martinez, owner and CEO of NetCollege. "This partnership provides us with increased opportunities for growth and access to many new groups of professionals."

NetCollege began in 2002 as a training provider in Chicago, educating clients on basic word processing, spreadsheet, database, and presentation programs. NetCollege now offers a wide range of high-level technology training, including courses on website design, CD/DVD production, interactive video streaming, and videoconferencing. In addition to live instructor-led programs, NetCollege also offers courses via the Web, through videoconferencing, and through customized CD/DVD programs. NetCollege prides itself on producing customer-driven customized courses focusing on the needs of the individual client.

"We have always tried to meet the unique needs of our clients, providing them with customized training they need at the time, both on the technology and the related interpersonal skills," Martinez added. "We have not wanted to offer identical cookie-cutter programs to all of our clients, but rather we want to help them target their specific needs. This provides a better outcome for our clients and helps them reach their goals. Hopefully for us, it encourages the client to return to us for later training when new needs arise."

For more information on NetCollege, contact Linda Boyd, vice president of corporate business development, at 708-555-0166 or Linda.Boyd@ubi-sw.com. For more information on UBI, contact Yan Huang, public relations director, at 708-555-0176 or Yan.Huang@ubi-sw.com.

 Professional organizations and journals are excellent resources for training professionals. Acquaint yourself with the training profession by visiting http://www.advancedapplications.swlearning.com. Click Links and click Project 5.

## TASK 2  EXECUTIVE SUMMARY WITH LINKED WORKSHEET

Jose Martinez, owner and CEO of NetCollege, has assigned you the responsibility of preparing the executive summary of the NetCollege business plan. This summary and business plan will accompany the application to join the UBI as an incubator company. You will use a *Word* file and an *Excel* file created by two NetCollege staff members to prepare the summary. Follow these guidelines to prepare a professional document. Save the document as *5-1task2*.

- Set margins for a leftbound report and apply **Heading 1** to the main heading and center; apply **Heading 2** to the side headings.

- Insert a footer with the company name at the left, the page number at center, and the current date at the right. Include a border above the information in the footer, and add a 3-point brown border after the main heading.

- Apply the **Table Web 1** format to the table summarizing management qualifications.

- Ensure there are no widows or orphans and no table rows split between pages.

## NetCollege, Inc. Business Plan

## Executive Summary

NetCollege, Inc., incorporated in March 2002, provides high-level information technology training to a wide variety of businesses, organizations, and industries. The vision of the company is to provide the best custom-designed technology training programs to clients whose business success depends on a qualified workforce prepared to meet the challenges of emerging technologies. The delivery vehicle of the instruction will be determined by the needs of each client but may include instructor-led instruction on site or via videoconferencing, Web-based instruction, and/or CD/DVD.

With this vision in mind, NetCollege believes it can generate $10M in annual sales and a 20 percent net profit margin. The goal is to increase revenue fourfold, double in staff size, and increase profits.

Market

The market is competitive with the rapid change in technology. However, NetCollege offers a unique opportunity for clients choosing to use its services. Our company has much-needed expertise in needs assessment and the ability to design custom training programs for adult learners in a variety of delivery formats with 24/7 support capabilities. Clients have already come to recognize our reputation of providing training for the 21st century and also training that gets results.

Product and Services

NetCollege, Inc. develops custom training programs that are designed after a thorough needs assessment of its clients' challenges. The learning outcomes of each training program are evaluated carefully by all stakeholders before specific training objectives are written for each goal. Grounded in adult learning theories and knowledge of a wide range of delivery media, our designers are able to ensure results when our custom training programs are acquired. Additionally, developers stay abreast of emerging technologies to ensure best delivery.

Management

The qualifications of NetCollege's management are impressive, totaling over 100 years of high-level technology and educational experience. A summary of their experience is outlined in the following table.

| Name/Title | Summary of Experience | Last Position |
|---|---|---|
| Jose Martinez, Owner and Chief Executive Officer | 15 years of high-technology business experience | Interim Chief Operating Officer at Telecommunications, Inc. |
| Rick Perez, Chief Financial Officer | 15 years of chief financial officer experience | Chief Financial Officer at NTC Systems, Inc. |
| Linda Boyd, Vice President of Corporate Business Development | 25 years in marketing and sales of education programs—both domestic and international | Director of International Corporate Relations at Simpson Communications, Inc. |
| Ralph Fugo, Vice President and Chief Learning Officer | 20 years as educator and pioneer in instructional technology | Senior Project Manager and District Manager for NTC Systems, Inc. |
| Debra Gross, Vice President of Technology and Development | 20 years of high-technology experience related to curriculum development | Director of Curriculum and Technology Department at Wellington University |

Customer Support

Supporting the customer through the entire process of training is a goal of NetCollege. The company realizes the initial support provided during the needs assessment stage is essential. But following through until the learning goals have been met and the client's employees are applying the skills in the workplace is an essential element of a successful training program. Our training staff is committed from the initial contact to the final evaluation of the training program. To further enhance this full service, the company offers clients a toll-free number for calls and a website for communication questions or problems.

Financial Projections

NetCollege presents the following financial projections as evidence of the company's ability to net profits and to show the rapid growth of the company since its inception.

*Open the Excel data file projections. Select the range A1:D13 and link it here. Add a border around the linked worksheet to make it more attractive.*

Capitalization

*Insert the data file capitalization provided by Rick Perez here.*

To link the file, in *Excel*, click **Edit, Copy**. In the *Word* file, click **Edit, Paste Special, Paste Link, Microsoft Office Excel Worksheet Object, OK**.

# Preparing a Training Proposal

### Objectives

- Combine subdocuments in master document
- Set a bookmark
- Compose a letter of transmittal
- Prepare an index
- Design a title page
- Generate a table of contents
- Update table of contents and index

---

## TASK 1  TRAINING PROPOSAL

Ralph Fugo, the chief learning officer, has assigned you to coordinate the preparation of the formal training proposal to be presented to Mr. Kevin Mayfield, President and CEO, Mayfield, Brown, and Associates, a public relations firm requesting training for their account executives.

Format the proposal as a leftbound report. Apply **Heading 1** style and center the main heading. Apply **Heading 2** style to the side headings. Below the last paragraph under *Projected Benefits*, link the cell range A3:E9 from the *Excel* data file *roi*.

Set a bookmark at the heading *Projected Benefits*; name it *Benefits*. Save the document as *5-2task1*.

### PRESENTATION TRAINING PROPOSAL

On March 2, Scott Johnson of Mayfield, Brown, and Associates met with Ralph Fugo, chief learning officer, to discuss the design of an electronic presentation training program for account executives in their public relations, marketing, and advertising firm. The following sections of this proposal address the needs assessment, learning outcomes of the training program, program outline, training materials required, development and delivery costs, and projected benefits.

Analysis of the Problem

To determine the specific needs for electronic presentation training, the following components were included in the needs assessment:

1. Administered pretest to account executives to determine current technology and delivery skills.

2. Interviewed account executives.

3. Interviewed vice presidents.

4. Videotaped one presentation delivered by each of the 18 account executives.

Projected Benefits

In analyzing time spent by executives on attracting new clients and preparation time spent in designing multimedia presentations, the following Return on Investment can be achieved by Mayfield, Brown, and Associates by implementing this training program.

## TASK 2  TRAINING PROPOSAL (MASTER DOCUMENT)

Today you have received the other sections of the training proposal from other staff members. Insert those files as subdocuments in your master document *5-2task1*. Follow these guidelines in preparing the master document.

In Outline View, place the insertion point just before the last section, *Projected Benefits*. Insert the following data files as subdocuments in the following order: *rationale*, *program outline*, and *materials and costs*. After the last paragraph under *Development and Delivery Costs*, link the range A4:C19 from the *Excel* data file *costs*.

Resave the document as *5-2task1*.

**THINK CRITICALLY**

- Do you think training is taking a large bite out of company budgets in the 21st century?
- Is the expense of training employees really a return on investment or is that money lost to the company?

## TASK 3  LETTER OF TRANSMITTAL

Prepare a letter of transmittal from Ralph Fugo to Mr. Kevin Mayfield, President and CEO, Mayfield, Brown, and Associates, transmitting the training proposal. Mr. Mayfield's address is 889 Winston Circle, Oak Park, IL 60301-0889.

The letter should be created as part of the training proposal and appear on a separate page before the table of contents. Resave the document as *5-2task1*.

Here is the proposal for an electronic presentation technology training program for 18 account executives at Mayfield, Brown, and Associates. This proposal, requested by you on March 12, is a result of collaboration among a number of outstanding learning and training specialists at NetCollege, Inc.

This proposal includes a thorough assessment of the needs of these employees and your organization, learning outcomes you wish to achieve, a detailed program outline, training materials and personnel required, development and delivery costs, and projected benefits. After your account executives complete this one-day training solution, you are expected to reap a return on investment of 250 percent.

Our formal meeting to discuss this proposal is scheduled for Monday, March 18. I look forward to this discussion and to assisting you in this training decision.

## TASK 4    INDEX

Create an index on a new page at the end of the master document. Add the main heading *Index*, apply **Heading 1** style, and center it. Format the index in the formal style. Include these words in the index: *benefits*, *costs*, *delivery*, *learning goals*, *materials*, *multimedia*, and *needs*.

Everyone has his or her own way of learning new information. Your learning style is how your brain works to learn new information. For more information on learning styles, visit http://www.advancedapplications. swlearning.com. Click **Links** and click **Project 5**.

## TASK 5     TITLE PAGE

You will now need to design an attractive title page as the first page of the master document. Include appropriate decorative elements such as WordArt, borders, or clip art. You are preparing the report for Mr. Kevin Mayfield, President and CEO, Mayfield, Brown, and Associates. The report is from Ralph Fugo, Chief Learning Officer.

## TASK 6     TABLE OF CONTENTS

Next you need to generate the table of contents, but first you must insert page numbers. Number the preliminary pages at the bottom center with small Roman numerals, and number the report and index at the top right with Arabic numerals.

Generate the table of contents to display on a separate page after the letter of transmittal. Use the formal style. Add the main heading *Table of Contents*, apply **Heading 1** style, and center it.

## TASK 7     UPDATE TRAINING PROPOSAL

The master document needs to be updated. Add *Return on Investment* to the index. Update the index.

Delete the heading *Development and Delivery Schedule*. Move the paragraph remaining in that section so that it is the first paragraph of the next section. Edit the heading to read *Development and Delivery Schedule and Costs*. Update the table of contents.

Save the master document. Display the Document Map; click on each heading. If headings do not display, go to Outline View, and expand the subdocuments. Print the training proposal.

> **SUCCESS TIP**
> Do your homework before delivering a training session.
> - Know your audience.
> - Know your content.
> - Know your technology.
> - Know what you want to achieve.

# Creating Training Materials

Objectives

- Prepare training program outline
- Prepare training worksheet
- Prepare instructional handout
- Send training materials to training director for review

## TASK 1  TRAINING PROGRAM OUTLINE

To fit the outline on one page, adjust the font size or the spacing between paragraphs.

Ralph Fugo, the chief learning officer, asks you to prepare the outline for the training session titled *Electronic Presentation Delivery and Design Skills*. Format the text that follows in an attractive outline that will be printed as the agenda for the training session. You may use a small amount of color for a professional image. Here are some guidelines:

- Use the table feature, but do not print borders. Fit the outline to one page.

- Use the NetCollege logo (*NC logo.tif* from the data files) and create a slogan to print at the top of the document. You will use this logo in other training materials.

- Create a footer with the name of the session at the left and page number at the right.

Insert an en dash between starting and ending times and save the document as *5-3task1*.

### Electronic Presentation Delivery and Design Skills

### April 15, 20--

### Schedule of Events

| Hours | Events | Minutes |
|---|---|---|
| 7:45–8:00 a.m. | Registration (Coffee and pastries available at 7:30 a.m.) | 15 |
| 8:00–8:10 a.m. | Introductions and Icebreaker | 10 |

| | | |
|---|---|---|
| 8:15–9:10 a.m. | Module 1 | 55 |
| | "Deliver Your Presentation with Finesse" Lecturette by Carol Rush, Trainer | 10 |
| | Exercise—Practice Selected Techniques | 40 |
| | Video Evaluation—Identifying Delivery Techniques | 5 |
| 9:15–10:15 a.m. | Module 2 | 60 |
| | "Apply Key Principles of Design in Your Presentation" Lecture by Candace White, Trainer and Author of presentation design book | 50 |
| | Exercise—Identifying Key Principles | 10 |
| 10:15–10:30 a.m. | Break | 15 |
| 10:30–Noon | Module 3 | 90 |
| | "Make Your Presentation Interactive with Hyperlinks" Hands-on workshop led by Marcus Alexander, Trainer | 60 |
| | Project—Job-Related Slide Show with Hyperlinks | 30 |
| Noon–1:00 p.m. | Lunch—On Your Own | 60 |
| 1:00–2:30 p.m. | Module 4 | 90 |
| | "Create Dynamic Charts" Hands-on workshop led by Marcus Alexander, Trainer | 60 |
| | Project—Job-Related Slide Show with Hyperlinks | 30 |
| 2:30–3:00 p.m. | Break | 30 |
| 3:00–5:00 p.m. | Module 5 | 120 |
| | "Edit Your Photographs" Hands-on workshop led by Phyllis Wilkerson, Trainer | 60 |
| | Project—Edit Photos for Use in Upcoming Presentation | 60 |

**THINK CRITICALLY**

- Why is it important to create such a detailed schedule?

# FOCUS ON THE WORKPLACE

## How Do You Like to Learn?

Designing an effective training program that will achieve the desired learning outcomes requires the training designer to understand how people in organizations prefer to learn.

- visual
- auditory (listening)
- read and write
- kinesthetic (hands on)

Research is available on learning styles and preferences for intake and output of information; however, without a conscious effort to consider employees' learning preferences, trainers will often teach according to their own learning preferences.

Let's take a look at your learning preferences. Go to http://www.advancedapplications.swlearning.com. Click **Links** and click **Project 5**. Click the appropriate link to complete the VARK questionnaire. Calculate your preferences using the scoring instructions to determine your learning preferences.

---

## TASK 2  TRAINING WORKSHEET

A detailed training worksheet must be designed for each of the five modules to ensure objectives and learning activities will accomplish the learning outcomes identified in the needs assessment. Ralph Fugo has asked you to prepare the training worksheet for Module 1. Your design will be used for the remaining four modules. You are provided these guidelines:

- Key the training worksheet in a five-column table in landscape orientation with these column headings repeated on each page—**Learning Objective**, **Procedure**, **Timing**, **Evaluation**, and **Materials and Costs**. The planning form for Learning Objective #1 is shown on the next page. For the remaining seven objectives, refer to the *module 1 objectives* data file.

- Create a header that includes **Module 1—Delivering Multimedia Presentations Seamlessly**; then create a footer that includes the company name, **Program—Electronic Presentation Delivery and Design Skills** at the left and Page # at the right.

- Use an AutoFormat to make the table attractive and add a main heading that includes the title of program, the date the worksheet was prepared (March 20, 20--), the module number, and the module name. Key the program goal as part of the heading section: **Program Goal #1 Employees must be able to deliver a multimedia presentation seamlessly**.

- Add a text box below the table on page 1 for reminders to the trainer.

  **Reminders:**
  **Lelia King will arrive at 8:15.**
  **Robert Deangelo will need a wheelchair-accessible computer.**

- After the last objective, add a row and key the following procedure and evaluation:

  **Procedure:** Closing: Trainer reviews techniques for presenting seamlessly.

  **Evaluation:** Participants are shown video of a speaker presenting with a slide show. Participants then evaluate seamless delivery skills.

- Add a new row labeled **Totals** after closing and calculate totals for the *Timing* and *Materials and Costs* columns. Check figures in the Timing column with the program outline prepared in *5-3task1*.

- Preview the table to ensure that rows don't break between pages. Save the document as *5-3task2*.

| PLANNING SHEET FOR TRAINING WORKSHEET MODULE 1 | | | | |
|---|---|---|---|---|
| Learning Objective | Procedure | Timing | Evaluation | Materials and Costs |
| The participant will understand what it means to deliver seamlessly. | Trainer lectures on presenting seamlessly. | 5 min. | Participants view video and evaluate electronic delivery skills of presenter. | Computer with projection device 18 zip disks 2-page handout Slide shows <br> • Demonstration <br> • Practice <br> • Video <br> • Video production <br><br> Costs <br> Zip disks     $180 <br> Handouts     $20 <br> Slide shows     $50 <br> Video production     $300 |

# TASK 3    INSTRUCTIONAL HANDOUTS

Check your keyboarding technique using the form on page 236.

Two very important elements of an effective training program are well-written and professional instructional handouts. You have been asked to design the layout for instructional handouts for this training program. Handouts for all five modules will be keyed in a file and then printed and placed consecutively in a three-ring binder that will be given to each participant at registration.

Prepare the handout for Module 1. You are provided these guidelines:

- At the top of the handout, include the company logo; the title, *Instructional Handouts for Electronic Presentation Delivery and Design Skills Training Program*; and a subtitle, *Module 1—Delivering Multimedia Presentations Seamlessly*.

- Below the heading information, add the following copy as two separate paragraphs:

  Program Goal #1: Employees must be able to deliver a multimedia presentation seamlessly.

  This handout presents the following techniques for presenting seamlessly: view slide show, advance forward and move backward, go to specific slide, annotate a slide, clear the screen for focus on audience, and end with black slide.

- Format the remainder of the handout in a two-column format (or another creative format). Include a footer with Module 1 with the title at the left and the page number at the right.

- Keep the handout to two pages by adjusting space after paragraphs or fonts (but keep it readable). Add clip art if necessary to balance the columns.

- Be creative with fonts and borders for the pages or sections. Use a small amount of color to add interest. Add a picture or clip art of a training situation.

- Save the handout as *5-3task3*.

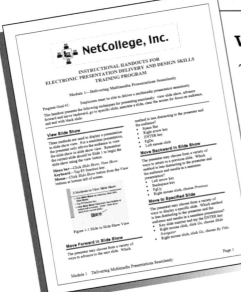

## View Slide Show

Three methods are used to display a presentation in slide show view. For a seamless presentation, the presenter only allows the audience to view the slide show in slide show view. Remember the current slide should be Slide 1 to begin the slide show using the view button.

**Menu bar**—Click *Slide Show, View Show.*

**Keyboard**—Tap F5 function key.

**Mouse**—Click *Slide Show* button from the View buttons at bottom left of screen.

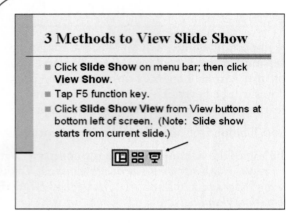

Insert the data file *slide 1.tif* here and add the caption.

Figure 1-1 Slide in Slide Show View

**Move Forward in Slide Show**

The presenter may choose from a variety of ways to advance to the next slide.  Which method is less distracting to the presenter and the audience?

- Space Bar
- Right arrow key
- ENTER key
- PgDn
- Left mouse click

**Move Backward in Slide Show**

The presenter may choose from a variety of ways to return to a previous slide.  Which method is less distracting to the presenter and the audience and results in a seamless presentation?

- Left arrow key
- Backspace key
- PgUp
- Right mouse click, choose *Previous*

**Move to Specified Slide**

The presenter may choose from a variety of ways to display a specific slide.  Which method is less distracting to the presenter and the audience and results in a seamless presentation?

- Key slide number and tap the ENTER key
- Right mouse click, click *Go*, choose *Slide Navigator*
- Right mouse click, click *Go*, choose *By Title*

**Change Cursor to Pen and Annotate**

Presenters may wish to draw and make notes on slides just as they might on a whiteboard or flip chart.  After the speaker moves from the annotated slide, the annotations are removed. Change the cursor to a pen as follows:

1. Right-click, click *Pointer Options*, and choose *Pen*.

2. Click and drag to draw with the pen. (*Hint:* Use Shift to draw a straight line.)

**Note:** Choose a contrasting pen color (right-click, *Pointer Options, Pen Color*).

### Clear Screen Using Black and White Techniques

When a question is raised by an audience member, the presenter will want to clear the screen so that the audience focuses on the question—not the slide. Use the black or white technique to clear the screen without going out of slide show view. Remember a seamless presentation is the goal.

### Black Technique

1. Tap the *B* key. Screen turns black.

2. Tap the *B* key to return to current slide in slide show view.

### White Technique

1. Tap the *W* key. Screen turns white.

2. Tap the *W* key to return to current slide in slide show view.

### End Slide Show with Black Slide

To prevent the presenter from clicking out of the slide show view when the last slide is shown, the presenter changes options so that each slide show ends with a black slide. To change options:

1. Click *Tools, Options, View*.

2. Choose option *End* with black slide.

---

### Module 1 Exercise

---

1. Open *Activity 1-1*.

2. Tap F5 to view slide show.

3. Tap ESC key to go out of slide show view.

4. Click *Slide Show* view button to display slide show.

5. Advance forward one slide as follows:
   a. Space Bar
   b. Right arrow key
   c. ENTER key
   d. PgDn
   e. Left mouse click

6. Move to previous slide as follows:
   a. Left arrow key
   b. Backspace key
   c. PgUp
   d. Right mouse click, click *Previous*
7. Move to Slide 2 (key 2; tap ENTER key).
8. Move to Slide 5.
9. Change cursor to pen.  Change pen color to magenta.  On Slide 5 underline the slide title.
10. Clear screen using the black technique; then display current slide again.
11. Clear screen using the white technique; then display current slide again.
12. Change options to end slide show with black slide.

| TASK 4 | E-MAIL WITH ATTACHMENTS |

E-mail the completed program outline, training worksheet, and instructional handout to Ralph Fugo (Ralph.Fugo@ubi-sw.com) for final approval.

 **For more information on icebreakers and free samples, search the Internet using keywords such as training icebreakers.  You may also visit http://www.advancedapplications.swlearning.com.  Click Links and click Project 5.**

# Completing Administrative Details

### Objectives

- Create an evaluation form
- Add registration information to database
- Prepare a class roster
- Create a custom name badge
- Create a training program checklist
- Create a certificate of completion

---

## TASK 1  EVALUATION FORM

Create as a table; print without gridlines. If necessary, use a smaller font.

To evaluate the Presentations Training Program, a printed evaluation form is given to each participant. Format the form attractively and adjust it as necessary to fit on one page. Use borders and shading to give emphasis to the sections. Include the NetCollege, Inc. logo at the top of the document. Save it as *5-4task1* and print.

### EVALUATION FORM

**Section 1:** *Please rate each of the following items to indicate your reaction to the training program. If your rating is less than average, please comment in the space provided below and, if necessary, continue on the back of this sheet.*

| | Poor | Adequate | Average | Good | Excellent |
|---|---|---|---|---|---|
| *Length of program* | ☐ | ☐ | ☐ | ☐ | ☐ |
| *Specific objectives of the training program were achieved.* | ☐ | ☐ | ☐ | ☐ | ☐ |
| *Environment was conducive to learning.* | ☐ | ☐ | ☐ | ☐ | ☐ |
| *Training materials were very well prepared.* | ☐ | ☐ | ☐ | ☐ | ☐ |
| *Training applied to job responsibilities and needs* | ☐ | ☐ | ☐ | ☐ | ☐ |
| *Which part of the program was of most value to you? Why?* | | | | | |

*Which part of the program was of least value to you?  Why?*

**Section 2:** *Please rate each of the following items regarding the trainer's ability to lead the program.*

| | Poor | Adequate | Average | Good | Excellent |
|---|---|---|---|---|---|
| *Knowledge of subject matter* | ☐ | ☐ | ☐ | ☐ | ☐ |
| *Organization/preparation of subject matter* | ☐ | ☐ | ☐ | ☐ | ☐ |
| *Clarity of instructions* | ☐ | ☐ | ☐ | ☐ | ☐ |
| *Ability to control time* | ☐ | ☐ | ☐ | ☐ | ☐ |
| *Ability to link content to your job* | ☐ | ☐ | ☐ | ☐ | ☐ |
| *Ability to create a productive learning environment* | ☐ | ☐ | ☐ | ☐ | ☐ |

**Section 3**

| | Poor | Adequate | Average | Good | Excellent |
|---|---|---|---|---|---|
| *Your overall reaction to the program* | ☐ | ☐ | ☐ | ☐ | ☐ |
| *Your level of skill after the program* | ☐ | ☐ | ☐ | ☐ | ☐ |
| *Comments* | | | | | |

**THINK CRITICALLY**

- Do you think evaluation forms such as these are really useful?
- Do you think that most participants would be truthful in their evaluations?  Why?

To sort, click in the last name field; then click Sort Ascending on the toolbar.

The participants of the Presentations training program need to be added to the database. Open the *Access* data file *training programs*. Open the table *Register* and input the following registrants. Sort participants by last name in ascending order. Save as *5-4task2 training programs*. Print the table in landscape orientation.

| No. | Last Name | First Name | Reg Date | Special Requests |
|-----|-----------|------------|----------|------------------|
| 01 | Moran | Valerie | 3/28/06 | |
| 02 | Modzelewski | Paul | 3/29/06 | |
| 03 | Pearson | Darlene | 3/29/06 | |
| 04 | Strickland | David | 4/1/06 | |
| 05 | Ashford | Charles | 4/1/06 | |
| 06 | Burroughs | Greg | 4/2/06 | |
| 07 | Novak | Andrew | 4/2/06 | |
| 08 | Ni | Tan | 4/3/06 | |
| 09 | Westfall | Kenneth | 4/3/06 | |
| 10 | Deangelo | Robert | 4/3/06 | Wheelchair-accessible computer table |
| 11 | Chitteni | Raja | 4/4/06 | |
| 12 | Sabatino | Suzanne | 4/4/06 | |
| 13 | Blake | Amy | 4/4/06 | |
| 14 | Barnet | Benjamin | 4/5/06 | |
| 15 | Raymond | Mary Ann | 4/5/06 | |
| 16 | Keene | Lelia | 4/5/06 | Will arrive at 8:15 |
| 17 | Flint | Anthony | 4/5/06 | |
| 18 | Givhan | Lynda | 4/5/06 | |

**TASK 3**      CLASS ROSTER (ACCESS REPORT)

The enrollment has reached the capacity of the computer lab scheduled for this session. You can now create the class roster using the *Access* database you updated in *5-4task2*. Open the *Access* file *5-4task2 training programs*, and follow these steps to create the report.

1. In the Objects column at the left, click **Reports**.

2. Double-click **Create report by using wizard**, and then click the double arrows (>>) to use all fields in the report. Click **Next**, and then click **Next** again.

3. Click the down arrow beside the first entry box and choose **Last Name**. Click the down arrow beside the second entry box and choose **First Name**. Click **Next**, and then click **Next** again.

4. Choose **Bold** from the list of styles, and click **Next**.

5. In the title entry box, key **Class Roster for Presentations Training Program**. Click **Finish**.

6. Select the report you just created and print it.

---

## TASK 4        ∏AME BADGES

Each participant in the Presentations training program will need a name badge. Use the *Access* database *5-4task2 training programs* for the recipient list and use the Mail Merge Wizard to prepare the badges. Sort by last name in ascending order. Use your creativity to customize the name badge and create a professional image. The name badge shown here is just an example; create your own design and slogan. Save the main document as *5-4task4 merge*. Save the merged labels as *5-4task4*.

NetCollege, Inc.

**Charles Ashford**

*...meeting your 21ˢᵗ century training needs*

---

**THINK CRITICALLY**

- Why is it important for the trainers to have a class roster?
- Why do you think the name badges will be helpful?

To ensure that everything goes smoothly, NetCollege uses an administrative checklist for each session. Create the administrative checklist for the April 15 training program. You will also need to create a diagram of the room as shown in the illustration using drawing tools. Use text boxes to key the five callouts (*Overhead Screen*, *VCR Cart*, etc.). Save the file as *5-4task5*.

## ADMINISTRATION CHECKLIST

Program Name:  Designing Presentations
Number of Participants:  18
Number of Instructors:  1
Number of Assistants:  1

Date:  April 15, 20--
Location:  Lab #1
Time:  8:00–5:00

Facilities Checklist — *Select square bullets*

☐ Computer laboratory

☐ Wall clock in computer laboratory

Equipment Checklist

☐ 18 computers

☐ Software—PowerPoint

☐ Data projection device

☐ Internet connectivity

☐ Remote mouse

☐ Microphones on each computer

☐ VCR (3/4") with monitor

Standard Materials

☐ 18 NetCollege logo pens

☐ 18 NetCollege logo writing pads

☐ 18 Participant binders

☐ Class roster

☐ Participant registration forms

☐ Participant name tags

☐ Paper clips

☐ Scissors

☐ Stapler

Special Materials

☐ Videotape "Multimedia Skills Unlimited"

☐ Bingo boards and board chips

☐ Door prize—Joey's Steak House Gift Certificate

Room Set-Up Diagram

☐ Lab arrangement—see layout on attached page.

Checked by _____     Date _____

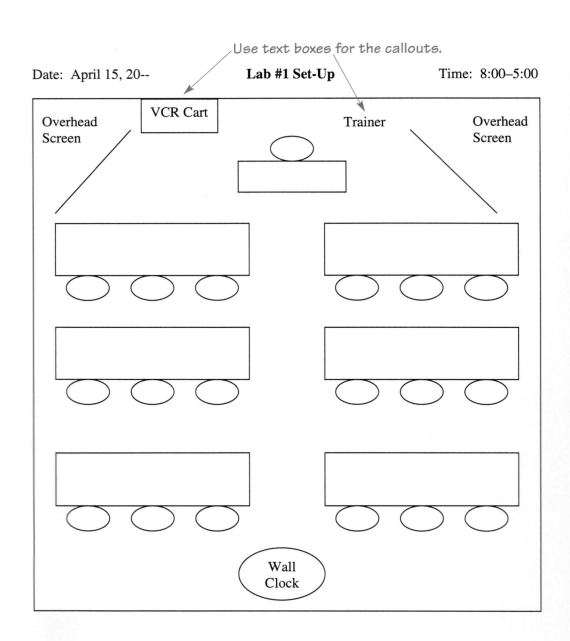

*Use text boxes for the callouts.*

Date: April 15, 20--                 **Lab #1 Set-Up**                 Time: 8:00–5:00

Overhead Screen          VCR Cart                    Trainer          Overhead Screen

Wall Clock

Design a certificate of completion to be presented to each participant by Ralph Fugo, the chief learning officer, at the conclusion of the training session. Open the data file *certificate* for a sample certificate. Use your creativity and add borders and fancy fonts.

Insert a merge field for the participant's name and use the *Access* database *training programs* as your recipient list. Sort by last name in ascending order. Assume all 18 participants completed the training.

Save the document as *5-4task6*. Save the main document as *5-4task6 merge*.

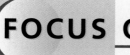

# FOCUS ON THE WORKPLACE

Training

## Will Any Icebreaker Do?

Getting off to a good start is very important for a successful training program. Thus, icebreakers are often used as a technique to get the class acquainted, to introduce the training topic, and to create interest in the training program.

Keep these points in mind when designing the icebreaker:

- Does it relate to the training content?
- Can participants apply the information to their jobs?
- Is it a waste of time?
- Is it just clever and fun to do or is learning really taking place?
- Will participants want to do the icebreaker—build an airplane, sing a song, throw a ball?

# PROJECT 5 CHECKPOINT

1.  What is a master document? What are subdocuments? In what situation would you use a master document and subdocuments?

2.  What information is keyed in the footer of the first page of a two-page news release? What is the purpose of this footer?

3.  What information is keyed in the header of the second page of a two-page news release? What is the purpose of this header?

4.  What notation indicates the end of a news release?

5.  What is an index? Can an index be updated if changes are made in the document? If so, how?

6.  How is the table of contents generated automatically?

7.  What command is necessary to number preliminary pages of a report with small Roman numerals (i, ii, iii) and to number other report pages with Arabic numbers (1, 2, 3)?

8.  Explain the steps to link an *Excel* worksheet in a *Word* document.

## Performance Assessment  Production Time: 20'

**Document 1**
**Inserting Subdocuments**
**in the Master Document**

1.  Open the data file *master*. Apply **Heading 2** style to the two side headings.

2.  After the last paragraph in the section labeled *sample test*, insert the data file *sample test* as the subdocument.

3.  After the last paragraph in the section labeled *practice test*, insert the data file *practice test* as the subdocument.

4.  Number pages at top right; print the document and save as *checkpoint5-d1*.

**Document 2**
**Prepare Diskette Labels**

1.  Create diskette labels for the participants in the Presentations training program. Include first name and last name on the label. Use the *Access* database *training programs* (used in *5-4task2*) for the data source, and use the Mail Merge Wizard to prepare the Avery 5196 diskette labels.

2.  Sort by last name in ascending order.

3.  Save the main document as *checkpoint5-d2 merge*. Print the merged labels and save as *checkpoint5-d2*.

**PRONOUN GUIDES**

## Pronoun Case

Use the **nominative case** (*I, you, we, she, he, they, it, who*):

1.  When the pronoun acts as the **subject of a verb**.
    Jim and *I* went to the movies.
    Mike and *she* were best friends.

2.  When the pronoun is used as a **predicate pronoun**. (The verb *be* is a linking verb; it links the noun/pronoun to the predicate.)
    It was *she* who answered the phone.
    The person who objected was *I*.

Use the **objective case** (*me, you, us, her, him, them, it, whom*):

3.  When the pronoun is used as a **direct** or **indirect object**.
    Jill invited *us* to the meeting.
    The printer gave Bill and *me* tickets to the game.

4.  When the pronoun is an **object of the preposition**.
    I am going with *you* and *him*.
    This issue is between *you* and *me*.

## Pronoun-Antecedent Agreement

1.  The **antecedent** is the word in the sentence that the pronoun refers to. In the examples, the antecedent is bold and the pronoun is in italic.
    **Players** must show *their* birth certificates.
    The **boy** lost *his* wallet.

2.  The antecedent must agree with the pronoun in **person** (first, second, third).
    **I** am pleased that *my* project placed first. (Both are first person.)
    **You** must stand by *your* display at the science fair. (Both are second person.)
    The ash **tree** has lost *its* leaves. (Both are third person.)

3.  The antecedent must agree with the pronoun in **gender** (neuter when gender of antecedent is unknown).
    **Gail** said that *she* preferred the duplex apartment.
    The adjustable **chair** sits firmly on *its* five-leg base.
    The **dog** looked for *its* master for days.

4.  The antecedent must agree with the pronoun in **number**. If the antecedent of a pronoun is singular, use a singular pronoun. If the antecedent is plural, use a plural pronoun.
    All **members** of the class paid *their* dues.
    **Each** of the Girl Scouts brought *her* sleeping bag.

Drill 1

**PRONOUN CHOICE**

1.  Open *pronoun* from the data files. Save it as *pronoun-drill1*.
2.  Follow the specific directions provided in the data file. Save again and print.

## Drill 2

Key the sentences, correcting the errors in pronoun case. Save as *pronoun-drill2*.

1. Marie and me have volunteered to work on the committee.
2. Give the assignment to George and I.
3. It is she who received the free airline ticket.
4. It was not me who sent in the request.
5. She has more time available than me for handling this project.
6. Did you see Cheryl and he at the opening session?

## Drill 3

Key the sentences, correcting the errors in pronoun and antecedent agreement. Save as *pronoun-drill3*.

1. Each student must have their own data disk.
2. Several students have his or her own computer.
3. Some of the employees were happy with their raises.
4. The company has not decided whether they will make profit sharing available.
5. All candidates must submit his or her résumé. (*To key the acute accent mark, press CTRL + apostrophe; then key* **e**.)
6. Napoleon organized their armies.

## APOSTROPHE GUIDES

### Apostrophes

1. Add *'s* to a singular noun not ending in *s*.
2. Add *'s* to a singular noun not ending in *s* or *z* sound if the ending *s* is pronounced as a syllable.

   **Sis's lunch, Russ's car, Buzz's average**
3. Add *'* only if the ending *s* or *z* is awkward to pronounce.

   **series' outcome, ladies' shoes, Delibes' music, Cortez' quest**
4. Add *'s* to a plural noun that does not end in *s*.

   **men's notions, children's toys, mice's tracks**
5. Add only *'* after a plural noun ending in *s*.

   **horses' hooves, lamps' shades**
6. Add *'s* after the last noun in a series to show joint possession of two or more people.

   **Jack and Judy's house; Peter, Paul, and Mary's song**
7. Add *'s* to each noun to show individual possession of two or more persons.

   **Li's and Ted's tools, Jill's and Ed's races.**

## Drill 4

Key the sentences, correcting all errors in apostrophes. DS between items. Save as *apostrophes-drill4*.

1. Mary Thomas, my neighbors sister, will take care of my son.
2. The assistant gave him the instructors telephone number.
3. The announcers microphone is never shut off.
4. His father-in-laws home will be open for touring next week.
5. Two hours time is not sufficient to set up the exhibit.
6. Someones car lights have been left on.

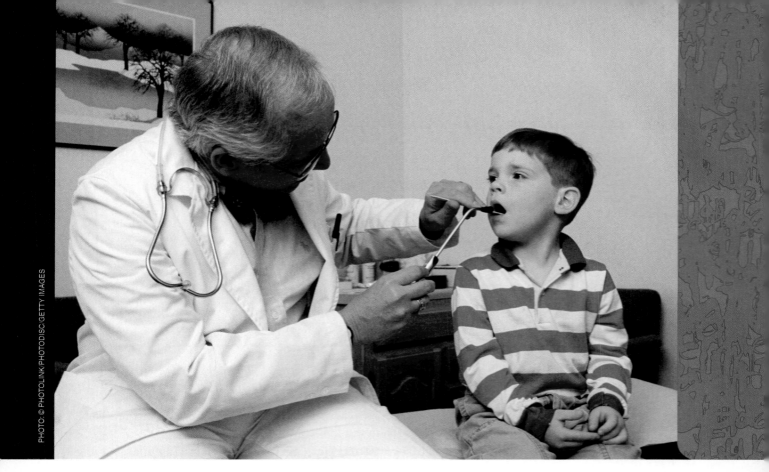

# PROJECT 6
# HealthCare Staff, Inc.

**6-1**  Getting Started

**6-2**  Creating Medical Office Documents

**6-3**  Preparing Web Pages and
PowerPoint Slides

**6-4**  Preparing Medical Reports

**6-5**  Designing Medical Forms

**FOCUS:** *Customer Service*

You report to the president and owner of HealthCare Staff, Inc., a company that joined the incubator on September 1, 2005. HealthCare Staff specializes in providing temporary staffing for a variety of administrative positions in physician offices, hospitals, and for other medical providers. It also provides temporary staffing for caregivers in home health-care situations. For several large clients, HealthCare Staff trains administrative workers using the specific forms and documents of the client. In most cases, work by HealthCare Staff is done in the provider's facility; however, in some cases, the work is sent as e-mail attachments to HealthCare Staff for completion. Your assignment requires you to work with a wide variety of medical documents for these different providers.

# Getting Started

## Objectives

- Design the company letterhead
- Create a macro incorporating the letterhead
- Develop an employment application form
- Customize a toolbar
- Display people-oriented traits

---

## TASK 1     LOGO

**caduceus:** an insignia bearing a caduceus and symbolizing a physician

Begin by creating the corporate logo and saving it as a separate file. The logo will be used repeatedly in future documents. The logo, created in WordArt, contains the name of the company encircling the **caduceus**.

1. Display the Drawing toolbar. Click the **Insert WordArt** button. Select the **WordArt** style in the first column, first row.
2. Key **HealthCare Staff, Inc.** Change the font to **Castellar**. Change the WordArt shape to **Circle (Pour)**. Change the height and the width of the WordArt to **1.3**.
3. Change the Fill Effects to **Gradient, Two colors**. Make Color 1 a shade of blue and Color 2 red. Select the **Horizontal Shading** style and use the variant that is in the second column, first row. Select **No Line**.
4. Change the layout of the WordArt to **In Front of Text**. Rotate the lettering as needed to place *HEALTHCARE* on the top half of the circle. Click the yellow diamond and move it slightly toward the lettering to make the inner circle wider.
5. Search in Clip Art for a **caduceus**. Size the caduceus to fit in the inner circle of the WordArt. Place it in back of the WordArt. Group the caducei and the WordArt.
6. Save as *HCS logo*. Print.

---

## TASK 2     LETTERHEAD

Use the **Insert, File** command to insert the logo.

You will now use the logo that you created in Task 1 to create a letterhead for HealthCare Staff, Inc. Use your creativity in making the letterhead. What follows is just an example. Include the logo, address, phone and fax numbers, and the website address in the letterhead. You will need to change the left and right margins to 1" and the top margin to .6" for the letterhead. HealthCare Staff, Inc. uses standard 1" side margins. Save the file as *6-1task2* and print.

# HealthCare Staff, Inc.

700 Lake Street, Suite 300, Oak Park, IL 60301-7984
708-555-0186   Fax: 708-555-0188
healthcarestaff@ubi-sw.com

THINK **CRITICALLY**

• Is the letterhead attractive and easy to read? Is it appropriate for a medical facility?

# FOCUS ON THE WORKPLACE

## Customer Service

### People-Oriented Employees

HealthCare Staff has adopted the slogan "Customer Service Is Our #1 Priority." Health care is a people-oriented profession. Caring for and a desire to help people are personal characteristics that workers in a medical environment must possess.

If you apply for a position in a medical field, you must let the potential employer know that you are "people oriented." Consider including the following information when writing your résumé or completing an application form.

- Mention any volunteer work you have done.
- If you hold a leadership role in an organization, note it on the résumé and application form.
- Include your desire to work with people as part of your career objective.
- List medical or professional organizations in which you are a member and any community activities in which you participate.

## TASK 3 — LETTERHEAD MACRO

Since the letterhead will be inserted at the top of many medical documents, you can save time by creating a macro to change the margins and insert the letterhead. Include these steps in your macro:

1. Change the left and right margins to 1" and the top margin to 6". Insert the letterhead you created in *6-1task2*.

2. Save the macro as *ltrhead*. Run the macro to verify that it works correctly.

## TASK 4 — EMPLOYMENT APPLICATION FORM

Click the **File** menu and then click **New**. Select **Templates on Office Online**. Key **Employment Application Form** in the Search box and click **Go**. View a sample form.

You have been asked to design an application form for those who apply for medical positions. Create the application form that is shown on the next two pages. To fit the application on two pages, use .5" margins and 9- and 10-point fonts. Use tables for the Education, Work Experience, and Reference sections. Insert graphic lines or borders to separate sections. Use the underscore and right leader tabs to add the write-on lines. Use tabs to align information attractively. Insert the logo at the top of the form. Key the company name and address. Do not insert the letterhead; it will take up too much space. Save as *6-1task4*.

# HealthCare Staff, Inc.
700 Lake Street, Suite 300, Oak Park, IL 60301-7984

## APPLICATION FOR EMPLOYMENT

TYPE OR PRINT CLEARLY _____

**PERSONAL INFORMATION**

NAME _____
         LAST                        FIRST                   MIDDLE

PERSENT ADDRESS _____
                  STREET            CITY          STATE       ZIP CODE

PERMANENT ADDRESS _____
                  STREET            CITY          STATE       ZIP CODE

PHONE NUMBER  (_____)_____    SOCIAL SECURITY NUMBER_____

CAN YOU, AFTER EMPLOYMENT, SUBMIT VERIFICATION OF YOUR LEGAL RIGHT TO WORK IN THE UNITED STATES?

**Circle One:**    YES   NO    (IF YES, VERIFICATION WILL BE REQUIRED.)

HAVE YOU EVER BEEN CONVICTED OF A CRIME?    YES   NO

**EMPLOYMENT DESIRED**

POSITION _____
DATE YOU CAN START_____
SALARY DESIRED_____

CIRCLE ALL THAT YOU ARE WILLING TO WORK:    DAYS     EVENINGS    NIGHTS     WEEKENDS    ON CALL

ARE YOU CURRENTLY EMPLOYED? _____
IF SO, MAY WE INQUIRE OF YOUR PRESENT EMPLOYER?_____

**EDUCATION**

|  | NAME AND LOCATION OF SCHOOL | DEGREE OR CERTIFICATE | SUBJECTS STUDIED |
|---|---|---|---|
| HIGH SCHOOL |  |  |  |
|  |  |  |  |
| UNIVERSITY OR COLLEGE |  |  |  |
|  |  |  |  |
| TRADE, BUSINESS, OR CORRESPONDENCE SCHOOL |  |  |  |
|  |  |  |  |

LIST ANY EXPERIENCE, SKILLS, OR QUALIFICATIONS THAT WILL BE OF SPECIAL BENEFIT IN THE POSTION FOR

WHICH YOU ARE APPLYING. _____

WHAT FOREIGN LANGUAGES DO YOU SPEAK FLUENTLY? _____

TO WHAT PROFESSIONAL ORGANIZATIONS DO YOU BELONG? _____

_____

LIST PROFESSIONAL LICENSES, CERTIFICATES, OR REGISTRATIONS. _____

_____

**WORK EXPERIENCE**

List all present and past employment, beginning with the most recent.

| Employer | Dates and Salary | Duties Performed | Reason for Leaving |
|---|---|---|---|
| Name: _____ <br> Address: _____ <br> City: _____ State: _____ ZIP: _____ <br> Phone: _____ Supervisor: _____ | From: _____ <br> To: _____ <br> Salary: _____ <br> _____ | | |
| Name: _____ <br> Address: _____ <br> City: _____ State: _____ ZIP: _____ <br> Phone: _____ Supervisor: _____ | From: _____ <br> To: _____ <br> Salary: _____ <br> _____ | | |
| Name: _____ <br> Address: _____ <br> City: _____ State: _____ ZIP: _____ <br> Phone: _____ Supervisor: _____ | From: _____ <br> To: _____ <br> Salary: _____ <br> _____ | | |

**REFERENCES:** List at least three people, who are not related to you, whom you have known at least one year.

| NAME | ADDRESS | TELEPHONE | BUSINESS |
|---|---|---|---|
| | | | |
| | | | |
| | | | |
| | | | |

In case of an emergency notify: _____
                                                      Name                                                          Phone No.

Address: _____

The above information is true and correct to the best of my knowledge. Misrepresentation or omission of material facts (i.e., facts related to my qualifications for the position for which I am applying) is cause for separation from the employer. I also authorize all former employers, schools, and persons named above to furnish references and any facts which may be pertinent to my employment. I understand that employment is also contingent upon passing a physical examination.

Signature: _____     Date: _____

You can customize a toolbar by adding buttons for tasks that you frequently perform. Ordinarily, you would save changes to the toolbar in the Normal template so that the custom toolbar is always displayed. However, since other people may use your computer, you need to save your custom toolbar in a document. You will use this document in the next job. Follow the steps below to customize your toolbar.

**Add a font button on your toolbar:**

1. Open a new document and save it as *custom-your last name*.

2. Click the **Tools** menu, select **Customize**, and click the **Commands** tab.

3. Click the **Save in** drop-list arrow and choose *custom-your last name*.

4. Choose **Fonts** in the Categories window. Select **Arial Black** in the Commands window and drag the name up to your Formatting toolbar. (If you do not have the Arial Black font, select another.) Close the Customize dialog box.

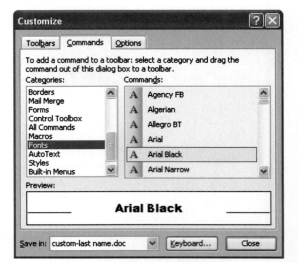

5. Click the **Arial Black** button on your toolbar. The font is now changed to the new font you selected.

**Add a button on your toolbar to go to the UBI website:**

1. Open the *custom-your last name* file you just created.

2. On the Commands tab of the Customize dialog box, select *custom-your last name* from the Save in box, and choose **Web** in the Categories window.

3. Select **Open Hyperlink** in the Commands box and then drag the **Open Hyperlink** command to the Standard toolbar. Close the Customize dialog box.

4. Click the **Open Hyperlink** button you just dragged to the toolbar. The Open Internet Address dialog box displays.

5. Key the address of the UBI website (http://www.ubi-sw.com) and then click **OK**. The Web page displays. Save your file and close.

# Creating Medical Office Documents

## Objectives

- Create a SOAP note form
- Create a SOAP note
- Create an Office Note form
- Create an Office Note
- Perform a mail merge

---

## TASK 1

## SOAP NOTE FORM

Remember that HealthCare Staff, Inc. uses standard 1" side margins.

Forms that include field headings and patient data should be formatted so that the headings are distinct and in a different font. First, key the headings and insert the text fields. Then apply a unique style to the field headings. When patient data is added later, it will be formatted in the Normal style (Times New Roman).

All medical facilities keep recorded notes of patients' office visits. These records are called chart notes, office notes, or SOAP notes. Whatever each office calls them, they all serve the same purpose.

The SOAP note format is the most commonly used. SOAP stands for:

**S** SUBJECTIVE (what the patient tells the physician)

**O** OBJECTIVE (the physician's findings as a result of a physical exam or evaluation)

**A** ASSESSMENT (the physician's diagnosis or impression of the problem)

**P** PLAN (the planned treatment for the patient)

Create a SOAP note as a protected form that can easily be filled in by each medical office. The form consists of the letterhead, text fields, and a table. Open the document *custom-your last name* that you created in 6-1task4 and save it as *6-2task1*. Insert the letterhead you created in *6-1task2*.

Create the form, leaving two spaces after each heading before inserting the fields. Set the text fields for unlimited length, except where a specific length is indicated. Tap TAB after each field to create the next heading and field. The headings will not always align, especially when the form is filled in. When you finish creating the form, format the headings (not the text fields) in Arial Black using the customized button.

Insert a graphic line below the headings, as shown on the next page. Then create a two-column table for the rest of the form. Increase the row height to 1". Align text vertically in the cells. Create a footer with a line for the physician's signature and date. When you finish, protect the form and save it as *6-2task1*.

# HealthCare Staff, Inc.

700 Lake Street, Suite 300, Oak Park, IL 60301-7984
708-555-0186    fax:  708-555-0188
healthcarestaff@ubi-sw.com

**Last Name:** *unlimited text field*    **First Name:**    **Patient No.** *number field, max. 5, format 0*

**Age:** *number field, 2, 0*    **Allergies:**    **Meds:**

**T:** *number field, 5, 0.0*    **P:** *number field, 2, 0*    **R:** *number field, 2, 0*    **B/P:** / *number field, 3/3, 0*

**C/O:**    **Date:** *m/d/yyyy*

| | |
|---|---|
| **S** | unlimited text field - Times New Roman |
| **O** | unlimited text field |
| **A** | unlimited text field |
| **P** | unlimited text field |

Physician's Signature                                         Date

# TASK 2      SOAP NOTE

To access AutoCorrect, click **Tools, AutoCorrect Options, AutoCorrect** tab.

Now that you have created the SOAP form, you can begin adding patient information. Since medical offices use common abbreviations when recording information, it will be easier if you add these abbreviations to AutoCorrect so that you do not have to key the complete medical term.

The following table shows some common abbreviations and what they stand for.

| Replace | With |
|---------|------|
| SOB | shortness of breath |
| NKDA | no known drug allergies |
| Pt | patient |
| URI | upper respiratory infection |

When you finish adding the abbreviations to AutoCorrect, fill in the form with the information that follows and save it as *6-2task2*.

---

Jacob Linden, age 19, Patient number 63679

Allergies: NKDA

Meds: None

T: 98.6      P: 84      R: 20      B/P: 124/86

C/O: Cough      Date: Current Date

S   Pt complains of cough and head congestion for the past 48 hours, SOB, lethargy, and low appetite.

O   Pt coughing up green sputum. Lungs clear, ears clear. Lymph nodes enlarged bilateral neck. Bilateral tonsils enlarged. CXR-WNL, PPD negative. CBC—elevated white count.

A   Acute URI

P   Pt is to take 333 mg E-Mycin, 1 tablet every 8 hours for 1 week. Increase fluids, increase rest. Pt is to remain off from work for 3 days. Recheck in 1 week or sooner if needed.

## THINK CRITICALLY

- What are the advantages of having standard forms in medical offices?
- What other tasks could be automated to save time?

## OFFICE NOTE FORM

Office notes serve the same purpose as SOAP notes. The office note does not have the letters SOAP spelled out, but as you can see from the illustration, the content of the two is very similar.

Open the SOAP note form you created as *6-2task1* and save it as *6-2task3*. Unprotect the form, and center and key **OFFICE NOTE** at approximately 2.1" in 14-point Arial Black and 12-point space after the paragraph. Delete the SOAP table. The body of the office note is keyed below the graphic line and should be created as an unlimited text field. Protect the form and save it again as *6-2task3*.

## OFFICE NOTE

Use the office note form you created in *6-2task3*, and fill it in with the following patient information. Save the completed form as *6-2task4*.

Jonathan Nolan, age 14, Patient number 3828

| Allergies | | Leave blank | | Meds | Leave blank |
|-----------|---|-------------|---|------|-------------|
| T | 98.6 | P | 84 | R | 20 | B/P | 110/50 |

C/O  Leave blank          Date

Jonathan Nolan (PF 3151-10-06) is a 14-year-old high school student who was in good health until February 21, 2007, when after four days of a flu-like illness, he awoke at 9 a.m. with numbness and tingling. By noon he had difficulty breathing and went to Children's Hospital of Chicago on a ventilator. He was initially treated with IV gamma globulin and later with steroids and subsequently transferred to St. John's for rehab. He is now at home. He has done very well but continues to have a major defect, particularly on his right side. He had some low back pain. He has the sensation of exaggerated temperature sensitivity on the right side and has horrific pains in the left posterior neck and suboccipital region, which last for half an hour and occur up to several times a day. He has had minor difficulties with bowel control. His MRIs have apparently shown myelopathy between C2 and C7.

> **SUCCESS TIP**   Keep a medical dictionary nearby to look up unfamiliar terms to ensure they are correctly spelled.

On examination, he has a blood pressure of 110/50. He is photophobic. He has some palpebral conjunctivitis bilaterally. He is uncomfortable in C3 on the right side and on the left side. The left triceps and left finger extensors are a little bit weak and the abductor pollicis brevis on the left was a little bit weak. On the right, these changes are markedly exaggerated but have a similar distribution. Repetitive movements are decreased on the left but are not easy to perform at all on the right. He has a weak right psoas and some moderate weakness of the quadriceps on the right. The right ankle is quite poor in terms of movement. There is some contracture of the Achilles tendon although it is rather mild. His right knee and ankle jerk are exaggerated. His finger jerks and triceps jerks are exaggerated. He has decreased biceps and supinator reflexes. Two-point discrimination is decreased on the right. Vibration sense is good. Position sense is good. His plantar responses are exterior. He has an exaggerated response to cold on the right but pin reduced on the left to T4.

It is clear that this was an autoimmune, postviral transverse myelitis. I feel strongly that he needs to be sustained in physical therapy and occupational therapy for many, many months. Because of his age, his prognosis is quite good. I asked him to start on Zanaflex beginning with one-half pill once a day and working up to as much as one or two pills twice a day. I gave him some Neurontin to try for his neck discomfort. For his headaches, I would try Advil or Midrin or Fiorinal. I also think that Claritin 10 mg once a day may help some of his symptoms in the eyes.

I will be happy to follow him. We will work on his continuing care as required.

**THINK CRITICALLY**

- How important is confidentiality in a medical office?
- What would you do if someone asked you for information about this patient?

# FOCUS ON THE WORKPLACE

## Customer Service

### Dealing with Difficult Patients

Patients expect office assistants working in a medical office, a hospital, or a clinic to show concern for their welfare and have a sincere desire to help them. Patients may be irritable, depressed, or angry due to their physical conditions. Dealing with patients requires tact. Both your verbal and nonverbal communication need to convey the message of care and concern.

- Greet patients by name when they enter the office.
- A gentle pat on the back can communicate a caring attitude.
- A smile on your face shows that you are happy to see them and you are willing to help.
- Face patients as they speak to you to show you are listening carefully.

---

**TASK 5**

## MAIL MERGE

Most medical facilities use a variety of form letters to remind patients of yearly exams and routine office visits, to inform patients of test results, and for collection notices. We need a new form letter to remind patients to schedule their mammograms. Prepare the following letter as a form letter. Be sure to include the letterhead, the current date, all appropriate letter parts, and your name as the writer. Key the patient number in a reference line. **Re: Patient No.: <<Patient No>>.**

Key the letter and merge it with the data that follows. Save the main letter as *6-2task5main*. Save the data file as *6-2task5data*. Save the merged letters as *6-2task5*.

You can search the Web for medical information using keywords such as myelitis. There are also a number of websites for looking up medical terminology. Try searching the Web for one of the terms in the previous report. You may also go to http://www.advancedapplications. swlearning.com. **Click Links and click Project 6.**

Our records indicate that your last mammogram was performed on <<Last Exam>>. It is time for your next routine mammogram. Statistics show that the mortality rate of breast cancer can be significantly reduced with routine mammography, an annual doctor's exam, and your own monthly breast self-examinations.

We recommend that you make an appointment for your next mammogram by <<Follow Up>>. Before making an appointment, please confer with your physician, <<Referring Dr>>.

Before making an appointment:

✓ Be sure you have a referral or prescription form from your doctor.

✓ HMO patients must have prior authorization from their insurer as well as referral from their primary care physician.

When you report for your exam, please do not wear powder or deodorant as they can interfere with the evaluation.

Sincerely

Student Name
Mammography Department

**Data Source**

Use the following data fields: Title, First Name, Last Name, Address Line 1, City, State, ZIP Code, Patient No, Last Exam, Follow Up, Referring Dr.

Ms. Helen Thomas, 2905 Alexandria Street, Oak Park, IL 60302; 59012
Last Exam: January 10, 2006              Follow Up: January 11, 2007
Lorianna Hernandez, M. D.

Ms. Patricia Bressler, 1502 Bixby Lane, Oak Park, IL 60301; 83215
Last Exam: February 2, 2006              Follow Up: February 3, 2007
Fredrick Stohl, M. D.

Ms. Lily Gates, 905 Tiffany Place, Oak Park, IL 60302; 89111
Last Exam: February 7, 2006              Follow Up: February 8, 2007
Stanley Moore, M. D.

SUCCESS TIP    Concern for others produces good results.

# Preparing Web Pages and PowerPoint Slides

Objectives

- Create a report and save it as a Web page
- Create a table and save it as a Web page
- Prepare *PowerPoint* slides
- Create a memo with links to Web documents
- Search files

---

## TASK 1

## WEB ARTICLE

HealthCare Staff maintains a website for the general public that contains articles relating to health and fitness. The site also contains reference material that only HealthCare staff members can access. One of your duties is to attractively format and key the articles written by the medical staff for the website.

Key the following article using the letterhead and WordArt for the title. Apply an appropriate theme for the Web page and save the document as a Web page named *6-3task1*.

On the menu bar, click **Format, Theme.**

### CONTROL HIGH BLOOD PRESSURE

High blood pressure (hypertension) is one of the most common diseases. Statistics show that 15–25 percent of adult Americans (60,000,000) have high blood pressure.

People often do not know that they have high blood pressure because it usually has no symptoms. It is important that high blood pressure is detected and treated; untreated high blood pressure can shorten life span or cause a stroke. People with high blood pressure are at greater risk of having a heart attack, angina pectoris (chest pain), heart failure, kidney failure, stroke, and rupture and blockage of major arteries. High cholesterol levels and cigarette smoking further increase the chances of having one of these major problems.

Blood pressure changes with exercise, body position (sitting, standing, lying down), diet (mostly salt intake), weight, stress, and time of day. Blood pressure is usually higher in the morning. It is often higher when measured in a doctor's office rather than at home. Oftentimes, blood pressure that is high will go back to the normal range if measured several more times.

Your doctor will advise you to take your blood pressure often if it is moderately high. Many times, higher blood pressure will return to normal without medication, simply by following these suggestions:

1. Cut down on the amount of salt and sodium you eat. Limit sodium intake to 1,800–2,400 mg/day. Read labels for sodium content on packaged foods.

2. If you are overweight, lose some weight.

3. Limit alcohol intake.

4. Avoid taking over-the-counter drugs that increase blood pressure such as ibuprofen (Nuprin®, Medipren®, Advil®, and Motrin®), decongestants with phenylpropanolamine, and antacids with high salt content.

5. Exercise moderately. Taking a brisk 30–45 minute walk 3–5 times per week can reduce your systolic blood pressure (the top number) by 10 mm.

If your blood pressure remains high after you have tried these measures, your doctor will most likely prescribe an antihypertensive medication (medicine to lower blood pressure). Even if you take medication, it is wise to follow these suggestions. Keeping your blood pressure under control lowers your risk of stroke or heart attack.

*Call 888-555-0180 to register for the free class*
*"Control Your Blood Pressure"*

 **Most major health-care providers have websites that provide health information, job opportunities, and links to valuable information. Search the Internet using keywords such as health care or health-care providers. For additional information, visit http://www.advancedapplications. swlearning.com. Click Links and click Project 6.**

## TASK 2        WEB TABLE

Create the table that will be placed in the reference section of the website. Home health nurses, medical assistants, and clinic assistants can refer to this chart when treating high blood pressure patients.

Key the table landscape as shown on the next page. Add the logo and company name (not the complete letterhead) centered at the top. Use WordArt to key **Stage** and the number in column A. Place the number in back of *Stage*. Format the table attractively, and save it as a Web page named *6-3task2*.

# HealthCare Staff, Inc.

## Asymptomatic Hypertension Algorithm

| | | | |
|---|---|---|---|
| Stage 1 | Systolic | 140 to 159 | 1. Patient instruction sheet.<br>2. Follow-up blood pressure **within 2 months** by already assigned primary MD. **Make appointment before patient leaves office.** |
| | Diastolic | 90 to 99 | |
| Stage 2 | Systolic | 160 to 179 | 1. Patient instruction sheet.<br>2. Follow-up blood pressure **within 1 month** by already assigned primary MD. **Make appointment before patient leaves office**. |
| | Diastolic | 100 to 109 | |
| Stage 3 | Systolic | ≥ 180 | 1. Patient instruction sheet.<br>2. Follow-up blood pressure **within 1 week** by already assigned primary MD. **Make appointment before patient leaves office**. |
| | Diastolic | ≥ 110 | |

## TASK 3 — POWERPOINT SLIDES

Part of HealthCare Staff's mission is to provide health education classes for the community. One of the staff cardiologists, Dr. David Beem, has asked you to assist him in preparing a few *PowerPoint* slides for his class "Control Your Blood Pressure."

A blank title slide displays when you open *PowerPoint*. Click the **View** menu, select **Master** and then click **Slide Master**. Click the **Insert** menu and select **New Title Master**. Insert the logo, **HealthCare Staff, Inc.**, and **Circulation Through the Heart**. Insert a graphic line separating the heading from the body of the slide. Group all the items in the heading. Save as *6-3task3* and click the **Close Master View** button on the toolbar.

Key **CONTROL HIGH BLOOD PRESSURE** in the title placeholder. Key **Dr. David Beem, Cardiologist** and your name as the assistant in the subtitle placeholder. Arrange placeholders attractively on the slide.

HealthCare Staff, Inc.
## Circulation Through the Heart

# CONTROL HIGH BLOOD PRESSURE

**Dr. David Beem, Cardiologist**
Student Name, Assistant

Switch to Slide Master View and click **Slide 1** to display the Master Slide. Move the top border of the *Object Area for AutoLayouts* placeholder down to make more room for the heading. Click the Title Slide (Slide 2); copy the heading. Paste the heading at the top of Slide 1. Save and click the **Close Master View** button. Add a new slide select the blank slide layout.

### Slide 2

Insert the diagram of a heart. You will find this clip art on the Microsoft site; access it by clicking **Clip art on Office Online** in the Clip Art task pane. Search for *heart chambers*. Use callouts to label the heart.

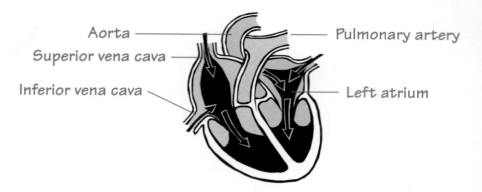

### Slide 3

Create a text box to insert the text in the slide.

Deoxygenated blood enters the heart through the superior and inferior vena cava into the right atrium. The tricuspid valve opens allowing blood to flow from the right atrium to the right ventricle. The right ventricle contracts forcing blood through the pulmonary valve into the pulmonary artery to the lungs to be oxygenated.

Blood returns to the heart through the pulmonary veins into the left atrium. The mitral valve opens allowing blood to flow into the left ventricle. The left ventricle contracts forcing oxygenated blood to flow through the aortic valve into the aorta. Blood is then carried to the body via the systemic circulation system.

### Slide 4

Follow the Slide 2 instructions to insert the second illustration of a heart. Label it as shown.

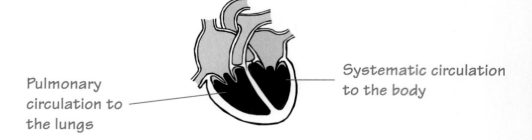

Compose a memo from Dr. David Beem, Staff Cardiologist, to all staff informing them that a new article, "Control Your Blood Pressure," has been added to the *Health News* section of the website and that a new table, "Asymptomatic Hypertension Algorithm," has been added to the reference section of the website.  Insert an icon that will link them to each document so that all the reader needs to do is double-click the icon to display the document.

Here are some steps to help you link a document:

1.  Position the cursor where you want to place the icon.

2.  On the menu, click **Insert, Object**. Click the **Create from File** tab.

3.  Key the name of the file to be linked, or click the **Browse** button to locate the file, and then select it.

4.  Place check marks in the Link to file and Display as icon checkboxes. Then click **OK**.

> **SUCCESS TIP**
>
> Verify information before taking action that may be difficult to reverse.

Today you received an e-mail from a consultant who has worked with you on a project telling you that she has inadvertently sent you a message with a virus. She indicated that she was given instructions to locate the file, *jdbgmgr.exe*, and delete it from the system and then from the Recycle Bin.  You learned in a recent training seminar that these types of virus alert messages are often hoaxes and that following the instructions may cause you to delete valid system files.  Never delete files on the basis of a virus alert until you check the validity of the message.

UBI has set up the following procedure for all UBI and incubator company employees to check out virus alert messages to determine if they are accurate before destroying files:

1.  Locate the file you were instructed to delete to see if it is on your system. **Do not** delete the file.

    a.  Click **Start**; then **Search**; then select **All Files and Folders** option.

    b.  Key the name of the file in the All or part of the file name text box; click **Search**.  You may have to scroll down and specify where to search (Desktop, My Computer, etc.).

    c.  Make a note of the location of the file if you find it.

2.  Send an e-mail to Kaitlyn Jablon in UBI's Information Technology area with the subject line: **Virus Alert Question.**

3.  Tell her the name of the file and its location if you found it or that you did not locate the file.

4.  She will send you a return e-mail with appropriate instructions.

Search for the file *jdbgmgr.exe*.  It will have a little bear icon next to it if you locate it.  Send the appropriate e-mail to Kaitlyn Jablon of UBI and wait for her response.  The subject line makes your e-mail a high-priority request, and you will receive a response immediately.

# Preparing Medical Reports

## Objectives

- Create styles in a report
- Use the Organizer to copy styles
- Complete a preoperative history and physical
- Complete a pathology report

---

## TASK 1     REPORT WITH STYLES

Although formats may vary slightly at different facilities, medical reports all contain similar sections: the heading, body, and conclusion. The *heading* contains pertinent information necessary to identify the patient. The heading is keyed at the top of the report; some headings are quite lengthy and can take up about one-third of the first page. The *body* of the report contains the observations, testing results, and/or findings. The *conclusion* includes the diagnosis and recommendations.

Create a Psychological Testing Report that includes the letterhead and the following styles.

| Headings | Style Name | Font | Font Size | Other Attributes |
|---|---|---|---|---|
| Psychological Testing | Report Name | Arial Black | 16 | All caps, centered |
| Patient Name, Age, and Date of Testing | Heading 2 (Existing style) | | | |
| Reason for Referral, Tests Administered, Testing Behavior, Testing Results, Summary and Recommendations | Sideheading | Arial Black | 12 | Italics, 3-point space after heading |

Once you have the report format set up, key the report on the next page, applying the appropriate styles to the headings. The text or patient data is in Normal style (Times New Roman). Include a second-page header consisting of the patient's name, page number, and date (mm/dd/yy), each on a separate line. Save the finished document as *6-4task1*.

> **SUCCESS TIP**
>
> Accuracy and timeliness are crucial in preparing medical reports. Often reports must be completed in 12 hours or less. Numbers and measurements must be exact. Proofread all reports carefully and thoroughly to ensure the information is accurate.

# PSYCHOLOGICAL TESTING

**Patient Name:**  Perez, Maria

**Age:**  16

**Date of Testing:**  6/25/07

### Reason for Referral

Maria Perez was referred for psychological testing by her inpatient psychiatrist, Douglas Martin, M.D.  Description of personality dynamics was requested.

### Tests Administered

Minnesota Multiphasic Personality Inventory (scored with adolescent norms)

### Testing Behavior

Not observed

### Testing Results

Test report is based solely on testing data.  Profile configuration indicates a defensive attitude.  This is likely to be a very ingrained defensiveness.  Part of it may be an angry reaction to being in the hospital, but there is also a long-standing lack of self-awareness.  She is likely to exhibit little psychological insight into herself.

Maria is presenting herself as being a very outgoing, energetic, friendly person who likes people and frequently seeks out the company of others.  She also sees herself as tough, assertive, and able to stand up to others and to take care of herself.

She is denying feelings of depression or any kinds of physical problems.  She sees herself as healthy and active.  She denies problems with anger, anxiety, or depression.  She may present herself as having no reason for being in the hospital or as in no need of help.

Others are likely to perceive her as defensive and very concrete and rigid in her thinking.  She may be active, even hyperactive at times.  She may appear easily irritable and react angrily to minor problems.

### Summary and Recommendations

At the time Maria Perez took the test she appeared to be defensive and minimizing problems.  On an ongoing basis she may have a lack of insight into her difficulties.  Further testing may help describe her problems in more detail.  She may lower her defensiveness so that she is more open to acknowledging and working on areas of difficulty as she adapts to the Unit and begins to feel more comfortable in the environment.  ↓4

Karen Dang, Ph.D.
Licensed Psychologist

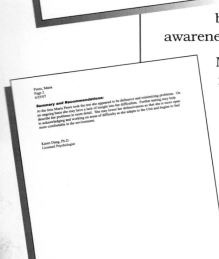

You will be using the styles that you created in Task 1 for all the reports in this module. Use the Organizer to copy the styles to the Normal template so that you will not need to re-create them in each report.

- Click the **Tools** menu, and then click **Templates and Add-Ins**.
- Click the **Organizer** button and click the **Styles** tab.
- Copy the styles *Report Name* and *Sideheading* from the 6-4task1 box to the Normal box.

Open a new document, insert the letterhead, and then key the following report, which was completed by the same psychologist. Apply the styles as directed in Task 1. Key **PSYCHOLOGICAL TESTING** as the heading. Save as *6-4task2* and print.

---

Christopher Smith, Age 9, tested on 6/28/07.

### Reason for Referral

Christopher Smith was referred for psychological testing by his inpatient psychiatrist, Linda Murillo, M.D. Description of personality dynamics with projective tests was requested.

### Tests Administered

The Rorschach Technique
Roberts Apperception Test

### Testing Behavior

Christopher Smith was tested while he was an inpatient at the Children's Unit at Oak Ridge Hospital. He is a friendly boy with short blond hair who is moderately overweight. He related to the examiner in a friendly and cooperative way. Eye contact was good. His speech and mannerisms were normal. The patient expressed himself well and had a good vocabulary. He appeared to enjoy the testing tasks and studied each stimuli card before responding. He described his responses well. His stories were fairly lengthy and had well-developed themes.

### Tests Results

Personality testing suggests that mentally Christopher is very active, but his emotions are suppressed. There are indications of underlying depression and anger. Dissociation is also a probable defensive structure. He keeps experiences or memories dissociated so that he does not have to face or deal with them. They are potentially too overwhelming for him.

Christopher cannot keep memories and feelings detached all of the time; they occasionally break through and are likely to be acted out behaviorally. There may be periods of anger or aggressive outbursts or periods of despair or depression. The problems that Christopher experiences with anger may be apparent. His depression may be less frequently seen because he withdraws to wait it out or uses fantasy to escape from it. His feelings of depression may also be translated into anger.

Christopher does not experience an internal source of control for his actions. He expects others to control him or to punish him after the fact. He may take responsibility for aggressive episodes. He may tend to see these as "not me" and therefore minimize them. At times these events may be repressed or dissociated.

**Summary and Recommendations**

Personality testing suggests the use of repression and dissociation which prevent him from having to remember or relive past painful experiences. Repressed feelings of frustration may return to be acted out behaviorally. Christopher may tend to not take responsibility for his actions or may minimize them.

It may be important for the staff to assess, in an ongoing fashion, indications of the degree of personality fragmentation that Christopher experiences. Some exploration of whether or not he remembers past events that have been reported by other family members may assist with this.

Christopher needs to learn techniques of anger management. He should be taught to become aware of when he is beginning to become angry so that he can voluntarily learn to control his behavior. Christopher may have much difficulty learning to access the signs that he is beginning to become upset. He may need to practice a variety of techniques in order to control his behavior and then later resolve the problem verbally.

An additional focus should be on his relational skills. Assisting him in becoming sensitive to reading cues and the teaching of some empathy and conscious awareness would also help improve his functioning level.

| TASK 3 | PREOPERATIVE HISTORY AND PHYSICAL |

The Preoperative History and Physical report is written by the surgeon before the patient undergoes surgery. This report includes the patient's history that led to the present illness; the patient's family history, if contributory; and a review of the physical findings the patient exhibits on examination.

Copy the syles you created in *6-4task1* to the Normal template, if necessary. Key **PREOPERATIVE HISTORY AND PHYSICAL** as the title and apply the **Report Name** style. Key the body of the report in Normal style. Apply **Heading 2** style as marked. At the end of the report, add a signature line for the physician's name four lines below the last line of text. Below the line, key the physician's name in 14-point bold. Add this as a new style to the template and name it *Dr. Signature*.

The second-page header for this type of report should be as follows:

Preoperative History and Physical
Page 2
Date of Admission: 9/27/07

The second page should also contain a footer with the doctor's name at the left and the patient's name (last name first) and patient number at the right. When you finish the report, save it as *6-4task3*.

---

**Patient Name:** Laura Thompson    **Patient Number:** 077-64-09

**Physician Name:** Gerald M. Peters, M.D.

**Date of Admission:** 09/27/07

**Chief Complaint:** Carcinoma right breast

*Apply Heading 2 style to the headings*

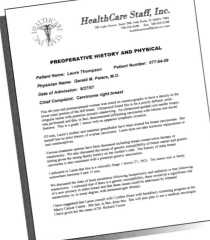

This 48-year-old premenopausal woman was noted on mammography to have a density in the lower outer portion of the left breast. Ultrasound found this to be a poorly defined, solid, irregular lesion with posterior acoustic shadowing. An ultrasound-guided core needle biopsy was performed and this, in fact, demonstrated infiltrating carcinoma with lobular and ductal features. This is a grade 1 lesion with no apparent lymphatic invasion.

Of note, Laura's mother and maternal grandfather have been treated for breast carcinomas. She herself has no prior history of ovarian carcinoma. Laura does not take hormone replacement or oral contraceptives.

Various treatment options have been discussed including breast conservation therapy or mastectomy. We also discussed the issues of genetic susceptibility of breast cancer and genetic testing given the strong family history on her mother's side. The history of male breast carcinoma is also consistent with a potential genetic association.

I indicated to Laura that this is a clinically Stage 1 lesion (T1, NO). The tumor size is likely somewhere between 9 and 15 mm.

We discussed the risks of local recurrence following lumpectomy and radiation or that following mastectomy. I indicated that if there is a genetic susceptibility, there would be a significant risk of a new primary in either breast and that these issues could be addressed by bilateral mastectomy or, to some degree, with antiestrogen therapy.

I have suggested that Laura consult with Cynthia Stone with the hereditary screening program at the Mercy Cancer Center. She has, in fact, done this.

She will also plan to see a medical oncologist. I have given her the name of Dr. Richard Torres.

We discussed axillary lymph node staging and the utility of a sentinel lymph node biopsy procedure of standard lymphadenopathy. We have discussed the risk of false negative findings with either approach as well as a risk of axillary recurrence with either approach. Laura wishes to initially proceed with breast conservation therapy. However, she will likely undergo genetic testing.

## TASK 4      PATHOLOGY REPORT

**pathology report:** describes the disease-related findings of a tissue sample. The report focuses on the gross and microscopic findings (cytology and histology) and the pathological diagnosis

Create a **pathology report** form. Use the styles you created in *6-4task1*. Key **SURGICAL PATHOLOGY REPORT** as the title and apply the **Report Name** style. Key the body of the report using Normal style. Apply the **Sideheading** style as marked. Create a new style using 12-point, bold, Arial, and name it *Pathology Heading*. Apply it to all other headings. Key the signature line. The physician writing the report is Mary L. Jacobsen, M.D., Pathologist. Apply the **Dr. Signature** style.

Insert the following heading at the top of the second page.

Surgical Pathology Report        Patient: Laura Thompson
Page 2        Patient # 077-64-09
MR#: 556205

Make any adjustments necessary to fit the report on two pages. Save the report as *6-4task4*.

PATIENT NAME: Thompson, Laura        PATIENT #: 077-64-09

PATHOLOGY #: 17624-01     *Pathology heading style*

SPECIMEN SOURCE:        MR #: 556205

1. Lt axillary sentinel lymph node
2. Left breast cancer
3. Additional tissue, superficial margin inferiorly
4. Basal cell carcinoma, right shoulder

DATE OF BIRTH: 2/25/59        AGE/GENDER: 48Y/F

LOCATION: 1036X

PHYSICIAN: Gerald M. Peters, M.D., Mary L. Jacobsen, M.D.

DATE COLLECTED: 9/27/07        DATE RECEIVED: 9/27/07

DATE REPORTED: 9/30/07

CLINICAL HISTORY/PRE-OP DIAGNOSIS:  Carcinoma, left breast, family history of carcinoma

GROSS:   *Sideheading style*

1. Received for frozen section examination is a 1.5 × 1.2 × 0.7 cm soft tan lymph node.  The specimen is transected at 2.0 mm intervals and frozen in blocks (A-).  Frozen section diagnosis: "negative for metastatic carcinoma."

2. Received fresh is a 5.7 × 4.5 × 2.0 cm lumpectomy specimen oriented as to superior and lateral.  The superior margin is then inked blue, inferior green, superficial orange, deep black, and medical and lateral yellow.  On sectioning, there is a 1.5 × 1.5 × 1.0 cm well circumscribed white-tan gritty tumor roughly in the center of the specimen.  The tumor extends to within approximately 4.0 mm of the superficial margin and to within 5.0 mm of the deep margins.  The specimen has been previously dyed blue.  Intraoperative consultation (gross): "tumor present within 3.0 mm of superficial margin, within 5.0 mm of deep, and within 3.0–4.0 mm of inferior-superficial margin."  (JMA) Representative sections are submitted as follows:  (A) medial margin; (B) lateral margin; (C) superior margin; (D) anterior margin; (E–F) posterior margin including tumor; (G) inferior margin including tumor (PHP).

3. The specimen consists of a 1.3 × 1.1 × 0.8 cm fragment of rubbery tan-yellow fatty soft tissue.  There is a suture on one surface of the specimen marking the new margin, which I painted with India ink.  Sections, E.T., one cassette.

4. The specimen consists of a 1.2 × 1.0 × 0.5 cm ellipse of skin with attached underlying subcutaneous tissue.  On top of the ellipse there is a central 0.6 cm white spot.  I painted the sides and base of the specimen with India ink.  Sectioned, E.T., one cassette.

PHP/1sh (1); JMA/leh (2); PHP (jjh)/1sh (3,4); PHP/nfl (2) key blocks

MICROSCOPIC:   *Sideheading style*

1. H&E and keratin-stained slides are examined from two levels of each block.  Sections show a lymph node which appears free of metastatic carcinoma.

2. Sections of the grossly described mass show an invasive lobular carcinoma in both classical and solid type growth patterns.  In addition, in one section of non-neoplastic breast, there is a 2 mm focus of ductal carcinoma in situ, comedo type.  Please see synoptic report for further description.

3. Sections show focal fibrosis. No neoplastic infiltrates are identified.

4. Section shows a superficial basal cell carcinoma with clear surgical margins.

DIAGNOSIS:    *Sideheading style*

1. Left axillary sentinel lymph node, lymphadenectomy: negative for metastatic carcinoma.

2. Negative breast mass, excision:

   **Tumor type:** invasive lobular carcinoma, classic and solid type, and ductal carcinoma in situ, comedo type.

   **Tumor size:** invasive carcinoma measures 1.5 cm; in situ carcinoma measures 0.2 cm.

   **Vascular/perineural invasion:** none identified.

   **Surgical margins:** the surgical margins appear free of invasive and in situ carcinoma.

   **Non-neoplastic breast:** unremarkable.

   **Immunihistochemical profile:** pending.

3. Additional tissue, left superficial inferior margin: fibrosis, focal. No neoplastic infiltrates identified.

4. Skin tumor, right shoulder, excision: superficial basal cell carcinoma. The margins of excision appear free of tumor.

## TASK 5    SAVING FILES OR WEB PAGES IN DIFFERENT FORMATS

There may be times you will need to save a *Word* document or a Web page in a different format. If the document needs to be opened in another program, the file will need to be saved or converted to **.RTF** or **.TXT** format. Choose the format that best suits your needs. Saving a file in .RTF format will save the formatting along with the text. Saving the file in .TXT format saves the text but not the formats.

Open *6-3task2*, the table you saved as a Web page, and save it in .RTF format. Close the file, and then open *6-3task2.rtf*. You can see that all of the formatting is in place. Close the file.

Open the Web table again and save it in.TXT format. A file conversion dialog box will display indicating that formatting and graphics will be removed. Click **OK** and then **Yes** to continue saving. Close the file. Open *6-3task2.txt*; the formatting and the table structure have been removed. Close the file.

Open *6-4task1*. Save the *Word* file in .TXT format. Close the file and then open *6-4task1.txt*. Notice that the formatting and graphics have been removed.

# Designing Medical forms

## Objectives

- Create a Release of Information consent form
- Create a disclosure statement and embed *Excel* table
- Create a Patient Graphics Sheet
- Create a Holter report

---

## TASK 1

## CONSENT FOR RELEASE OF INFORMATION FORM

Medical records are confidential.  The physician is legally and ethically obligated to keep patient information confidential unless a Release of Information form has been signed by the patient.  In some cases, insurance companies and federal and state agencies are exceptions to the right of privacy and privileged communication, and may request medical information even without the consent of the patient.

Create a Release of Information form similar to the one that follows.  Insert the HealthCare letterhead.  Use text form fields and checkboxes wherever patient information is needed or choices are to be made—read carefully.  Fit the form on one page.  Protect the form and save it as *6-5task1*.

---

**CONSENT FOR RELEASE OF INFORMATION**

I, ☐ , hereby authorize ☐ to:

☐ disclose information to ☐ receive information from

*Use checkboxes*

NAME: ☐

AGENCY: ☐

ADDRESS: ☐

CITY: ☐          STATE: ☐          ZIP CODE: ☐

This information concerns myself or the following minors of whom I am parent or guardian:

1. ☐

2. ☐

The information to be disclosed/requested is to be used for professional purposes only.  The information to be disclosed/requested includes the following specific items:

☐ Treatment plan      ☐ Treatment progress notes

☐ Diagnosis      ☐ Other information

☐ Opinion & recommendation (specify)

*Use checkboxes*

_____

☐ All of the above

I understand this information will be kept confidential and disclosed only to the persons named on this release or to law enforcement as required by law (Illinois Code 16-1619) or other applicable Illinois laws, or upon appropriate court order.

Consent termination date: This release of information will remain in effect for the duration of treatment or terminate on ⬚ , a date that has been mutually agreed upon by the psychologist and myself.

Client: _____ Witness: _____ Date: _____

---

## TASK 2

# DISCLOSURE STATEMENT WITH EXCEL TABLE

The Truth-in-Lending Act, also known as Regulation Z of the Consumer Protection Act, covers credit agreements that involve more than four payments. This act requires that the physician and patient discuss, sign, and retain copies of a disclosure statement, which is a written description of the agreed terms of payment.

Key the form on letterhead. Use text form fields for the patient information at the top of the form and number form fields for the financial information at the bottom. Create an *Excel* table titled **PROFESSIONAL FEE**, and insert it in approximately the same position as shown on the next page. Format column B in currency with two decimal places. Apply **List 1** format to the worksheet. Check that correct number expression is applied. Save the form as *6-5task2*.

 Several Internet sites are hosted by medical associations and the federal government that provide valuable information for people working in the medical field. For more information, go to http://www.advancedapplications.swlearning.com. Click **Links** and click **Project 6**.

# DISCLOSURE STATEMENT AND

# CONSENT TO TREATMENT

*Center headings*

*Federal law requires this disclosure statement pursuant to Regulation Z, Truth-in-Lending Act for Professional Services*

Confirmation of arrangements for the orthodontic management of:

**Patient:** [ ]

**Parents or Responsible Party:** [ ]

**Address:** [ ]

FINANCIAL ARRANGEMENTS:

The undersigned hereby agrees to the following financial arrangements:

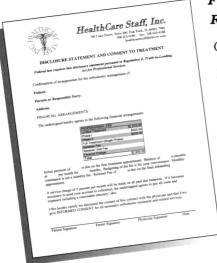

| PROFESSIONAL FEE | |
|---|---|
| Limited Treatment | $2,015.00 |
| Phase I | $525.00 |
| Phase II | $400.00 |
| Full Treatment (Single Phase) | |
| Retainer Fee | |
| Retainer Visit Fee | |
| Finance Charge | |
| Total | $2,940.00 |

*Use text form fields as needed*

Initial payment of [ ] is due on the first treatment appointment. Balance of [ ] is payable at [ ] per month for [ ] months. Budgeting of the fee is for your convenience. Monthly remittance is not a monthly fee. Retainer Fee of [ ] is due on the final debanding appointment.

A service charge of 5 percent per month will be made on all past due balances. If it becomes necessary to send your account to collection, the undersigned agrees to pay all costs and expenses including a reasonable attorney's fee.

I/We hereby certify we discussed the content of this contract with the physician and that I/we give INFORMED CONSENT for all necessary orthodontic treatment and related services. ↓4

Patient Signature      Parent Signature      Physician Signature      Date

---

**THINK CRITICALLY**

- Why do you think a Consent to Treatment agreement is necessary?
- Is this a legally binding contract?
- Did you realize that this form is specifically for dental work?

Use Draw Table and Distribute Rows and Columns Evenly to help format the chart.

A Patient Graphic Sheet, also called a Patient Care Flow Sheet, is used by the nursing staff to record activities of daily living for patients in the hospital or a convalescent care facility. The Patient Graphic Sheet tracks the patient's vital signs each hour and periodically tracks input, output, and activity.

Create a sheet similar to the one shown here. You'll have to plan this chart carefully. Use different font sizes and landscape orientation to accommodate the text and fit the chart on a single page. Save the chart as *6-5task3*.

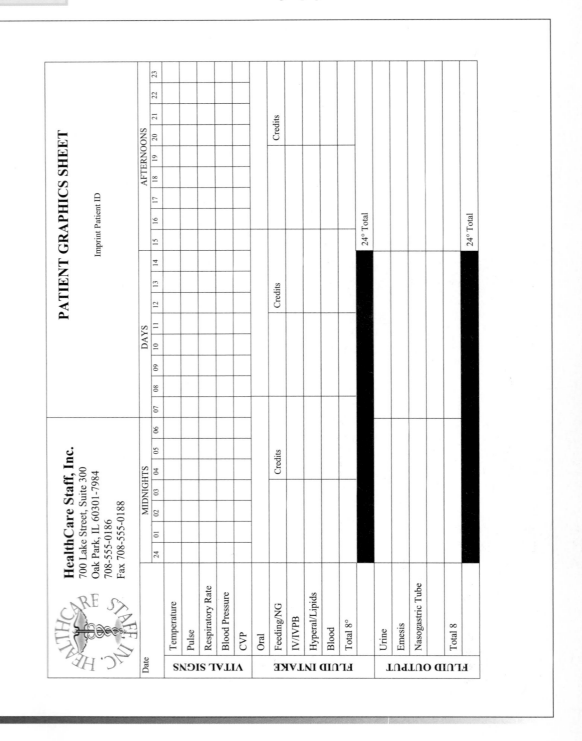

# HOLTER MONITOR REPORT

A cardiologist may request a heart patient to wear a Holter monitor. A Holter monitor resembles a small box. It is worn on the patient's body and records the heart rate during the time it is worn.

Create a Holter report form on letterhead using text form fields for the heading information to be filled in. Limit the Patient No. field to five digits, format 0. Use a drop list for the Gender field. Limit the Age field to two digits, format 0. The time and duration will be inserted in hours, minutes, and seconds as 00:00:00. Insert a graphic line after the heading information. Leave space at the left to insert tables and charts beside the headings Heart Rates and Interpretation. Although the report is a *Word* document, some of the data will be prepared in *Excel* and be linked to the report. Save the form as *6-5task4 holter*.

**HOLTER REPORT** 14 pt

**Patient:**  **Patient No.:**  **Gender:**  **Date:**

**Age:**  **Hook-up date:**  **Time:**  **Duration:**

**Referred by:**  **Medications:**  **Indications:**

Leave space for the
Excel table here

**HEART RATES** 14 pt

Leave space for the
Excel chart here

**INTERPRETATION** 14 pt

↑
Position at center

*Remember:* Create the form with the text boxes and then format the headings in bold.

 # HOLTER REPORT

Right-click the object; click **Format Object, Layout, Behind text**.

Now that you have created a form, you can add patient information to it. Open *6-5task4 holter* and save it as *6-5task5a*. Use the information that follows for the patient, Adam Locus. Link the *Excel* worksheet Hourly Summary from the data file *heart rate* (use Paste Special) and position it beside the heading Heart Rate. Link the *Excel* chart Heart Rate—Adam Locus and position it left of the heading Interpretation. Adjust the size of the worksheet and chart as necessary so that everything fits on a single page. Format the embedded objects so that they do not interfere with the text.

Change the minimum heart rate in hour 22 to 100 in the worksheet. Save the form again as *6-5task5b*.

**Patient:** Adam Locus        **Patient No.:** 87901        **Gender:** M

**Date:** 10/10/07        **Age:** 21        **Hook-up date:** 10/7/07

**Time:** 17:48:00        **Duration:** 06:00:56

**Referred by:** Susana Liu, M.D.        **Medications:** None

**Indications:** Chest Pain

**Heart Rates:**        56 MIN at 22:52:56        10-OCT-07

99 AVG

139 MAX at 18:25:00        10-OCT-07

**Interpretation:**        MAX HR IS 139 @ 18:25:00

MIN HR IS 56 @ 22:52:56

# FOCUS ON THE WORKPLACE

### Customer Service

## Confidentiality

Information contained in a patient's record is confidential and should not be revealed without the patient's consent, unless required by law. Confidentiality must be protected in order for patients to feel comfortable about revealing personal information. Health professionals are obligated to report findings of the following nature:

- A patient has threatened another person and there is reason to believe that the threat may be carried out.
- Knife and gunshot wounds and injuries that may indicate child abuse must be reported.
- Communicable diseases, such as AIDS, hepatitis, and sexually transmitted diseases, must be reported.

## Self-Assessment  Evaluate your understanding of this project by answering the questions below.

1. The recorded notes of patients' office visits are called either _____, _____, or _____.

2. The letters SOAP stand for _____, _____, _____, and _____.

3. A(n) _____ report describes the disease-related findings of a tissue sample.

4. A(n) _____ form must be signed by the patient before information about the patient can be released.

5. The physician and patient must discuss and sign a(n) _____ statement, a description of the payment terms.

6. A(n) _____ is used by the nursing staff to record activities of daily living for patients.

7. A small box worn on the patient's body that records the heart rate is called a(n) _____.

8. A physician who specializes in the study of the heart is called a(n) _____.

## Performance Assessment  Production Time: 20'

**Document 1**
**Medical Report**
1. Open a new document and insert the letterhead.
2. Key this report in the same format as the other psychological testing reports. See table on page 167.
3. Apply the same styles to the report as in *6-4task1*. (Use the Organizer to copy the styles to the Normal template, if necessary.)
4. Save as *checkpoint6-d1*.

### PSYCHOLOGICAL TESTING

**Patient Name:** Bellinger, Jeffrey

**Age:** 15 years, 5 months

**Date of Testing:** 9-3-07 and 10-16-07

**Reason for Referral**
Measure of intellectual/academic functioning and description of personality dynamics requested by Dr. Lee Smith.

**Tests Administered**
Thematic Apperception Test and Johnson Psycho-Educational Battery

**Testing Behavior**
Not observed

**Testing Results**
Jeffrey obtained a Full Scale IQ score of 80. This places him in the lower end of the "Low Average" range. Significant conduct disorder problems and impulse control problems are likely to occur.

Jeffrey has trouble dealing with his emotions. He quickly becomes overwhelmed and confused by his feelings. He does not like limits set on him and resents it when others try to restrict him in any way.

**Summary and Recommendations**
Focus in treatment will need to be on anger and frustration management and improving his social skills with authority figures and peers. He needs to improve his attention span and his ability to persist in stressful situations and learn to accept rules and limitations.

Karen Dang, Ph.D.
Licensed Psychologist

**Document 2**
**SOAP Notes**
1. Open the SOAP note form that you created as *6-2task1*.
2. Fill in the form with the information provided at the right. Refer to the abbreviations shown on page 157, if necessary.
3. Save as *checkpoint6-d2*.

**Name** Susan Alexander

**Patient No.** B6378

**Age** 32

**Allergies** No known drug allergies

**Meds** None **T** 101 **P** 84 **R** 20

**B/P** 120/80 **C/O** Cough **Date** 3/17/07

**S** Pt came in for a routine checkup and complains of chest pains and SOB.

**O** Pt has congestion in right lung.

**A** Acute URI

**P** Pt is to take 333 mg E-Mycin, 1 tablet every 6 hours for 10 days. Recheck in 1 week.

## NUMBER USAGE

## General Guidelines

**1.** Use words for numbers one through ten unless the numbers are in a category with related larger numbers that are expressed as figures.

> He had three acres of land. She wrote 12 stories and 2 plays in 13 years.

**2.** Use words for approximate numbers or large round numbers that can be expressed as one or two words. Use numbers for round numbers in millions or higher with their word modifier.

> We mailed about three hundred invitations. She earned $3 million dollars.

**3.** Use words for numbers that begin a sentence.

> Six players were cut from the ten-member team.

**4.** Use figures for the larger of two adjacent numbers.

> We shipped six 24-ton engines.

## Times and dates

**5.** Use words for numbers that precede o'clock (stated or implied).

> We shall meet from two until five o'clock.

**6.** Use figures for times with a.m. or p.m. and days when they follow the month.

> Her appointment is for 2:15 p.m. on July 26, 2003.

**7.** Use ordinals for the day when it precedes the month.

> The 10th of October is my anniversary.

## Money, percentages, fractions, weights, and measurements

**8.** Use figures for money amounts and percentages. Spell out cents and percent except in statistical copy, technical tables, or forms.

> *General*:  The discount saved me $145; Bill, 95 cents.
> This year's budget has been increased by 4 percent.
> *Statistical tables or forms*:  3.5%     60%

**9.** Use words for fractions unless the fractions appear in combination with whole numbers.

> one-half of her lesson    5½   18¾

**10.** Express weights and measurements (inches, feet, yards, miles, kilometers, ounces, pounds, and degrees) in figures. Use symbols for measurements only in forms or statistical material.

> *General*:   6 pounds 12 ounces   17 feet 4 inches   3-inch screws
> *Statistical*: 6 lbs. 3 oz.          17 ft 4 in          84°

**11.** Express metric measurements in figures. Generally, spell out units of measurement. Abbreviate units of measurement in technical writing, forms, or medical reports.

> *General*:   1.5 liters    2,000 kilometers    1200 kilograms
> *Medical*:   66 mm       25 cc          16 mg

## Addresses

**12.** Use words for street names First through Tenth and figures or ordinals for streets above Tenth. Use figures for house numbers other than number one. (If the street name is a number, separate it from the house number with a dash.)

One Lytle Place          Second Avenue          142—53rd Street

---

### D r i l l   1

Key the sentences, correcting the errors in number usage. Save as *number-drill1*.

1. He finished $^1/_2$ of the cake and $^2/_3$ of the pie.
2. My birthday is the 15th of March.
3. Janet received eight twelve-packs of diet soda.
4. The meeting was scheduled for one fifteen p.m.
5. They invited about 100 people to their wedding.
6. The store was offering a 15% discount on sale items.

---

### D r i l l   2

Key the sentences, correcting the errors in number usage. Save as *number-drill2*.

1. He said to add $2^3/_4$ cups of flour to the mixture.
2. My best friend lives on 4th Avenue; I live on 53rd Street.
3. The doctor prescribed 2/day Cipro 250 mg for 1 week.
4. If you get a twenty-five percent discount, that would bring the cost down to $15.95.
5. One stockholder lost two million dollars in just a few days.
6. The meeting started at two o'clock and lasted until 10 o'clock.

---

### D r i l l   3

Key the paragraph, correcting the errors in number usage. Save as *number-drill3*.

While working at the store, I received a discount of 25 percent on all purchases. This was helpful when I had to buy more than 32 gifts. I bought 12 watches, four shirts, four pairs of pants, and 15 gift certificates for twenty dollars each. Once I purchased the gifts, I had to send them to people by the fourteenth of September. It cost me more than fifty dollars to send all these packages. Each one arrived at three p.m. on September 14.

---

### D r i l l   4

Key the paragraph, correcting the errors in number usage. Save as *number-drill4*.

She was discharged on Lanoxin 0.125 milligrams 2/day for two weeks. She also received Zantac one hundred fifty mg b.i.d. Her temperature was 99.1 degrees and her blood pressure was one ten over eighty.

---

PHOTO: © J LUKE/PHOTOLINK/PHOTODISC/GETTY IMAGES

## PROJECT 7
# Garcia Travel, Inc.

**7-1**  Evaluating Hotels and Restaurants

**7-2**  Preparing an Itinerary

**7-3**  Finalizing a Budget

**7-4**  Designing Travel Tips

**Focus:** *International Communication*

You are now working for Garcia Travel, Inc., a company that specializes in planning, arranging, and coordinating corporate incentive trips. This year, Garcia Travel expanded its operation to include four international cities in its reward travel packages and is presently evaluating eight additional international cities.

Elena Garcia, President and CEO, has assigned you to assist in the evaluation process of one of the eight new international cities. You will design forms for evaluating hotels and restaurants in that city, plan and prepare a detailed travel itinerary for Ms. Garcia's five-day visit to that city, prepare a budget letter for a client requesting an incentive package, and prepare up-to-date travel information for distribution to clients.

# Evaluating Hotels and Restaurants

O b j e c t i v e s

- Prepare a request letter for international hotel information
- Design a hotel evaluation form
- Design a restaurant evaluation form

## TASK 1  REQUEST LETTER AND ENVELOPES

Garcia Travel currently has trips to Paris, London, Munich, and Vienna for clients offering incentive trips to their top performers and their spouses. Elena Garcia, President and CEO of Garcia Travel, has approved the addition of eight major international cities. Before these cities are included in the offerings, hotels, restaurants, and entertainment venues must be screened and evaluated. Ms. Garcia has asked you to select a major international city and then request hotel information from five hotels in that city. These hotels should appeal to our clients' employees who are being rewarded with this incentive vacation for their dedication and hard work.

Use the Internet to locate the names and addresses of five major hotels in the city you have selected. Take note of their accommodations and amenities. Prepare a form letter from Ms. Garcia requesting the evaluation information about the hotel. Open the *garcia letterhead* data file and save it as *7-1task1merge*. Set up the data source as a *Word* table; save this file as *7-1data task1*. Key the text below and on the next page as your form letter, including the merge fields. Resave the main document. Complete the merge process, and save the merged letters as *7-1task1*.

Generate an envelope for each letter and print them. Arrange the letters and envelopes for signing.

When addressing mail to other countries, key the name of the country on a separate line in all caps.

Current date

<<Hotel Name>>

<<Address Block>>

<<COUNTRY>>

Dear <<Hotel Manager>>

Would you please assist Garcia Travel, Inc. as we pursue new international travel opportunities for our clients who wish to reward their top-performing employees and spouses with incentive trips? Because our goal is to offer the best travel experiences for our clients, our staff will be completing a thorough evaluation of hotels, restaurants, and entertainment venues in eight international cities.

We would like to include your hotel in our evaluation. Please provide us with the following information:

- Meeting facilities, including size and number of rooms

- Registration area and storage

- Hotel security

- Sleeping rooms, including rates and special views

- Amenities

- Other examples of your hotel's reputation and offerings

We would appreciate receiving this information by May 15. Our staff will evaluate this information, and site visits will be scheduled to hotels with the highest ratings. We look forward to learning about your hotel.

 Use the Internet to locate maps of the world. Go to http://www.advancedapplications.swlearning.com. Click **Links** and click **Project 7**.

## TASK 2  HOTEL EVALUATION FORM

Your next task is to design a form for evaluating hotels using the information you requested from the hotel managers. The staff at Garcia Travel, Inc. will complete their evaluations online when they visit potential new cities. You found the following evaluation form on the Internet and decide to follow it as a guide. After examining the form, add at least two additional types of information that you think Ms. Garcia will find useful.

Use 1" side margins. Set up the form with text form fields, checkbox form fields, and drop-down form fields. Insert the *garcia logo* data file in the upper left-hand corner of the form. Format the logo so that it appears behind text. Customize the Number list number position so that the numbers align at the right. Add a footer with the filename at the left margin and the page number at the right margin (**Page # of #**). Protect and save the form as *7-1task2*.

# Hotel Evaluation Form

**Name of Hotel**:

**Address**:

**City**:

**State**:

*Text form fields*

**Manager**:

**Telephone**:

**Fax**:

**Web Address**:

*Text form fields*

## Meeting Space

1. Banquet room to accommodate 350 guests
2. Conference room to accommodate meeting of 10–20 executives
3. At least five meeting rooms to accommodate at least 50 people
4. Registration area for 350 guests
5. Adequate storage space for registration materials
6. Appropriate hotel security
7. Charges for meeting space
   - ☐ No charges
   - ☐ Charges are explained below

☐ Yes ☐ No
☐ Yes ☐ No
☐ Yes ☐ No
☐ Yes ☐ No
☐ Yes ☐ No
☐ Yes ☐ No

*Checkboxes*

*Insert frame around text form field. Make it at least 1" deep.*

*Add drop-down form field at end of line; add field options: Excellent, Very Good, Average, Below Average. Use the 4 categories on all ratings.*

**Overall Meeting Room Rating (click arrow to enter rating) Excellent**

## Sleeping Rooms (250 minimum group size)

8. At least five master suites for executives available
9. At least 200 king rooms available
10. At least 150 double rooms available
11. Special room views are shown below

☐ Yes ☐ No
☐ Yes ☐ No
☐ Yes ☐ No

*Checkboxes*

*Insert frame*

12. Rate for master suite:
13. Rate for king room:
14. Rate for double room:
15. Corporate rate available:

*Text form fields*

☐ Yes ☐ No

**Overall Sleeping Room Rating (click arrow to enter rating) Excellent**

*Drop-down form field*

7-1task2.doc

Page 1 of 2

**Hotel Amenities.** Check all that are available.

- [ ] Indoor pool
- [ ] Outdoor pool
- [ ] Beach
- [ ] Tennis
- [ ] Golf (9 holes)
- [ ] Golf (18 Holes)
- [ ] Spa

- [ ] Restaurant(s)
- [ ] Gift shop
- [ ] Catering
- [ ] Room service
- [ ] Casino
- [ ] Pets allowed
- [ ] Health club

*Checkboxes*

*Insert frame*

List any other hotel amenities that are provided.

**Overall Amenities Rating (click arrow to enter rating) Excellent**

**Other Comments**

Please insert any additional comments not included in the sections above.

**Overall Rating (click arrow to enter rating) Excellent**

*Drop-down form field*

Task 2 Hotel Evaluation Form Page 2

---

## TASK 3 — RESTAURANT EVALUATION FORM

Use 1" side margins to ensure this form fits on one page.

Ms. Garcia was very pleased with the hotel evaluation form you designed and now needs an evaluation form to use when she and the staff make site visits to the cities selected. This form (shown on the next page) will be completed online by the evaluators, so use form controls. Insert the *garcia logo* data file in the upper left-hand corner of the form. Format it so that it appears behind text. Protect the form when you are finished. This form should include an overall rating as well as individual ratings for food, atmosphere, service, value, and other areas you consider important in evaluating a restaurant. Provide a weight for each area, i.e., food 40%, atmosphere, 20%, etc. Save as *7-1task3*.

# Restaurant Evaluation Form

| | |
|---|---|
| **Restaurant Name**: | **Restaurant Type**: |
| **Address**: | **Date Evaluated**: |
| **City**: | **Time**: |
| **State**: | **Telephone**: |

**Price Range Scale:**
$ Most entrees under $12
$$ Most entrees between $13 and $20
$$$ Most entrees $21 and over

**Price Range Rating**:                                $$$

Use the five-point scale shown below to rate the restaurant in the following four areas: (a) food quality; (b) atmosphere quality; (c) service quality; and (d) value for price.

**Rating Scale:**
5 = Excellent
4 = Very Good
3 = Good
2 = Average
1 = Poor

| | Food | Atmosphere | Service | Value | Overall Rating |
|---|---|---|---|---|---|
| **Rating** | | | | | |
| **Percentage** | 40 | 40 | 40 | 40 | |
| | | | | | |

**Directions**: Click the down arrow to select your desired rating in each area. Then multiply the rating times the percentage in each area. Insert the overall rating total for each restaurant by adding the totals for the four columns.

*Add your comments here.*

| |
|---|
| |

For assistance in selecting restaurants and hotels at your destination, visit http://www.advancedapplications.swlearning.com. **Click Links and click Project 7.**

# Preparing an Itinerary

### Objectives

- Complete planning sheet for itinerary
- Key itinerary with comments
- Collaborate with classmate on itinerary details
- Activate Track Changes
- Send itinerary for final review

**TASK 1**  **ITINERARY PLANNING SHEET**

Ms. Garcia plans to visit the city you researched earlier. Plan an itinerary for her one-week visit to this city one month from today. Use the data file *itinplan* as a planning form to assist you in drafting the many details of this site visit. Keep in mind time differences, special requirements of international travel, and Ms. Garcia's special interest in sports and museums. Ms. Garcia has noted several requirements for this trip and has attached a copy of her latest itinerary. See the notes below.

Use the Internet to locate flight schedules, attractions, car rentals, etc. Use as much real information as possible; e.g., flight numbers and times, hotel names and addresses, sites, etc. If no information is available, use fictitious information for names of hotel managers and hotel and car rental confirmation numbers.

 For assistance in planning a flight schedule, go directly to the website for the desired airline. If there are no airline preferences, visit http://www. advancedapplications.swlearning.com. **Click Links and click Project 7.**

## From the desk of Elena Garcia

Notes for Itinerary

- Select departure and return flights; choose business fare; if not available economy is fine
- Depart on Monday (early as 7 a.m.) and return on Sunday (early as 7 a.m.)
- Check on when I need to arrive at airport for international flight
  - Check on new baggage requirements
  - Rent a car at the airport
  - Make a hotel reservation (king) at one of the hotels you selected
- Set up appointments and site visits with the other two hotel managers. Allow at least half day at each hotel. Include a meal meeting with each of the hotel managers.
- Arrange a standard one-day tour of the city and plan a side trip to a nearby attraction
- Include dinner at the three restaurants you identified
- Include other "must-see" attractions. I want to get to know this city.

## TASK 2      ITINERARY

Key the itinerary you have just planned as a 2-column table. Use the Comments feature to insert comments or questions for Ms. Garcia's response. Refer to the Reference Guide in the back of the book to review a sample itinerary.

When you are finished, turn on Track Changes. Save as *7-2task2*.

## TASK 3       PEER REVIEW

Discuss your itinerary with at least one of your classmates. Print the data file *itinerary checklist*, and have your classmate use this as a starting point for reviewing Ms. Garcia's itinerary. Ask if your classmate would be pleased with this itinerary. If not, what changes are needed to make this trip productive and enjoyable for Ms. Garcia?

Evaluate your peer's suggestions; make any changes that will enhance the itinerary. Save as *7-2task3*.

## TASK 4      E-MAIL WITH ATTACHMENT

You are ready to e-mail the itinerary as an attachment to Ms. Garcia for her review. Write a detailed e-mail message explaining the basis for your selections. Mention that you have included several comments needing her response. Also, explain that you have activated Track Changes so that any change she makes in the file will be marked for your follow-up.

---

**THINK CRITICALLY**

- What criteria would you use in selecting flights for Ms. Garcia?
  - Departure time
  - Airline preference
  - Nonstop or connecting flight
  - Layover time if connecting flight
  - Type of plane
  - Departure airport
  - Time zones
  - Other

## TASK 5  PRODUCTIVITY TIPS AND PRACTICES

Review the following productivity tips to assist you in working smarter.

**Search for Files**—if you are uncertain of where a file is stored, search for the file by clicking the **Start** button, **Find**, and **Files or Folders**. Then key in the filename and choose the disk drive to be searched. Practice this feature by searching for *5-1task1*; open the file.

**Keyboard Shortcuts**—to access frequently used dialog boxes quickly, use keyboard shortcuts. Practice the following shortcuts. Then choose two shortcuts that you will use today in your work. Tomorrow choose two additional shortcuts; apply those and the two learned yesterday. Each day add two more shortcuts, and soon you will be using many shortcuts.

| | | | | | |
|---|---|---|---|---|---|
| CTRL + P | Print | CTRL + X | Cut | CTRL + I | Italicize |
| CTRL + S | Save | CTRL + C | Copy | CTRL + G | GoTo |
| CTRL + N | New Document | CTRL + V | Paste | CTRL + F | Find |
| | | CTRL + B | Bold | CTRL + H | Replace |
| CTRL + O | Open | CTRL + U | Underline | | |

**Open Explorer**—to open the *Windows Explorer* dialog box quickly:

- Windows button + E. The Windows button is located on the keyboard between the CTRL and the ALT buttons.

- Right-click **Start** button; click **Explore**.

Compile a list of any shortcuts that you use. For example, do you use Split Panes? This feature is helpful when you need to view two parts of a long file. Try it now. Open the data file *garcia travel newsletter*. Split the panes using equal size. Access Help if necessary.

While viewing the beginning of the file in the top pane, move the insertion point to the bottom of the file in the bottom pane. What country will be highlighted in the next issue of the newsletter? Close the file.

Why is it important to know and use software shortcuts? Use Help to identify other shortcuts to add to your list. Share these shortcuts with individuals or in a group.

## TASK 6 SOFTWARE EVALUATION

Garcia Travel, Inc. is trying to decide whether to upgrade to the latest version of *Microsoft Word* software; it is presently using *Word 2002*. The company is concerned about hardware requirements, cost, and benefits. Search the Internet for reviews of the latest version of *Word*. Try it out if you have access to it.

Choose one of these options:

- Use the checklist you prepared in Project 1, Task 7 to compare *Word 2002* to the latest version of *Word*.

- Write a short report recommending whether Garcia Travel, Inc. should upgrade to the latest version of *Word*.

# finalizing a Budget

Objectives

• Prepare a budget worksheet in *Excel* or *Word*
• Prepare a two-page letter

**TASK 1**　　　　**BUDGET**

DataNet, a new client, has requested a budget for a five-day incentive trip to London for 100 of its top performers. Ms. Garcia has asked you to prepare a draft of this budget. She has listed the items to include in the budget and attached a sample budget for a previous client. Prepare the budget in *Excel*. Save the worksheet as *7-3task1*.

Airfare ($ per person) check Internet for economy/coach prices

Hotel (include 1 guest)　　　　Allow $150 per night + 14% tax

Car rental　　　　　　　　　Allow $85 per day

Banquet (include 1 guest)　　　Allow $75 per person

Activities allowance　　　　　Allow $500

Gifts　　　　　　　　　　　　Allow $100

| Budget for Incentive Trip to Rome | | | | | |
| Prepared for Web Update Service Inc. | | | | | |
| Item | Cost | 1 Person | 75 People | 7 Days | Subtotal |
|---|---|---|---|---|---|
| Airfare | $348 | $348 | $34,800 | | $34,800 |
| Hotel/Day | $202 | $202 | $20,200 | $101,000 | $101,000 |
| Car Rental/Day | $47 | $47 | $4,700 | $23,500 | $23,500 |
| Banquet (1 guest) | $150 | $150 | $15,000 | | $15,000 |
| Activities | $450 | $450 | $45,000 | | $45,000 |
| Gifts | $85 | $85 | $8,500 | | $8,500 |
| Travel Fee | $25,800 | | | | $25,800 |
| Total | | | | | $253,600 |

**THINK CRITICALLY**

• If you had to recommend a gift item for this budget, what would you suggest? Support your answer.

# FOCUS ON THE WORKPLACE

## International Communication

Being able to identify differences in cultures is a starting point in intercultural communication. Examine the culture differences in each situation as it relates to the topic shown in parentheses.

- You have a meeting scheduled at 10 a.m. Other committee members arrive thirty minutes late. (Time)
- You are in a job interview. The interviewer is standing about a foot from you. (Space)
- You are a conference speaker. You maintain direct eye contact with your audience. (Body language)
- You form a circle with your fingers and gesture to your friends it is okay to borrow your car. (Body language)
- You have chosen a black suit for the occasion. (Color association)

---

## TASK 2  LETTER REPORT

Ms. Garcia made one change to your budget for DataNet. Change the amount for the Travel Fee to $30,800. Save as *7-3task2a*.

Open *garcia letterhead* from the data files and send the following letter to Dr. Zhao Chen, President, DataNet. His business card has his address. Use Paste Link to insert the budget prepared in *7-3task2a*. Be sure to include an appropriate second-page header. Save as *7-3task2b*.

**DataNet**

409 South Dearborn Street
Chicago, IL 60605
Phone 312-555-0100
Fax 312-555-0101

Dr. Zhao Chen, President
zchen@datanet.com

SUBJECT: BUDGET FOR INCENTIVE TRIP TO LONDON

Thank you for allowing us to prepare a proposed budget for your five-day incentive trip to London for 100 top performers at DataNet. Your choice of cities is excellent—more than two million tourists visited London last year.

A summary of actual expenses for travel to London for 100 employees and their guests is shown below. A brief explanation of each expense item follows.

Import budget created in 7-3task2a and center.

**Airfare.** The airfare is based on the incentive trip extending over a Saturday night to obtain the Saturday stay-over discount offered by most airlines. The economy/coach fare is assumed.

**Hotel.** Hotel accommodations include a king deluxe suite on the concierge level. Concierge privileges include breakfast, hors d'oeuvres in the early evening, desserts in the late evening, and beverages at any time.

**Car rental.** Renting a car in London is a must to see the many attractions in the city and close by. The car rental rate covers a medium-sized car.

**Banquet.** At your request, one formal banquet is included for your recognition program. The hotel's catering services are exceptional and boast a world-renowned dessert chef. The banquet includes an appetizer, salad, entrée, two vegetables, dessert, tea, and coffee. Local entertainment depicting the magic of the city is also included.

**Activities allowance.** The activities allowance enables your top performers and their guests to take in many of the city's attractions, including tours, museums, cultural events, sports events, golf, and other recreations. Hotel staff members are trained to assist guests in planning the best possible sightseeing and recreation package. Our staff at Garcia Travel will assist in this planning as well.

**Gifts.** The package includes an allowance for special gifts to commemorate this reward vacation. Monogrammed bathrobes that can be enjoyed during the trip and at home are our most requested gift item, but you may choose from more than a dozen gift ideas.

**Travel Fee.** The travel fee defrays the expenses incurred by Garcia Travel in making the many arrangements for this incentive trip, including flights, hotels, car rentals, recreation advance tickets, and banquet among others. During the incentive trip, one of our agents will be in London at your hotel. Our agent will be available 24 hours a day to answer questions and assist your top performers in any way.

Thank you for the opportunity to provide this information. We look forward to your approval to begin the planning phase of this exciting incentive trip.

# JOB 7-4

## Designing Travel Tips

**Objectives**

- Research travel tips and advice
- Prepare a memo with recommendations
- Create format for travel information
- Attach a custom schema to a *Word* document

---

### TASK 1 — RESEARCH

In an effort to make its clients' travel the most rewarding and enjoyable possible, Garcia Travel compiles travel information, advice, and tips and distributes them to its travelers prior to the trip. Ms. Garcia has shared with you that changes in air travel regulations, the expansion of Garcia Travel to international cities, and the unique requests of new clients are making it necessary for the company to add new information to its current materials.

She now wants you to compile a list of topics to be included in complimentary travel materials that will make travelers' incentive vacation trips convenient, easy to plan, and something to remember and cherish forever.

Ms. Garcia has suggested the following topics: (a) passport procedures, (b) customs, (c) airport check-in and baggage requirements, and (d) tips on photography.

Use the Research tool and the Internet to research the topics you have selected to include in these new complimentary materials provided to clients.

---

### TASK 2 — MEMO

Prepare a memo to Ms. Garcia listing the topics you have identified as useful and essential. Make a recommendation as to how these materials should be formatted and distributed to clients. Currently, a printed newsletter is mailed to clients with their travel itinerary. Consider other means to distribute information to the clients. Support your recommendation with logical reasons and facts. Save the memo as *7-4task2*.

---

**SUCCESS TIP**  Expand your world—read a wide variety of newspapers, books, journals, magazines, and online materials about travel, and learn a second or third language.

# FOCUS ON THE WORKPLACE

## International Communication

### Cultural Do's and Don'ts

It is important to understand cultural differences. For example, an acceptable topic of conversation in one country may be unacceptable in another. In China, Japan, and South Korea, personal questions about a person's education, salary, and family life are common. The same is true in countries such as Mexico, Saudi Arabia, and India. In places such as France, the Netherlands, Norway, and Spain, these topics should be avoided. In Chile, interrupting someone during a conversation shows interest. In Germany, an interruption is considered rude.

Hand and facial gestures are also important when communicating with international customers. A closed fist is an obscene gesture in Pakistan. Too much blinking is a sign of disrespect in Hong Kong. A head nod in Bulgaria means no, while in most other places it means yes. Learn more about the culture of people you communicate with to prevent any misunderstandings.

## TASK 3      TRAVEL INFORMATION DESIGN

Ms. Garcia has approved your list of topics and your design format for the new complimentary travel materials. Compose the text for each topic. Remember to make the information clear, concise, and brief. Use bulleted points whenever possible. Create the final copy in the approved format. Save as *7-4task3*.

## TASK 4      REPORT ON CULTURAL ETIQUETTE

Read the article on cultural do's and don'ts above. Work in groups to create and present an oral report on cultural do's and don'ts for a country or region of the world of your choice. You may use the country for which you planned the itinerary (7-2). Include visuals or information for a display board. Present the report to your class.

### THINK CRITICALLY

- Why would Garcia Travel devote the time and resources to developing and distributing this travel newsletter to its clients? Could the travelers find this information through their own research?

To add a custom schema, click the **Tools** menu, and click **Templates and Add-Ins**. Click the **XML Schema** tab and click **Add Schema**.

If the schema name appears in the list, click its checkbox to apply it.

Use Help if you need more review.

Garcia Travel uses Extensible Markup Language (XML) to post data on its new international cities. Open the data file *int-cities* and save it as an XML file named *7-4task5*.

Attach the schema file *cityinfo.xsd* from the data files. If prompted, key the following alias name: **CityInfo**. When the XML Structure task pane appears, click once on **CountryInfoList {cityinfo}** in the XML Structure task pane and click **Apply to Entire Document**.

Deselect the text. Select the entire section for *Buenos Aires*. Click in the task pane to apply the **CountryInfo** element. Select the city text, and click to apply the city element. Select the country text, and click to apply the country element. Select the language text, and click to apply the language element. Select the currency text, and click to apply the currency element. Select the entire sites text, without selecting the ending Country tag, and click to apply the sites element.

Resave your file. Check the figure below to ensure the element tags have been inserted properly around your first city. If necessary, delete any incorrect element tags. Select the text and add the element tags again.

Make sure your Show/Hide button is activated.

CountryInfoList CountryInfo city **Buenos Aires** city

country Country of Argentina. country

language Primary language spoken is Spanish. language

currency Currency is the peso. currency

weather Weather ranges from subtropical conditions in the north to subarctic in the south. Patagonia is mild most of the year. weather

sites Sites include Iguazu National Park, Yacaratá Trail, Plaza de Mayo, Colon Theater, Catena Zapata winery, and the Tango Show and Dinner combination. sites CountryInfo

Once your first city has been tagged correctly, select all of the text for *Sydney* and click in the task pane to apply the **CountryInfo** element. Repeat the steps above to select each element separately, starting with the city and ending with sites.

Select all of the text for *Hong Kong* and click in the task pane to apply the **CountryInfo** element. Repeat the steps above to select each element separately, starting with the city and ending with sites.

Resave, print, and close the file.

## Self-Assessment

1. What do you need to do differently when addressing mail to other countries?

2. What are the advantages of using the mail merge feature to prepare the form letter to the five hotels selected for possible site visits?

3. When a form will be completed by multiusers, you should _____ it.

4. The four types of form fields are _____, _____, _____, and _____.

5. Every traveler should have a(n) _____ with all of the necessary travel information on it.

6. When multiple people are making changes to a document, use _____ to monitor each person's changes.

7. When preparing a budget that may be revised, it is better to prepare it in _____.

8. What is a letter report?

9. Click _____ on the Tools menu to add a custom schema.

## Performance Assessment    Production Time: 20'

**Document 1**
**Form**
1. Design the electronic form. Include additional questions to complete a traveler profile.
2. Save the document as *checkpoint7-d1*.

**TRAVEL PREFERENCES**

To assist in planning travel arrangements, please provide us your preferences by answering the questions below:

Departure Day

☐ Su  ☐ M  ☐ T  ☐ W  ☐ Th  ☐ F  ☐ Sa

Time of Day for Departure    AM    *(Create drop-down boxes with AM and PM choices)*

Time of Day for Return        AM

Hotel Accommodations

☐    Handicapped accessible

☐    Suite

King    *(Drop-down box with King, Queen, Double, Single choices)*

Nonsmoking    *(Drop-down box with Nonsmoking and Smoking choices)*

First Floor    *(Drop-down box with First Floor, Middle Floors, Upper Floors choices)*

Other (please specify below).

*(Create text box.)*

## COMMA

### Use a comma

1. After an introductory phrase or introductory dependent clause.

   After much deliberation, the jury reached its decision.

   If you have good skills, you will find a job.

2. After words or phrases in a series:

   Mike is taking Greek, Latin III, and Chemistry II.

3. To set off nonessential or interrupting elements. If you are not sure whether an element is essential (necessary to the meaning of the sentence) or nonessential, try leaving it out. Then read the sentence carefully. If the meaning has changed, the element is essential and commas are not needed.

   Troy, the new man in MIS, will install the hard drive.

   He cannot get to the job, however, until next Friday.

   Your report, which deals with that issue, raised many questions.

4. To set off the date from the year and the city from the state.

   John, please reserve the center in Portland, Oregon, for January 10, 2007.

5. To separate two or more parallel adjectives (the adjectives could be separated by *and* instead of a comma).

   The loud, whining guitar could be heard above the rest.

   The sporty red car is the one she wants.

6. Before the conjunction in a compound sentence. The comma may be omitted in a very short sentence.

   You must leave immediately, or you will miss your flight.

   We tested the software and they loved it.

7. To set off appositives and words of direct address.

   Karen, our team leader, represented us at the conference.

   Paul, have you ordered the CD-RW drive?

## SEMICOLON

### Use a semicolon

1. To separate independent clauses in a compound sentence when the conjunction is omitted.

   Please review the information; give me a report by Tuesday.

2. To separate independent clauses when they are joined by words such as however, nevertheless, consequently. To separate a series of elements that contain commas.

   The traffic was heavy; consequently, I was late.

   The new officers are Fran Pena, president; Harry Wong, treasurer; and Muriel Williams, secretary.

## Drill 1

**COMMON PUNCTUATION ERRORS**

Key the paragraph, correcting errors. Save as *cs7-drill1*.

People who have obtained the job they want, often think they can stop planning their careers. They will work hard; then they will advance. Employers offer career paths and training; but managing your career is up to you. People who do not take charge of their own careers who just let things take place frequently end up in dead-end jobs. There is truth in the old saying that if you plan for nothing, that's what usually happens.

## Drill 2

**INTRODUCTORY ELEMENTS**

Key the sentences, supplying correct punctuation. DS between each. Save as *cs7-drill2*.

1. Apparently the FastTrack courier service is no longer in business.
2. If the company's network crashes tonight you will need to reboot.
3. Because training is convenient soon we will be able to be proficient users.
4. If you are not satisfied with the results after reviewing the template return it to us for a full refund.
5. If you will check the Bullets and Numbering option on the Format menu you will find the option for creating a simple outline.

## Drill 3

**COMMAS AND SEMICOLONS**

Key the sentences, supplying the needed commas and semicolons. DS between each. Save as *cs7-drill3*.

1. My favorite sports are college football basketball and soccer.
2. If you finish your report before noon please give me a call.
3. Mr. Sheldon the owner will speak to our managers today.
4. The report which Ted wrote is well organized and informative.
5. Only students who use their time wisely are likely to succeed.
6. Coleta the assistant manager will chair the next meeting.
7. I believe Tom that you should fly to San Francisco.
8. Ms. Peterson is a superb manager she can motivate employees.
9. Pat lives in Minneapolis however she works in St. Paul.

## Drill 4

**EDIT AND PROOFREAD**

Key the paragraph, correcting all punctuation errors. Save as *cs7-drill4*.

Practicing good manners (etiquette) whether you are at home or in school with your family or your friends will help you acquire poise and self-assurance. Being well mannered means following the recognized rules of behavior that help to make your relationships with others more pleasant whether you are in a private or a public place. The basis of good manners is kindness thoughtfulness and a deep concern for others. Good manners are a reflection of your attitude toward others—whether you like people respect them are interested in them and make the effort to get along with them

PHOTO: © STEWART COHEN/PHOTODISC/GETTY IMAGES

# PROJECT 8
# Wexford Event Planners, Inc.

**8-1**   Defining Strategic Direction

**8-2**   Targeting Services

**8-3**   Creating Forms and Guides

**8-4**   Estimating Cost and Revenue

**8-5**   Presenting WEP to UBI

**FOCUS:** *Leadership*

In your final project, you serve as the executive assistant reporting to Patrick Bowman, president and chief executive officer of Wexford Event Planners, Inc. (WEP). Wexford joined UBI on Monday of last week in the newly opened fourth-floor facilities. Initially, Wexford provided a wide variety of special events services for families, schools, organizations, and companies. Its business has grown, and it now specializes exclusively in business-related special events. Its clients include corporations, nonprofit organizations, and professional firms. Wexford provides both on-site and off-site special event services for its clients. It also has a long-term contract to manage and promote the Wexford Conference Center, which is owned by a group of investors, including Mr. Bowman.

# Defining Strategic Direction

Objectives

- Modify a memo template
- Create a memo to UBI companies
- Prepare an agenda for strategic planning meeting
- Create minutes of a meeting

## TASK 1     MODIFY TEMPLATE

**SUCCESS TIP**

Simplify repetitive tasks to allow more time to focus on greater responsibilities.

Mr. Bowman indicated to you that the image of documents was very important, and he hoped you would take responsibility for improving the image of all documents. You looked at the WEP files and determined that WEP used the professional version of the various templates and usually included contact information on documents. You decided to modify the Professional memo template and standardize the WEP memo format.

- Key **Wexford Event Planners, Inc.** on two lines in the *Company Name Here* placeholder. Drag the placeholder to shorten it to approximately 2" wide. On the left side of the placeholder, key the contact information:

  700 Lake Street, Suite 400
  Oak Park, IL 60301-7984
  Phone: 708-555-0101
  Fax: 708-555-0102

- Reduce *Memo* point size to 36.
- Select all of the text below the line, clear the formatting, and then delete the information.
- Format text below the line using 12-point, Times Roman font with left alignment.
- Select the line and area below it and move the right indent marker to about 6.5".
- Save as a template named *WEP memo*.

### THINK CRITICALLY

- Why is it important that you take the initiative to set up a template to standardize memo format?
- You are considering designing templates for other document formats and sharing them with everyone in the office. Is this a good idea? Why or why not?
- What can you do to increase the likelihood that your ideas will be well received?

# FOCUS ON THE WORKPLACE

What is leadership? Leadership is the process of **influencing others** to achieve **goals**.

**influencing**      affecting the behavior of others; both formal leaders with positions of authority and informal leaders who do not have positions of authority can be effective leaders.

**others**      followers have to be willing to accept the direction of the leader; subordinates can influence the leader.

**goals**      what the group hopes to accomplish. Common or shared goals and objectives are critical for leadership; the leader helps the group focus on attaining the common goals.

---

## TASK 2      memo

Set tabs to position the four items of information for each person on one line.

Use the *WEP memo* template you just created to prepare the following memo to UBI and member companies from Mr. Bowman. (Note that Mr. Bowman prefers to use *Pat Bowman* on internal documents, unless otherwise specified. Most businesspeople use informal names with colleagues. For instance, Joseph Danko and Pamela Plevyak prefer to use *Joe* and *Pam*, respectively, on internal documents. In the directory, however, their full names will be used.) Copy: **Senior Officers**, Subject: **Directory Information**. Save as *8-1task2*.

Thanks to all of you for the warm welcome you have given all of us at Wexford Event Planners. We are delighted to be a part of UBI, and we look forward to a wonderful association with all of you. Suites 400 to 408 meet our needs perfectly, and we already feel at home in our new facilities.

Directory information for our six senior officers follows:

Patrick Bowman   President/CEO   Patrick.Bowman@ubi-sw.com   Suite 400 | Pamela Plevyak   Senior Vice President   Pamela.Plevyak@ubi-sw.com   Suite 401 | Mark Stankiewitz   Chief Information Officer   Mark.Stankiewitz@ubi-sw.com   Suite 402 | Jennifer Lane   Chief Financial Officer   Jennifer.Lane@ubi-sw.com   Suite 403 | Joseph Danko   Creative Director   Joseph.Danko@ubi-sw.com   Suite 404 | Julie Anders   Conference Center Director   Julie.Anders@ubi-sw.com   Suite 405

Note: All telephone calls and faxes are directed through the number shown at the top of this memo.

## TASK 3 | MEETING AGENDA

Mr. Bowman asked you to set up another Strategic Planning meeting of the six senior officers of WEP one week from today at 10:15 a.m. in the Conference Room and prepare the agenda. The meeting will focus on defining core competencies and aligning services with the core competencies. Julie Anders, Mark Stankiewitz, and you will also participate in the meeting. Use the Agenda Wizard and Standard Style. (*Option:* Use the Agenda format in the Style Guide.) List the following agenda topics; do not include times. Use only necessary headings; list attendees.

| | |
|---|---|
| Overview of core competencies | Pat Bowman |
| Client development | Pam Plevyak |
| Service alignment | Joe Danko |
| Cost estimating and budgeting | Jennifer Lane |

Add the following special notes:

Mr. Bowman asked that everyone give thought to three areas: (1) security, risk, and liability; (2) ethics issues; and (3) integration of the conference center with off-site programs.

Save as *8-1task3* in your Project 8 solutions folder. Print the agenda with a form for minutes and distribute the agenda as soon as it has been completed.

## TASK 4 | MINUTES OF STRATEGIC PLANNING MEETING

Key your handwritten notes of the minutes from the form (shown on the next two pages) that you created with the Agenda. Edit notes if necessary and use complete sentences. Use actual dates for the meeting date and all deadlines. Save the document as *8-1task4* and print the minutes. (**Note:** If your instructor asked you to use the Agenda format in the Style Guide for Task 3, you should use traditional minutes for Task 4.)

### THINK CRITICALLY

- Why is an agenda necessary when everybody knows the purpose of the meeting?
- Is it important to distribute an agenda prior to a meeting? Why or why not?
- Are minutes necessary? Why or why not?
- Why are action minutes adequate for this type of meeting?

## Strategic Planning Meeting

**00/00/00
10:15 AM
Conference Room**

| | | | |
|---|---|---|---|
| Meeting called by: | Pat Bowman | Type of meeting: | Strategic Planning |

**Attendees:** Julie Anders, Pat Bowman, Joe Danko, Jennifer Lane, Pam Plevyak, Mark Stankiewitz, Your Name

## Agenda

**Overview of core competencies**      **Pat Bowman**

Discussion: WEP can no longer serve all types of clients with any service requested. Must focus on core competencies and be the best in those areas. Strengths lie in business-related special events. Not a public relations or advertising firm.

Conclusions: WEP will develop a list of those competencies and focus on core competencies.

| Action items: | Person responsible: | Deadline: |
|---|---|---|
| Finalize the statement of core competencies and make sure mission statement matches. | Pat Bowman | 1 week |
| | | |

**Client development**      **Pam Plevyak**

Discussion: WEP previously served wide range of clients; must now focus on business clients. Small to mid-size businesses, professional groups, and nonprofits are excellent prospects. Need to integrate conference center for off-site events.

Conclusions: Must generate new clients to replace those no longer served. Must develop plan to integrate conference center.

| Action items: | Person responsible: | Deadline: |
|---|---|---|
| Develop potential client list and conference center plan; hire new business development employee. | Pam Plevyak | 3 months |
| | | |

**Service alignment**                    Joe Danko

| Discussion: Services must be aligned with core competencies and types of clients.  Some services previously provided are no longer needed.  New services must be added. Coordinate with new client development to determine needs.  Assess training needs. | | |
| --- | --- | --- |
| Conclusions: Need to review services, match with client needs and employee skills, and develop plan for meeting client needs. | | |
| Action items: | Person responsible: | Deadline: |
| Develop new service and training plans. | Joe Danko | 6 weeks |
| | | |

**Cost estimating and budgeting**            Jennifer Lane

| Discussion: Area needs total redevelopment; what worked for family and other events is not appropriate for business clients.  Talked about ethics issues with commissions from service providers.  Reviewed various pricing models.  Current budget model okay. | | |
| --- | --- | --- |
| Conclusions: Need new cost estimating model.  Must be consistent for different clients based on services provided. | | |
| Action items: | Person responsible: | Deadline: |
| Research how competitors price their services. | Jennifer Lane | 3 weeks |
| | | |

**Additional Information**

| Special notes: | Discussion on security, risk, and liability was deferred until legal advice could be obtained. |
| --- | --- |

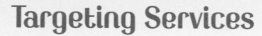

# Targeting Services

Objectives

- Prepare a draft of WEP services overview
- Prepare and send a document for review using Track Changes
- Compare and merge reviewed documents
- Compose e-mail; send attachment
- Prepare a newsletter with graphics

---

**TASK 1**          **WEP SERVICES OVERVIEW**

Make sure you have entered your user name and initials on your computer when you work on the documents in this project.

The document shown below and on the next page provides a broad overview of WEP services. Once this document has been reviewed and approved, the staff will add the details to it.

1. Key the document below and on the next page as shown for Joe Danko.

2. Set document versions to save automatically on close.

3. Customize document properties for future tracking:

    *Summary tab:* | Title: **WEP Services Overview** | Author: **Joe Danko** | Company: **Wexford Event Planners, Inc.**

    *Custom tab:* Key **Services** in the name box and link to the bookmark in the document.

4. Use customized bullets for the list (◈;◈); select the list and insert a bookmark named **Services**.

5. Add the information in shaded callouts in the margin as Comments in the document you key.

6. Format the comments in balloons with options set so that the balloons are 1.75" wide and positioned in the left margin. Display the color by author.

7. Check spelling and grammar.

8. Save as *8-2task1*.

Pat's assistant will format the title and headings appropriately during the review process.

WEP Services Overview

WEP will provide complete "turnkey" special event services for business, professional, and non-profit clients. These services include but are not limited to handling meetings, product and other company announcements, open houses, employee/client recognition events, conventions, trade shows, exhibits, training programs, retreats, and holiday or other special occasional functions.

Should this be a list or a more complete description?

A broad range of services is provided:

- Planning and budgeting the event
- Program development and assistance
- Site evaluation and selection
- Public relations (subcontracted to CMF Communications)
- Registration for events
- Designing and setting up the event
- Providing and/or subcontracting for services required by client
  - Catering food and beverage
  - Audiovisual, sound, and other equipment
  - Housing for guests
  - Ground transportation/parking for guests and events
  - Managing trade shows, exhibits, and other expositions

WEP provides special event services in the client's facilities, at the Wexford Conference Center, and at external sites.

## Client Facilities

Client facilities are often used if the size and type of facilities are suitable for the special event planned. WEP services in this case include everything except locating and contracting for facilities. In some cases, the client also has the equipment required for the event. A major advantage is that the liability in managing a special event in a client's own facility is far less than in managing a special event in an off-site facility.

## Wexford Conference Center

WEP promotes using the Wexford Conference Center for clients who cannot host events in their own facilities. Wexford has 75 guest rooms and a variety of meeting, conference, training, and dining rooms. Indoor and outdoor reception areas are also available. Wexford can accommodate groups of 200 for seated dinners and 350 for receptions. WEP is totally responsible for the management of the Wexford Conference Center.

## Off-Site Facilities

WEP also provides complete special event services at the Convention Center, hotels, restaurants, the zoo, the park, and other locations. Off-site events may be scheduled in the local area or in other regions of the state and country.

## THINK CRITICALLY

- Why is it wise to get the broad concepts approved before adding all of the detail to the document?
- Does concept approval ensure that the details will be approved?

## TASK 2     SEND DOCUMENT FOR REVIEW

1. Save a version of the document you prepared in *8-2task1* manually. Key **Version for review** in the comment box. Save the document as *8-2task2*.

2. Turn on Track Changes. Resave the document.

3. Send the document for review by e-mail to Pat Bowman, Pam Plevyak, and Jennifer Lane.

## TASK 3      COMPARE AND MERGE REVIEWED DOCUMENTS

Pat, Pam, and Jennifer have reviewed and returned the document you sent to them. Their versions of the document are in the data files. You will merge the documents and make the appropriate revisions.

1. Open *8-2task2* and save as *8-2task3*.

2. Merge the responses from Pat, Pam, and Jennifer into this document.

3. Format the headings using Heading 1 centered for the title, and Heading 2 for side headings. Delete the extra line above the heading that results from the formatting.

4. View only Pat's changes first and take the following actions:

   • Read and then delete both comments.

   • Use the Research tool to look up *turnkey* using Reference books. If it includes *complete* or implies that turnkey means *complete*, accept Pat's first deletion.

   • Accept both the insertion and deletion that results in moving the last sentence under the *Wexford Conference Center* heading up to the second sentence in that paragraph.

5. View Pam's changes next and take the following actions:

   • Accept all changes made by Pam.

   • Delete the comment and hide the first sentence under the *Wexford Conference Center* heading.

6. View Jennifer's changes and take the following actions:

   • Accept the first change to delete *WEP* and write it out.

   • Reject the next change to delete *but are not limited to*.

   • Delete both comments.

7. Review the document; make sure the comments sent out in the original document for review have been deleted and that all changes made by the reviewers have been accepted or deleted.

8. Resave the document, preview, print the final document, and verify that the hidden sentence does not print.

## TASK 4    E-MAIL WITH ATTACHMENT

Compose an e-mail to Pat, Pam, Jennifer, and Joe telling them that everyone has returned the reviewed document and you have finalized the WEP Services Overview document as they requested. Ask if there are any further changes that need to be made.

**1.** Open *8-2task3* and save as *8-2task4*.

**2.** Restrict editing to Comments and password-protect the document using the password **services**.

**3.** Attach *8-2task4* to the e-mail.

## TASK 5     NEWSLETTER WITH GRAPHICS

Click the **WordArt Vertical Text** button on the WordArt toolbar to rotate the vertical text to horizontal text.

Prepare a newsletter with graphics that will be sent to Wexford Conference Center clients informing them that Wexford Event Planners now has a long-term contract to manage the center. The center has been very popular with clients, and the goal of the newsletter is to reassure clients that the same staff will be serving them in the future and that they will have many more service options available to them in the future.

**1.** Use .5" side margins; adjust the document to fit on one page.

**2.** Use WordArt to create a masthead for the newsletter. Select the style in column 6, row 5 to insert **WCC** as vertical text. Then use the same WordArt style to key **Wexford Conference Center**. Rotate *Wexford Conference Center* to horizontal text.

**3.** Set a continuous break at approximately 2.5" and then format in two equal columns.

**4.** Use Heading 3 for all headings in the newsletter.

**5.** Insert the conference center picture from the data files.

**6.** Format the picture as follows:

- Crop the picture .25" from the right side.
- Change the brightness to 55%.
- Size the picture 4" wide.
- Wrap text on both sides.
- Position the picture approximately as shown in the illustration.

**7.** Key the text shown on the next page.

**8.** Save as *8-2task5*, preview, and print.

## Successful Opening Year

Wexford Conference Center recently completed its first year of operation. Results for the first year exceeded expectations on all measures. Goals for the first year were set at 60 percent for guest rooms and 45 percent for meeting and dining rooms. Occupancy exceeded 70 percent for guest rooms and 55 percent for meeting and dining facilities.

Feedback forms completed by clients and by individual participants in events at the center indicated that the facilities were ideal for the events participants attended. Food and service ratings were also extremely high.

## Outstanding Staff

Julie Anders, Wexford Conference Center director, and her entire staff did an outstanding job in making the center's first year so successful. In fact, the center has been so successful that it has outgrown the capabilities of the small management staff.

## New Management Contract

Wexford Event Planners, Inc. has signed a long-term contract to manage the Wexford Conference Center. The great news is that Julie and her entire staff will continue to manage the center. Wexford Event Planners has hired Julie Anders as one of its senior officers, and she retains the title of Conference Center Director.

## Wexford Event Planners

Wexford Event Planners, which recently joined the University Business Incubator, is an exciting young company that is growing rapidly. The company has focused its strategic direction on corporate, professional, and nonprofit organizations. It provides a wide range of both client and administrative services that are not currently available at the Wexford Conference Center.

Several of the Wexford Conference Center owners are senior partners in Wexford Event Planners; therefore it is logical to combine these two extremely successful groups. A tremendous amount of synergy will result from this partnership.

## Outlook for Next Year

The outlook for next year is extremely bright. Advance reservations for both guest rooms and conference facilities are already 20 percent ahead of where they were last year at this time. Wexford Planners select meeting sites for many clients and will be using the conference center for many of those events. In addition, the company will be promoting the use of the center to bring in new business.

Thank you for being a significant part of Wexford Conference Center this year. We hope to serve as your hosts again this year.

## ...ng Forms and Guides

...ves

...minary event planning form
...liminary event planning form
...ninary event planning form
... capacity table
... facilities guide

---

## TASK 1     PRELIMINARY EVENT PLANNING FORM

Design an online fill-in form that can be used with the initial discussion with clients to plan an event. This form collects general information that will later be transferred to a comprehensive service request form. In some cases, the form will be completed by the client; in others, a representative of WEP will complete the form.

1. Prepare the form shown on the next page. Three types of fields are used: text box fields ⬚, checkbox fields ☐, and drop-down fields. Options for drop-down fields are shown below:

   Type of event: **Meeting/training | Trade show/exhibit | Product/special announcement | Reception**

   Type of service desired: **Turnkey | On-site planning and management | Special services**

   Venue location: **Client facilities | Wexford Conference Center | Other off-site facility**

   Special needs: **Program assistance | Event promotion | Entertainment | Decoration**

2. Protect the form; use the password **pepform**. Save as *8-3task1*.

---

## TASK 2     FILL-IN PRELIMINARY EVENT PLANNING FORM

Test the form you completed in Task 1 by filling it out. Use the rough notes below to complete the form. You should be able to extract enough information to complete most sections. If you have difficulty completing any section, make a note of it so that the form can be revised. Save as *8-3task2*.

**GLENN & VANHUSS DEVELOPERS**

William R. (Bill) Glenn, President
1298 Forest Avenue
Oak Park, IL 60302-1204
Phone: 708-555-0137 Fax: 708-555-0159
Bill.Glenn@Glenn&VanHuss.com

Bill Glenn of Glenn & VanHuss Developers wants WEP to handle a turnkey job for an Investment Opportunity Seminar at Wexford Conference Center designed to attract investors in a new subdivision they are planning to develop. They would like the two-hour seminar to be held three weeks from today. A reception will follow the seminar. About 20 local investors will be invited. They would like WEP to provide program assistance and event promotion. Bill has not yet formalized a budget for the event. Bill has been a regular client of WEP (see business card).

# Preliminary Event Planning

## Client Information

Company/organization: [_____]

Key contact person: [_____]

Address: [_____]

Telephone and Fax: [_____]

E-mail: [_____]

## Event Information

Name: [_____]

Type of event: [_____ ▼]

Date(s) and approximate length of event: [_____]

Venue location: [_____ ▼]     Venue: ☐ Indoor ☐ Outdoor

Approximate number of attendees: [_____]

Housing required: ☐ Yes ☐ No

Ground transportation required: ☐ Yes ☐ No

Type of service desired: [_____ ▼]

Catered meal service: ☐ Yes ☐ No

Other food and beverage service: ☐ Yes ☐ No

Special needs: [_____ ▼]

Budget established: ☐ Yes ☐ No

If yes, approximate amount: [_____]

Other information: [_____]

## Is There a Leader?

Many teams are ad hoc; that is, they are set up to accomplish a specific purpose, and no one person is designated as the leader. The members may not have authority over each other in the organization or they may consist of a variety of ranks. The leader simply emerges from the group.

**Who might become the unofficial leader of a team?**

- Person with the highest rank
- Person with the closest association to the person who set up the team
- Person who brings the group together and coordinates the meetings
- Person with the best leadership skills may become the natural leader
- Person who takes the initiative to do things

---

**TASK 3**

## MODIFY PRELIMINARY EVENT PLANNING FORM

Unprotect the form you prepared in Task 1 and make the following modifications in it.

1. Add **Employee function** to the drop-down options on Type of Event. Reorder the list so that it will be in alphabetical order.
2. Change Special Needs from a drop-down list to a checkbox list so that multiple items can be selected. Use the following options:

   Special needs: ☐ Program/materials assistance ☐ Event promotion Entertainment ☐ Decoration/plants/floral
3. Protect the form using the same password.
4. Save as *8-3task3*.

---

## Influencing Others

Effective leaders can influence individuals to do things even though they have no authority over them. An example is getting individuals who own their own companies to participate in the UBI Annual Report.

Effective leaders use the following techniques:

- Approach the situation from the perspective of the other person.
- Show the benefits to the other person.
- Use good human relations skills and make it easy for the other person to grant requests.

Julie Anders, director of the Wexford Conference Center, has asked you to prepare a Room Capacity Guide. This guide will be part of a Wexford Conference Center promotion package. WEP employees and clients can use the guide as a tool in planning and utilizing space effectively.

1. Key the table shown below.

2. Apply **Table Contemporary** AutoFormat.

3. Save as *8-3task4*, preview, and print.

| Wexford Conference Center Facilities | | | | | | | | |
|---|---|---|---|---|---|---|---|---|
| **Room** | **Size** | **Capacity Based on Seating Type** | | | | | | |
| | Square Feet | Banquet Rounds | Reception | Classroom | Conference | Theater | U-Shape | Hollow Square |
| Nord Boardroom | 850 | | | | 24 | | | |
| Wexford Ballroom | 3,600 | 200 | 350 | | | 350 | | |
| Salons A, B, C, D | 900 | 50 | 75 | 30 | 26 | 60 | 22 | 26 |
| Salons A & B | 1,800 | 100 | 150 | 60 | 40 | 120 | 40 | 50 |
| Salons C & D | 1,800 | 100 | 150 | 60 | 40 | 120 | 40 | 50 |
| Oak Room—Fixed | 2,000 | | | 80 | | | | |
| Rex Computer Lab | 1,000 | | | 30 | | | | |
| Summit Room | 1,250 | 72 | 100 | 50 | 30 | 80 | 30 | 40 |
| Lakeview Room | 2,025 | 128 | 175 | 65 | 40 | 140 | 50 | 60 |

**THINK CRITICALLY**

- Why is it important to list capacity by seating type?
- What are the advantages and disadvantages of each type of seating type?

For more information on effective seating arrangements, visit http://www.advancedapplications.swlearning.com. Click **Project 8** and click **Links** or use the **Research** tool to find additional information.

Julie Anders was pleased with the table you prepared and asked you to incorporate it in a more complete Wexford Conference Center Facilities Guide. You have been working on that draft and are now ready to complete it.

1. Open *facility guide* from the data files and save it as *8-3task5*.

2. Format the document using SS; number the pages.

3. Use heading style indicated in comments.

4. Position the inserts shown below where indicated by comments in the data file.

5. Insert the table you created in *8-3task4* where indicated.

6. Resave your changes, preview, and print.

Insert #1

In addition to the on-site fitness center, extensive fitness and recreations facilities are available at the nearby Oak Park SportsPlex. Guests can access tennis, swimming, golf, walking trails, and a host of other activities with less than a five-minute ride on the free Wexford shuttle.

Insert #2

Outdoor Functions

The patios and large gazebo area provide excellent venues for receptions and picnics when the weather is appropriate for outdoor functions. Large climate-controlled tents can also be rented for special functions.

Other Amenities

The Wexford dining room provides full breakfast and lunch buffets for residential guests and for conference functions that do not have group meals for participants. Chef Pat receives rave reviews for the theme buffets he offers in the evening. The Wexford lounge is open daily from 5:00 p.m. until 11:00 p.m.

# Estimating Cost and Revenue

Objectives

- Complete WCC guest room projection
- Prepare WEP revenue sources projection
- Prepare a budget checklist
- Prepare slides for WCC strategic pricing decisions

## TASK 1  GUEST ROOM PROJECTION

Julie asked you to complete the *Excel* spreadsheet projecting the guest room revenue for the Wexford Conference Center. You decided to prepare a column chart to give a better picture of the revenue based on projected occupancy rates.

1. Open *guest room projections* from the data files and save it as *8-4task1*.

2. Complete the spreadsheet as follows:

   - Complete row 7 (Total Income) by summing rows 4 and 5 for each column.

   - Complete row 13 (Total Allocated Expense) by summing rows 10 and 11 for each column.

   - Complete row 21 (Total Unallocated Expense) by summing rows 16 through 19 for each column.

   - Compute the Profit (row 23) for each column by using the following formula:

     Total Income minus the sum of the Total Allocated Expenses plus the Total Unallocated Expenses. For example, the formula for column B would be: =B7-(B13+B21) and for column C would be: =C7-(C13+C21).

   - Bold the title and column heads; format gridlines and an external border.

3. Select the Profit row (row 23) and use the Chart Wizard to create a Clustered Column chart with 3D Visual Effects in a new Chart sheet.

4. Format the chart as follows and

   - Do not show the legend.

   - Key **Profit** as the title of the chart; format it in bold, 18-point type.

   - Key **75%**, **80%**, and **85% Occupancy** as the Category Axis title; format it in bold, 16-point type.

   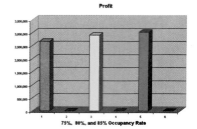

   - Format each tall column (data point for 1, 3, and 5) with a different color. Format the flat columns (profit per room data points for 2, 4, and 6) with one color.

5. Resave the document.

# PROJECTED SOURCES OF REVENUE CHART

This morning you attended a meeting in which WEP sources of revenue for this year were projected. You were asked to summarize the sources in a table or chart. You decided that a pie chart would be the best way to summarize the sources of revenue since they total 100 percent. Use *Microsoft Graph* to prepare the chart and save it as *8-4task2*.

Your notes from the meeting are shown below:

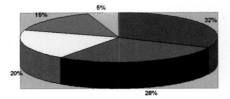

**Projected Sources of Revenue**

| Wexford Conference Center guest rooms | 32% |
| Wexford Conference Center services | 28% |
| Client on-site special events | 20% |
| Client off-site special events | 15% |
| Other special event services | 5% |

**Note:** Use abbreviated titles for the legend.

# BUDGETING CHECKLIST

Use Heading 1, centered for the title; then key the paragraph shown at the top of the next page. Insert a 3-column table below the paragraph. Save as *8-4task3*.

1. In the first column, insert a checkbox form field.
2. In the second column, key the budgeting activities listed on the next page.
3. Leave the third column blank for cost estimates.

### Budgeting Checklist

The budget for special events can range from hundreds of thousands of dollars to a few dollars depending on the type of event, where it is held, and what is involved in staging and producing the event. This budgeting checklist focuses on programs offered in the client's facilities. An event staged in a client's own facilities is easier to budget than other alternatives. However, many clients do not have facilities available that can accommodate the type of special event being considered.

Only an illustration, see next page for text. →

| Checkbox | Checklist Items | Estimated Costs |
|---|---|---|
| **Planning and Preparation** | | |
| ☐ | Client staff salaries and benefits | |
| ☐ | Labor charges special events planners | |
| ☐ | Planning meeting costs | |
| **Promotion and Printing** | | |
| ☐ | Design and production of invitations/promotional pieces | |
| ☐ | Advertising/public relations costs | |

The budget for special events can range from hundreds of thousands of dollars to a few dollars depending on the type of event, where it is held, and what is involved in staging and producing the event. This budgeting checklist focuses on programs offered in the client's facilities. An event staged in a client's own facilities is easier to budget than other alternatives. However, many clients do not have facilities available that can accommodate the type of special event being considered.

## Planning and Preparation

Client staff salaries and benefits
Labor charges special events planners
Planning meeting costs

## Promotion and Printing

Design and production of invitations/promotional pieces
Advertising/public relations costs
Printing registration and other forms, guest lists, programs, tickets, handouts, announcements, menus, special materials
Directional materials and signs
Telephone and mailing expenses
Design and production of invitations/promotional pieces

## Overhead Expenses

Office supplies
Telephone/fax
Shipping/storage
Taxes, insurance, security

## Program

Honoraria and expenses for speakers
Expenses of special guests
Entertainment of speakers and guests
Program entertainment
Audiovisual resources

## Staging and Production of Event

Coordinator expenses
Decorations/flowers
Special furnishings
Registration
Housing for speakers/guests
Food and beverage costs
Food and beverage service costs
Ground transportation
Parking for guests
Furniture/equipment rental
Cleaning charges
Coordinator expenses

## Spouse/Family Program

Gifts, amenities
Childcare arrangements
Special activities

Senior managers are meeting to discuss appropriate pricing for Wexford Conference Center facilities and services. Julie Anders has asked you to prepare slides for use in that meeting.

1. Select a design of your choice. Make sure it is appropriate for a meeting designed to make strategic pricing decisions. The design illustrated is Studio. Use transitions and animations you think appropriate.

2. Prepare slides with the information shown below and on the next two pages. Insert slide numbers. Key the notes shown.

3. Save as *8-4task4* and preview the slides.

**Slide 1 Notes:**

The objective of this presentation is to present current pricing structure and alternatives that might be considered. Since many events are already booked for this year, changes can be implemented only on new business.

**Slide 2 Notes:**

Recommend that no changes be made in the rates this year. Projections for revenue were made on an average daily rate of $160 with occupancy expected to reach 80 percent. Consider a 5 to 15 percent increase for next year.

**Slide 3**

Link chart created in *8-4-task1*.

**Slide 3 Notes:**

Occupancy rates currently exceed original expectations; therefore, profit will be higher than originally expected.

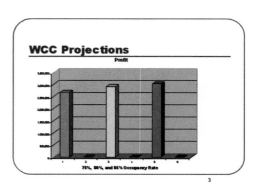

## Slide 4

Embed chart created in *8-4-task2*.

### Slide 4 Notes:

Note that WCC guest rooms are expected to produce 32 percent of WEP revenue this year. WEP conference services are expected to produce 28 percent of WEP revenue this year. This situation resulted from no longer serving private clients and not yet having time to develop business customers.

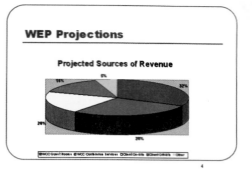

## Slide 5

1. Choose the Title and Table layout to create a 4-column, 8-row table.

2. Adjust font size of column headings to fit on one line. Bold headings.

3. Adjust column size so that all entries fit on one line.

**Price Per Meeting Room**

| Meeting Room | Full Day | Half Day | Evening |
|---|---|---|---|
| Boardroom | $1,500 | $1,200 | $1,000 |
| Ballroom | $2,500 | $2,000 | $2,200 |
| Salons | $1,000 | $ 600 | $ 800 |
| Summit Room | $1,500 | $1,000 | $1,000 |
| Lakeview Room | $1,800 | $1,400 | $1,200 |
| Oak Room | $2,000 | $1,250 | $1,000 |
| Rex Computer Lab | $2,000 | $1,500 | $1,250 |

### Slide 5 Notes:

Many conference centers price rooms on a price per person within ranges and with a specified minimum rather than a per-room basis. Generally, more revenue is created using the price-per-person approach.

### Slide 6 Notes:

Clients like the fact that they are not charged for individual items and do not have to pay high rental fees for the extensive, state-of-the-art audiovisual equipment that is available in each meeting room.

**Meeting Room Price Includes**

- All WCC audiovisual resources
- Registration
- All day beverage station – coffee, tea, cold drinks, bottled water
- Morning – pastries; afternoon – snacks
- Notepads and pens
- Access to a computer and printer
- Printing supplies

**Slide 7 Notes:**

Prices shown in ranges vary depending on menu selection. Prices are very competitive.

**Meal Charges Per Person**

- Lunch buffet in dining room    $10
- Lunch in separate room    $12 – $18
- Theme buffet – evening    $20
- Seated dinners    $25 – $75
- Receptions    $15 – $50

7

**Slide 8 Notes:**

Examples of additional services include providing speakers, decorations, entertainment, ground transportation, obtaining gifts for participants, event promotion, etc.

**Additional Services**

Wide range of services available

Quotes provided depending on services requested

8

**THINK CRITICALLY**

- Why is it important to present current pricing to this group?
- Why is it important to have competitive information?

 **For more information on conference center rates, use the Research tool or keywords *Conference Center Rates* to search the Web.**

# FOCUS ON THE WORKPLACE

## Leadership

### Results of Team Leadership

Team leaders are usually judged by the results of their team members. Good leaders focus on the way team members participate in the work of the team and try to ensure that:

- Each team member is committed to the work of the team and to doing a fair share of the work or even more than that.
- Each team member is given and must accept the opportunity to participate actively in making decisions that affect the team.
- Each team member supports team decisions once they have been made.

# Presenting WEP to UBI

## Objectives
- Prepare presentation
- Revise presentation
- Make team presentation

---

## TASK 1  PRESENTATION FOR UBI OWNERS

Remember to use all of the previous jobs in this project for information about WEP.

Mr. Bowman was very pleased with the slides you prepared for Julie Anders and asked you and two team members to prepare slides for a presentation that he was asked to make at the next meeting of the owners of UBI companies. Owners of new companies are asked to make a presentation about their company to other companies. Originally he planned just to talk about WEP, but now he would like slides as well. You will be able to incorporate some of the slides you did in the last presentation. He met with the team and talked about things he would like to include in the presentation. He emphasized that he would like the slides to use a graphic approach rather than a lot of bulleted text. He will critique the presentation, and then you can revise it. One of your team members keyed the notes from your meeting. They are stored in the data files as *bowman notes*.

1. Review the notes from Mr. Bowman carefully.

2. Prepare a presentation that follows the suggestions given in the notes. Brainstorm and try to supplement ideas when appropriate.

3. Save as *8-5task1*.

---

## TASK 2 REVISE PRESENTATION

A sample presentation is shown on the next page that you can use to compare to your presentation. Mr. Bowman reviewed this presentation and made a couple of suggestions:

1. Move the Mission slide before the organization chart.

2. Hide slides 7, 8, 9, and 10. He will use them if questions are asked about these topics.

3. Add callouts to slide 14 as follows:

    CMF      Subcontractor for public relations and advertising

    CSV      WCC uses SportsPlex as recreational facilities for guests

    UBI      Provides business planning and legal assistance for contracts, liability issues, and insurance needs

4. Review the presentation shown on the next page and the presentation you prepared. Revise your presentation to include the best of both presentations.

5. Use the animation or transitions of your choice.

6. Save as *8-5task2*.

### Wexford Event Planners, Inc.

A Corporate Overview

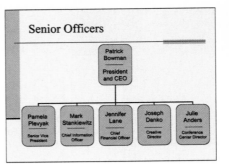

### Senior Officers

Patrick Bowman — President and CEO

- Pamela Plevyak — Senior Vice President
- Mark Stankiewitz — Chief Information Officer
- Jennifer Lane — Chief Financial Officer
- Joseph Danko — Creative Director
- Julie Anders — Conference Center Director

### Mission

*Our mission is to provide creative and unique special events as well as extraordinary service to our business, professional, and nonprofit clients.*

### Core Competencies

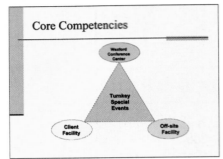

Wexford Conference Center

Turnkey Special Events

Client Facility — Off-site Facility

### Revenue Sources

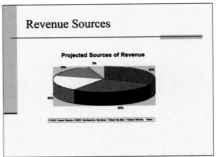

Projected Sources of Revenue

### Wexford Conference Center

- 75 guest rooms including 10 two-bedroom suites
- World-class boardroom with state-of-the-art audiovisual resources
- Ballroom—200 for a seated dinner; 350 for a reception (4 salons)
- Two multipurpose meeting rooms
- Fixed classroom
- Computer training room for 30

### WCC Guest Rooms

King/queen double — $160
- Full breakfast for up to two guests
- Area shuttle service

Deluxe two-bedroom suites — $205
- Full breakfast for up to four guests
- Buffet lunch for up to four guests
- Concierge lounge — 6:30 a.m. to 11:00 p.m.
- Area shuttle service

### Price Per Meeting Room

| Meeting Room | Full Day | Half Day | Evening |
|---|---|---|---|
| Boardroom | $1,500 | $1,200 | $1,000 |
| Ballroom | $2,500 | $2,000 | $2,200 |
| Salons | $1,000 | $ 600 | $ 800 |
| Summit Room | $1,500 | $1,000 | $1,000 |
| Lakeview Room | $1,800 | $1,400 | $1,200 |
| Oak Room | $2,000 | $1,250 | $1,000 |
| Rex Computer Lab | $2,000 | $1,500 | $1,250 |

### Meeting Room Price Includes

- All WCC audiovisual resources
- Registration
- All day beverage station – coffee, tea, cold drinks, bottled water
- Morning – pastries; afternoon – snacks
- Notepads and pens
- Access to a computer and printer
- Printing supplies

### Meal Charges Per Person

| | |
|---|---|
| Lunch buffet in dining room | $10 |
| Lunch in separate room | $12 – $18 |
| Theme buffet – evening | $20 |
| Seated dinners | $25 – $75 |
| Receptions | $15 – $50 |

### Events in Client's Facility

Events in Client's Facility: Meetings, Product Introduction, Employee Recognition, Management Briefing, Training Program, Holiday Events, Open House, Retreat

### Off-Site Facilities

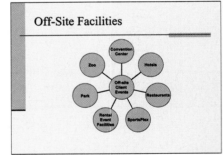

Off-site Client Events: Convention Center, Hotels, Restaurants, SportsPlex, Rental Event Facilities, Park, Zoo

### Special Event Process

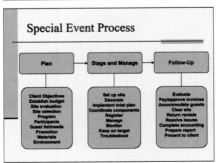

Plan — Stage and Manage — Follow-Up

Plan: Client Objectives, Establish budget, Site evaluation, Site selection, Program, Participants, Guest listmeads, Promotion, Materials, Environment

Stage and Manage: Set up site, Decorate, Implement total plan, Coordinate components, Register, Manage, Monitor, Keep on target, Troubleshoot

Follow-Up: Evaluate, Pay/approve invoices, Accommodate guests, Clear site, Return rentals, Resolve issues, Complete accounting, Prepare report, Present to client

### Strategic Partners

- CMF Communications, Inc.
- Champion Sports Venues, Inc.
- University Business Incubator

- How do these changes improve the presentation you designed?

Mr. Bowman gave the presentation to the UBI owners/presidents, and he indicated it was well received. Several members of the group asked if someone from WEP could give the presentation again for some of their management team at a meeting that is scheduled later this week.

Mr. Bowman indicated that your team would be happy to make the presentation.

1. You and your team should prepare Notes Pages and divide up the presentation.

2. Practice presenting before your class.

3. Save the presentation with the notes you added as *8-5task3*.

# FOCUS ON THE WORKPLACE

### Leadership

## Team Leadership

The success of a team without an officially designated leader depends on every team member accepting responsibility for the success of the team project. Self-motivation is critical. Each team member must demonstrate initiative and work smart.

Highly effective teams demonstrate the following leadership characteristics:

- Each member is empowered and controls his or her own responsibilities.
- Each member accepts ideas of others.
- Each member respects and trusts other members.

## Self-Assessment   Evaluate your understanding of this project by answering the questions below.

1. A(n) _____ provides the structure and style of a document and is used to enhance productivity.

2. A form to prepare minutes can be produced automatically by using the _____ Wizard.

3. Key statistics about a document can be located in the _____.

4. The feature used to integrate several documents that have been returned by reviewers is _____.

5. _____ is a graphic feature frequently used to prepare mastheads for newsletters.

6. Click the _____ button to add alternatives in a drop-down form field.

7. Use the _____ editing restriction to allow users to complete a form but not change the form.

8. A(n) _____ chart can be used to summarize data that total 100 percent.

9. An *Excel* chart that is _____ to a *Word* or *PowerPoint* document will be updated in the *Word* or *PowerPoint* document when the *Excel* file is updated.

10. If you do not want an *Excel* chart updated in a *Word* or *PowerPoint* file, you should _____ it.

## Performance Assessment   Production time: 15'

**Document 1**
**Memo**
1. Prepare a memo to the other five senior officers from Joe Danko using the *WEP memo* template. Indicate a copy to you. Use a distribution list. Attach the finalized WEP Services Overview you created in *8-2task3* and the table from Document 2.
2. Check spelling and grammar; proofread, preview, and print. Save as *checkpoint8-d1*.

**Document 2**
**Table**
Create Document 2 using the instructions at the right.

Everyone has reviewed the WEP Services Overview document and made comments on it. All of the comments have been incorporated in the document, and the final copy is attached.

A copy of this document will be provided to the staff, and they will be asked to complete the detailed service plan. We estimate that it will take four weeks for the first draft and another two weeks to finalize the plan.

I have also attached the Wexford Conference Center meeting room pricing chart that several of you requested. I highlighted the Boardroom and Computer Lab prices; we need to review them.

**Document 2**

1. Open the *8-5task2 PowerPoint* presentation you prepared and convert the table on slide 8 to a *Word* table.

2. Copy the table to a new *Word* document. Use Paste Special and paste the table in HTML format. Center the table about 2" from the top of the page.

3. Center, bold, and shade row 1 (column heads) 10% gray. Insert a row above the column heads, merge the cells, and bold and center on two lines the heading **Wexford Conference Center | Price Per Meeting Room**.

4. Select the data in all but the first column and center it. Use the Table Properties to vertically align the data in all cells at the center.

5. Use yellow to make the highlights noted in the memo.

6. Preview and save as *checkpoint8-d2*.

# KEYBOARDING SKILLS TRAINING

## Drill 1

### PROGRESSIVE WRITINGS

1. Set the timer for 1'.

2. Practice each paragraph in a set until you can complete it in 1' with no more than one error.

3. Take a 3' writing; strive to maintain your 1' rate.

4. Move onto the next set. Notice that each set progresses by 5 words.

  all letters

The Writing number refers to MicroPace Pro. To access writings on MicroPace Pro, key **W** and the timing number. For example, key **W26** for Writing 26.

**Writing 26: 40 gwam**

gwam   1' | 3'

"An ounce of prevention is worth a pound of cure" is really | 12 | 4 | 31
based on fact; still, many people comprehend this statement more | 25 | 8 | 35
for its quality as literature than on a practical, common-sense | 38 | 12 | 39
philosophy. | 40 | 13 | 40

Just take health, for example. We agonize over stiff costs | 12 | 17 | 44
we pay to recover from illnesses; but, on the other hand, we give | 25 | 22 | 48
little or no attention to health requirements for diet, exercise, | 38 | 26 | 53
and sleep. | 40 | 27 | 53

**Writing 27: 45 gwam**

gwam   1' | 3'

Problems with our environment show an odd lack of foresight. | 12 | 4 | 34
We just expect that whatever we may need to support life will be | 25 | 8 | 38
available. We rarely question our comforts, even though they may | 38 | 13 | 43
abuse our earth, water, and air. | 45 | 15 | 45

Optimism is an excellent virtue. It is comforting to think | 12 | 19 | 49
that, eventually, anything can be fixed. So why should we worry? | 25 | 23 | 53
A better idea, certainly, is to realize that we don't have to fix | 38 | 28 | 58
anything we have not yet broken. | 45 | 30 | 60

**Writing 28: 50 gwam**

gwam   1' | 3'

Recently, a friend of mine grumbled about how quickly papers | 12 | 4 | 37
accumulated on her desk; she never seemed able to reduce them to | 25 | 8 | 42
zero. She said some law seemed to be working that expanded the | 38 | 13 | 46
stack today by precisely the amount she reduced it yesterday. | 50 | 17 | 50

She should organize her papers and tend to them daily. Any | 12 | 21 | 54
paper that needs a look, a decision, and speedy, final action | 24 | 25 | 58
gets just that; any that needs closer attention is subject to a | 37 | 29 | 62
fixed completion schedule. Self-discipline is the key to order. | 50 | 33 | 67

1' | 1 | 2 | 3 | 4 | 5 | 6 | 7 | 8 | 9 | 10 | 11 | 12 | 13
3' | 1 | 2 | 3 | 4

**Writing 29: 55 gwam**

A crucial life skill is the ability to put things in proper 12 4 41
perspective. Individuals often fail to realize that many things 25 8 45
are just not worth fighting about. A quick way to know whether 38 13 50
an issue is worth fighting for is to look at the situation from a 51 17 54
long-term perspective. 55 18 55

If you will care five or six years from now that you de- 11 22 59
fended an issue, it is a principle worth defending. If you will 24 26 63
not even remember, the situation does not justify the effort 36 31 67
required for defending it. The odds of winning are also impor- 49 35 72
tant. Why fight a losing battle? 55 37 74

**Writing 30: 60 gwam**

Why do we remember some things and forget others? Often, 12 4 44
we associate loss of memory with aging or an illness such as 24 8 48
Alzheimer's disease. However, the crux of the matter is that we 37 12 52
all forget various things that we prefer to remember. We tend to 50 17 57
remember things that mean something special to us. 60 20 60

For many people, recalling dates is a difficult task; yet 12 24 64
they manage to remember dates of special occasions, such as anni- 25 28 68
versaries. Processing requires one not only to hear but to 36 33 72
ponder and to understand what has just been said. We recall 49 37 77
things that we say and do longer than things we hear and see. 60 40 80

**Writing 31: 65 gwam**

Humor is very important in our professional and our personal 12 4 47
lives. Fortunately, we realize that many things can and do go 25 8 52
wrong. If we can learn to laugh at ourselves and with other 37 12 56
people, we will get through the terrible times. Adding a little 50 17 60
extra laughter can help put the situation in proper perspective 63 21 64
much quicker. 65 22 65

Maintaining our sense of humor lets us enjoy our positions 12 26 69
to a greater degree. No one is perfect, and we cannot expect 24 30 73
perfection from ourselves. However, the quality of our perfor- 37 34 77
mance is greater when we do the things we like. We realize our 50 38 82
prime time is devoted to work. Thus, it is important that we 62 42 86
enjoy this time. 65 43 87

**Writing 32: 70 *gwam***

    Foreign study and travel take extra time and effort, but 11 | 4 | 50
these two activities quickly help us to understand people. Much 24 | 8 | 55
can be learned from other cultures. Today, business must think 37 | 12 | 59
globally. Learning about the culture of others is not a luxury. 50 | 17 | 63
Even the owner of a small business realizes that he or she cannot 64 | 21 | 68
just focus on the domestic scene. 70 | 23 | 70

    Many examples can be used to show how a local business may 11 | 27 | 74
be influenced by global competition. A hair stylist may be re- 24 | 31 | 78
quired to learn European styles because customers may want to try 38 | 36 | 83
a style just like they saw on their travels. Or salons may want 51 | 40 | 87
to offer other services such as facials that people have tried 63 | 44 | 91
while they were traveling abroad. 70 | 47 | 93

**Writing 33: 75 *gwam***

gwam   1' | 3'

    Getting a job interview is certainly a triumph for the job 12 | 4 | 54
seeker. Yet anxiety quickly sets in as the applicant becomes 24 | 8 | 58
aware of the competition. The same attention to details that was 37 | 12 | 62
used in writing the successful resume will also be needed for the 51 | 17 | 67
interview. Experts often say that the first four minutes are the 64 | 21 | 71
most crucial in making a strong impact on the interviewer. 75 | 25 | 75

    First, people focus on what they see. Posture, eye contact, 12 | 29 | 79
facial expression, and gestures make up over half of the message. 26 | 33 | 84
Next, people focus on what they hear; enthusiasm, delivery, pace, 39 | 38 | 88
volume, and clarity are as vital as what is said. Finally, 51 | 42 | 92
people get to the actual words that are said. You can make a 63 | 49 | 96
good impression. But, realize, you have just four minutes. 75 | 50 | 100

**Writing 34: 80 *gwam***

gwam   1' | 3'

    Would a pitcher go to the mound without warming up? Would 12 | 4 | 57
a speaker go to the podium without practice? Of course not! These 25 | 8 | 62
experts have spent many long hours striving to do their best. 38 | 13 | 66
Similarly, the performance of business employees is rated. The 51 | 17 | 70
manager's evaluation will include a record of actual performance 64 | 21 | 75
and a list of new goals. A good mark in these areas will demand 77 | 26 | 79
much hard work. 80 | 27 | 80

    Many work factors can be practiced to help one succeed on 12 | 30 | 84
the job. Class attendance and punctuality can be perfected by 24 | 35 | 88
students. Because work is expected to be correct, managers do 37 | 39 | 92
not assign zeros. Thus, students must learn to proofread their 49 | 43 | 96
work. A project must also be completed quickly. Students can 62 | 47 | 101
learn to organize work and time well and to find ways to do their 75 | 52 | 105
work smarter and faster. 80 | 53 | 107

| 1' | 1 | 2 | 3 | 4 | 5 | 6 | 7 | 8 | 9 | 10 | 11 | 12 | 13 |
|----|---|---|---|---|---|---|---|---|---|----|----|----|----|
| 3' | | 1 | | | 2 | | | 3 | | | 4 | | |

## D r i l l  5

**SPECIFIC FINGERS**
Key each set twice;
DS between groups.

1st
1 fun gray vent guy hunt brunt buy brunch much gun huge humor vying
2 buy them brunch; a hunting gun; Guy hunts for fun; try it for fun

2nd
3 cite decide kick cider creed kidded keen keep kit idea ice icicle
4 keen idea; kick it back; ice breaker; decide the issue; sip cider

3rd
5 low slow lax solo wax sold swell swollen wood wool load logs doll
6 wooden dolls; wax the floor; a slow boat; saw logs; pull the wool

4th
7 quip zap Zane zip pepper pay quiz zipper quizzes pad map nap jazz
8 zip the zipper; jazz at the plaza; Zane quipped; La Paz jazz band

1. Key three 1' writings on each paragraph.

2. Key one 5' or two 3' writings.

**Option:** Practice as a guided writing.

| | | | gwam |
|---|---|---|---|
| 1/4' | 1/2' | 3/4' | 1' |
| 8 | 16 | 24 | 32 |
| 9 | 18 | 27 | 36 |
| 10 | 20 | 30 | 40 |
| 11 | 22 | 33 | 44 |
| 12 | 24 | 36 | 48 |
| 13 | 26 | 39 | 52 |
| 14 | 28 | 41 | 56 |
| 15 | 30 | 45 | 60 |
| 16 | 32 | 48 | 64 |
| 17 | 34 | 51 | 68 |
| 18 | 36 | 54 | 72 |

  all letters

**Writing 38**

*gwam* 3' 5'

How much power is adequate?  Is more power always better | 4 | 2 | 50
than less power?  People often raise the question in many differ- | 8 | 5 | 52
ent instances.  Regardless of the situation, most people seem to | 12 | 7 | 55
seek more power.  In jobs, power is often related to rank in an | 17 | 10 | 57
organization, to the number of people reporting to a person, and | 21 | 13 | 60
to the ability to spend money without having to ask someone with | 25 | 15 | 63
more power.  Most experts indicate that the power a person has | 30 | 18 | 65
should closely match the responsibilities (not just duties and | 34 | 20 | 68
tasks) for which he or she can be held accountable. | 37 | 22 | 70

Questions about power are not limited to jobs and people. | 41 | 25 | 72
Many people ask the question in reference to the amount of power | 45 | 27 | 75
or speed a computer should have.  Again, the response usually | 50 | 30 | 77
implies that more is better.  A better approach is to analyze how | 54 | 32 | 80
the computer is to be used and then try to match power needs to | 58 | 35 | 82
the types of applications.  Most people are surprised to learn | 62 | 37 | 85
that home computer buyers tend to buy more power than buyers in | 67 | 40 | 87
offices.  The primary reason is that the computers are used to | 71 | 43 | 90
play games with extensive graphics, sound, and other media appli- | 75 | 45 | 93
cations.  Matching the needs of the software is the key. | 79 | 47 | 95

3' | 1 | 2 | 3 | 4 |
5' | 1 | 2 | 3 |

**SPECIFIC ROWS**
Key each set of
lines twice.

Reach to the first and
third rows with a
minimum of hand
movement; keep hands
quiet; don't bounce on
the keys.

Key two 3' or one 5'
writing; key with fluency
and control.

 all letters

**Rows 3, 2, 1**

1 you we quip try pot peer your wire put quit wet trip power toy to
2 salad fad glad lass lag has gall lash gas lad had shall flag half
3 comb zone exam man carve bun oxen bank came next vent zoo van cab

4 we try to; you were; put up your; put it there; you quit; wipe it
5 Gail asked Sissy; what was said; had Jake left; Dana sold a flag
6 Zam came back; can Max fix my van? a brave man, Ben came in a cab

7 Peter or I will try to wire our popular reports to Porter or you.
8 Ada Glass said she is glad she had half a kale salad with Dallas.
9 Zack drove a van to minimize expenses; Ben and Max came in a cab.

**Writing 39**                                                     *gwam*  3' | 5'

Sports are very big business today; that is, those sports  4 | 3 | 62
competitions in which men participate are very big business.  What  9 | 5 | 65
about sports for women?  At the professional level, women have made  13 | 8 | 67
real progress in golf and tennis; they, as well as their sponsors, can  18 | 11 | 70
make big money in both of these events.  The other sports for women  22 | 13 | 73
still are not considered to be major revenue sports.  The future  26 | 16 | 75
may be much better, however, because sports for women at all levels  31 | 19 | 78
are gaining in popularity.  Programs that are designed to help  35 | 21 | 81
young girls develop their athletic skills and interest are having  40 | 24 | 83
an impact.  The result is that girls now expect to play for organ-  44 | 26 | 86
ized clubs as well as in school programs just as boys do.  Club  48 | 29 | 88
sports often will lead to varsity teams.  51 | 31 | 90

Many people wonder how much impact the current emphasis on  55 | 33 | 92
gender equity will have on sports at the college level.  Most  59 | 35 | 95
people agree that this new emphasis is very positive for women.  63 | 38 | 97
Some people feel, though, that it either has had or could have a  68 | 41 | 100
negative impact on sports for men.  They believe that resources  72 | 43 | 103
that would have been spent on sports such as football, basketball,  77 | 46 | 105
and baseball for men are now being spent on the Olympic sports for  81 | 49 | 108
women.  Overall, most people believe that both men and women who  85 | 51 | 111
have the ability to excel in an athletic event as well as in the  90 | 54 | 113
classroom should have the opportunity and should be encouraged to  94 | 56 | 116
do so.  Success for both women and men is better than success for  98 | 59 | 118
either.  99 | 59 | 119

3' | 1 | 2 | 3 | 4
5' | 1 | 2 | 3

# Drill 7

**OPPOSITE-HAND COMBINATIONS**
Key each line once;
repeat four-line groups.

br/rb
1 break barb brawn orbit brain carbon brakes barbecue brazen barber
2 Barbara Brady brought us a new brand of barbecue to eat at break.

ce/ec
3 cease decide cent collect cell direct cedar check center peck ice
4 Cecil recently received a check for his special barbecue recipes.

mu/um
5 mull dumb must human mud lumber mulch lump mumps slump music fume
6 Bum Muse must have dumped too much muddy mulch on the bumpy lawn.

nu/un
7 nut sun fun nurse gun sinus number punch nuzzle pound lunch until
8 Uncle Gunta, a nurse, was uneasy about numerous units unionizing.

gr/rg
9 grade merge grand purge great large grab organ green margins gray
10 Margo, our great grandmother, regrets merging those large groups.

ny/yn
11 Wayne any shyness many agony balcony Jayne lynx penny larynx myna
12 Wayne and Jayne fed many skinny myna birds on that sunny balcony

Key fluently,
without rushing.

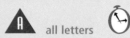 all letters

**Writing 40**

*gwam*   1' | 5'

    The job market today is quite different than it was a few   12 | 2
years ago.   The fast track to management no longer exists.   24 | 5
Entry-level managers find that it is much more difficult to   36 | 7
obtain a promotion to a higher-level position in management than   49 | 10
it was just a few years ago.   People who are in the market for   61 | 12
new jobs find very few management positions available.   In fact,   74 | 15
many managers at all levels have a difficult time keeping their   87 | 17
current management positions.   Two factors seem to contribute   99 | 20
heavily to the problem.   The first factor is the trend toward   112 | 22
self-managed teams.   The second factor is that as companies   124 | 25
downsize they often remove entire layers of management or an   136 | 27
entire division.   140 | 28

    Layoffs are not new;   but, what is new is that layoffs are   12 | 30
affecting white-collar workers as well as blue-collar workers.   24 | 33
Coping with job loss is a new and frustrating experience for many   38 | 35
managers.   A person who has just lost a job will have concerns   50 | 38
about personal security and welfare, and the concerns are com-   63 | 40
pounded when families are involved.   The problem, however, is   75 | 43
more than just an economic one.   Job loss often damages an in-   87 | 45
dividual's sense of self-worth.   An individual who does not have   100 | 48
a good self-concept will have a very hard time selling himself   112 | 50
or herself to a potential employer.   120 | 52

| 1' | 1 | 2 | 3 | 4 | 5 | 6 | 7 | 8 | 9 | 10 | 11 | 12 | 13 |
| --- | --- | --- | --- | --- | --- | --- | --- | --- | --- | --- | --- | --- | --- |
| 5' | | 1 | | | | 2 | | | | 3 | | | |

Combination response drills contain both word- and letter-response sequences. Use top speed for easy words and phrases and lower speed for words that are more difficult to key. (Key phrases marked with a line as a unit.)

  all letters

1 it to the us me you so go now we my he two in can her by of do no

2 it is | it is the | is it | is it you | he can | can he | he can go | can he go

3 who is | who is it | is it you | you can go | can you go | you can go to it

4 car mail two you may just can lake ask sail sign his form her who

5 who can sail | you can sail | you may sign | can you sign | sign his form

6 sign the form | mail the form | sign and mail | sign and mail that form

7 it was | was it so | if she can go to | can he go to the | can she go to the

8 she can | she may not | she may not go | can you go to the | so we may go

9 sign the | sign the form | they may sign that | they may sign that form

*gwam* 3' | 5'

**Writing 41**

| | 3' | 5' |
|---|---|---|
An essential part of analyzing a career option is to de- | 4 | 2 | 65
termine the type and extent of education that are required for a | 8 | 5 | 67
selected career. A main factor to consider about an education is | 12 | 7 | 70
how long it will take to get the skills that are needed to com- | 17 | 10 | 73
pete successfully for a job. This factor includes any other | 21 | 12 | 75
training that may be essential at the outset of employment. Be- | 25 | 15 | 78
cause jobs change, also assess how an educational program is | 29 | 17 | 80
structured to meet work changes. | 31 | 19 | 81
Many people choose a career without considering how well | 35 | 21 | 84
they may be suited for it. For example, a person who is outgoing | 39 | 24 | 86
and enjoys being around people probably should not select a | 43 | 26 | 89
career that requires spending long hours working alone. A job | 48 | 29 | 91
that requires quick, forceful action to be taken probably should | 52 | 31 | 94
not be pursued by a person who is shy and contemplative. Just | 56 | 34 | 96
because one has an aptitude for a specific job does not mean he | 60 | 36 | 99
or she will be successful in that job. Thus, be sure to weigh | 65 | 39 | 101
individual personality traits before making a final career | 69 | 41 | 104
choice. | 69 | 42 | 104
Money and inner satisfaction are the two leading reasons | 73 | 44 | 106
why most people work. For most persons, the need for money | 77 | 46 | 109
translates into food, shelter, and clothing. Once the basic | 81 | 49 | 111
needs of a person are met, satisfaction is the greatest motivator | 85 | 51 | 114
for working. To the average person, a job is satisfying if he or | 90 | 54 | 117
she enjoys the work, likes the people associated with the work, | 94 | 56 | 119
and feels a sense of pride in a job well done. Because you may | 98 | 59 | 122
not be the average person, analyze yourself to discover what will | 103 | 62 | 124
provide job satisfaction. | 104 | 63 | 125

3' | 1 | 2 | 3 | 4
5' | 1 | 2 | 3

# TECHNIQUE RATING SHEET

**Rating Periods**

| | 1 | 2 | 3 | 4 | 5 | 6 | 7 | 8 |
|---|---|---|---|---|---|---|---|---|

**Position at keyboard.....................** **Rating**

1. Sits in a comfortable, relaxed position directly in front of keyboard.....................
2. Keeps feet on floor for proper body balance............
3. Keeps elbows in relaxed, natural position at sides of body.....................
4. Keeps wrists low and relaxed but off frame of keyboard.....................

**Keystroking.....................** **Rating**

1. Keeps fingers well curved and upright over home keys.....................
2. Taps each key with proper finger.....................
3. Keeps hands and arms quiet; wrists low.................
4. Makes quick-snap keystrokes with immediate key release.....................

**Space Bar.....................** **Rating**

1. Keeps right thumb curved and close to Space Bar..
2. Taps Space Bar with a quick, down-and-in (toward palm) motion of thumb.................
3. Releases Space Bar instantly.................
4. Does not pause before or after spacing stroke.........

**Enter key.....................** **Rating**

1. Returns quickly wherever a hard return is required.
2. Taps Enter key with right little finger, then returns finger to home key.....................
3. Keeps eyes on source copy during and following return.....................
4. Starts new line without a pause.................

**Shift keys.....................** **Rating**

1. Reaches quickly with little fingers; keeps other fingers on home row.....................
2. Depresses Shift key as the character key is struck..
3. Releases Shift key quickly after character is struck..
4. Does not pause before or after Shift-key stroke........

**Tab key.....................** **Rating**

1. Reaches quickly with controlling little finger.............
2. Keeps other fingers near home keys.................
3. Keeps eyes on source copy as Tab key is used.......
4. Continues keying after Tabl stroke—without pauses.

**Total**

## Proofreading Procedures

Always proofread documents so that they are free of errors. Error-free documents send the message that you are detail oriented and capable of doing business. Apply these procedures after you key a document.

1. Use the Spelling and Grammar feature.

2. Proofread the document on screen to be sure that it makes sense. Check for these types of errors:
   - Words, headings, or amounts omitted.
   - Extra characters, words, or lines not deleted during the editing stage.
   - Incorrect sequence of numbers in a list.

3. Preview the document on screen using Print Preview. Check the vertical placement, presence of headers or footers, page numbers, and overall appearance.

4. Save the document again and print.

5. Compare the printed document to the source copy. Check all figures, names, and addresses against the source copy. Check that the format of the document is consistent throughout.

6. If errors exist on the printed copy, revise the document, save, and print.

7. Verify the corrections and placement of the second printed copy.

| | | |
|---|---|---|
| # | Add horizontal space | / or *lc* Lowercase |
| ‖ | Align | ⌐ Move left |
| ~ | Bold | ¬ Move right |
| *Cap* or ≡ | Capitalize | Γ Move up |
| ⌣ | Close up | L Move down |
| ℓ | Delete | ¶ Paragraph |
| ∧ | Insert | *sp* Spell out |
| ⌄ ⌄ | Insert quotation marks | ◡ or *tr* Transpose |
| ... or *stet* | Let it stand; ignore correction | Underline or italic |

## Addressing Procedures

Use the Envelopes function (**Tools, Letters and Mailings, Envelopes and Labels, Envelopes** tab). The envelope feature inserts the delivery address automatically if a letter is displayed. Title case, used in the letter address, is acceptable in the envelope address.

Ms. Amy Vreede
Communications Limited
57 Santa Ynez Street
Santa Ana, CA 92708-1537

## Folding and Inserting Procedures

Large envelopes (No. 10, 9, 7 3/4)

| Step 1 | Step 2 | Step 3 |
|---|---|---|
|  |  | |

**Step 1:** With document face up, fold slightly less than 1/3 of sheet up toward top.

**Step 2:** Fold down top of sheet to within 1/2" of bottom fold.

**Step 3:** Insert document into envelope with last crease toward bottom of envelope.

1" margins      **AGENDA** ↓2    ←14-point bold

**UBI SYSTEMS REVIEW**

**March 4, 20--**
**9:30 a.m.-10:30 a.m.**
Set tab at 1.5" ↓   **UBI Conference Room 101A** ↓2

Meeting called by:   Nicole Cox ↓2

Facilitator:   Yan Huang ↓2

Attendees:   Jacob Hudson, Emily Brown, Devin Cross, Nathan Shultz ↓2

| Topic | Person Responsible | Time |
|---|---|---|
| Welcome | Nicole Cox, UBI President | 5 minutes |
| Overview of UBI Systems | Emily Brown | 10 minutes |
| E-mail System<br>   Incoming e-mail<br>   Outgoing e-mail | Seth Lourie | 10 minutes |
| Payroll System | Jacob Hudson | 10 minutes |
| General Discussion | All | 20 minutes |
| Action Plan | Yan Huang | 5 minutes |

3-column table

↓2

**Special Notes:** ↓2

Attendees should be prepared to report on the successes and problems they have encountered with the e-mail and payroll systems. ↓2

Similar meetings will be held quarterly. All employees should track data for discussion at the next meeting.

> Adapt this standard format to fit the information in the agenda.
> Insert a row between topics in the table to create white space.
> Adjust the heading and font size as needed; try to keep the agenda to one page.

---

Tap ENTER 6 times

14-point bold → **ITINERARY FOR JOSHUA FOSTER** ↓2

Hanging indent 1.5"    May 9-11, 20-- ↓2

**Monday, May 9**    **Chicago to Montreal** ↓2

7:15 a.m.    Leave Chicago O'Hare Airport, Canadian Flight 983 (Boeing 737 jet nonstop business class); snack/brunch; arrive Montreal at 10:14 a.m.; pick up Riser rental car at airport (#C389-112); king deluxe reservation at Montreal Resort (Confirmation #573658). ↓2

12:30 p.m.    Lunch with Clifton Boyette, Hotel Manager, Montreal Resort.

2:00 p.m.    Tour of resort

7:30 p.m.    Dinner at La Chalet (restaurant known for seafood and skyline)

**Tuesday, May 10**

7:30 a.m.    Breakfast with Shelley Matta, Hotel Manager, Loews Hotel

9:00 a.m.    Tour of Loews Hotel

12:30 p.m.    Lunch at La Café (bistro famous for its pastries and desserts and casual atmosphere)

2:00 p.m.    City tour

8:00 p.m.    Dinner at Versailles (French restaurant known for its authentic menu and festive atmosphere)

**Wednesday, May 11 Montreal to Chicago**

7:45 a.m.    Leave Montreal, Canadian Flight 343 (Boeing 737 Jet nonstop economy class); arrive Chicago O'Hare Airport at 9:03 a.m.

Hanging indent

---

```
1   Brick Vandersnick Law Firm
    3829 Spring Street
2   Chicago, IL 60630-2948

3   Attorney for Plaintiff

4

5   SUPERIOR COUT OF THE STATE OF WASHINGTON

6

7   Judith R. Robinson, et. al.,        ) Case No.: No. 01-37-97-36
                                         ) RIGHT TO PRIVACY
8            Plaintiff,                  )
                                         )
9        vs.                             )
                                         )
10  Steven Johnson, et. al.,             )
                                         )
11           Defendant                   )

12

13      Defendants operate a company website that contains a database listing

14  employee names, addresses, telephone numbers, social security numbers, and

15  other personal information.

16      Plaintiffs assert that publication of this personal information invades

17  their privacy interests and is causing them undue exposure to identify theft

18  since the site is susceptible to intrusion by unauthorized users.

19      The Issue for this Court.  No challenge is raised at this time to the

20  legality of defendants' access to plaintiffs' private information.  The only

21  question presented in this Motion is whether plaintiffs can, by asserting a

22  right to privacy, stop the dissemination of any or all personal information

23  that has come into the defendants' hands.

24      Washington State Law Addresses Only the Question of Access to

25  Information.  In the State of Washington there is a Constitutional provision
```

Right to Privacy - 1

---

```
1   that appears to address privacy.  Article 1, Section 7, which was adopted in

2   1889, states simply, "No person shall be disturbed in his private affairs, or

3   his home invaded, without authority of law." This Constitutional provision has

4   been interpreted as relating solely to possible governmental intrusion into

5   private affairs.  See, e.g., State v. Myrick, 102 Wn.2d 506 (1984).  It

6   therefore provides no assistance in resolving this dispute.

7       May plaintiffs seek other forms of relief?  This case was filed

8   recently.  No significant discovery has occurred.  Damages may be available to

9   a plaintiff who proves that the defendant had the specific intent to cause the

10  plaintiff severe mental or emotional distress by his invasion(s) of the

11  plaintiff's privacy.  This Court does not yet have a record on which any

12  finder of fact could determine whether that level of specific intent could be

13  proved in this case.

14      The parties are therefore to prepare for trial, and to develop evidence

15  concerning all of plaintiffs' legal and equitable claims of injury and

16  defendants' defenses thereto.

17

18

19                              Dated this 7th day of April, 20--

20

21                                       Brick Vandersnick Law
                                         Firm
22                                       3829 Spring Street
                                         Chicago, IL 60630-2948
23

24

25
```

Right to Privacy - 2

**Oncology Associates, Inc.**
1000 Jasonway Avenue, Suite 356
Columbus, OH 43206

Dateline    May 21, 20-- ↓4    Tap ENTER 6 times or .5" below letterhead

At 2.1"   Ln 8   Col 1

Letter
address
William Tremblay, M.D.
Oncology Associates, Inc.
324 Washington Avenue, Suite 2000
Columbus, OH 43230  ↓2

Dear Dr. Tremblay  ↓2

Salutation    RE: Lynn Ackerman  ↓2

Subject
line
You will be pleased to know that I was able to meet with Ms. Ackerman today.  Ms.
Ackerman is a 46-year-old woman who was referred urgently by Dr. Pratt with a
diagnosis of inflammatory breast cancer for which surgery was not employed as the
initial therapeutic modality.  ↓2

Her examination was remarkable for a large and deep breast mass measuring at least 6
cm in diameter in the inner aspect of the upper outer quadrant of her left breast.
Overlying this area and extending beyond its margins was an area of erythema, warmth,
and classic peau d'orange character.  There were no signs of metastatic disease.

Body
I told Ms. Ackerman that I concurred with the diagnosis of inflammatory breast cancer.
From her visit with you this morning and with me this afternoon, she understands that
chemotherapy rather than surgery is the initial therapeutic modality in this form of breast
cancer.  I explained to her that this form of cancer was initially treated with
chemotherapy (and not surgery) because of its very aggressive nature and proclivity for
early systemic spread.  She now knows that chemotherapy will be followed by surgery,
which will then be followed with additional chemotherapy and radiation.

As I plan to use an Adriamycin-based chemotherapy regimen for this purpose, I have
asked that she make an appointment with you again for placement of a single lumen
MediPort catheter and to undergo a resting MUGA scan.  She understands that these
studies and consultations are designed to assess possible metastatic disease, to facilitate
administration of systemic chemotherapy, and to assess her cardiac status before potential
use of Adriamycin which has possible cardiac complications.  She will receive a flu shot
today and a Pneumovax inoculation when I see her again next week.  In the meantime,
she will immediately stop the use of estradiol as the hormone receptor status of her tumor
is unknown and undergo a complete imaging evaluation in search of possible sites of
metastic disease.

William Tremblay
Page 2
Current date       2ⁿᵈ page heading

Inflammatory breast cancer certainly poses therapeutic challenges, but we will treat her
aggressively and expect the best.  I will be in touch with you again after her visit next
week.  ↓2

Complimen-
tary close
Sincerely  ↓4

Writer's
name and
title
Lawrence Faulkner, M.D.
Medical Oncology  ↓2

Typist's
Initials
xx  ↓2

Copy
notation
c  Dr. James Pratt

Left tab 0.15"

Tap ENTER 6 times

Heading

**TO:**     All Incubator Companies  ↓2

**FROM:**   Nicole Cox ↓2

**DATE:**   Current ↓2

**SUBJECT:**  Grand Opening ↓2

Body
We are finally ready for our grand opening!  Everyone has worked so long and so hard to
complete everything on schedule.  Thank you everyone for everything that you have done
to make this day a success.  ↓2

We're expecting a large turnout, and none of this would be possible without your help.
Thank you for providing information, staff, and other resources for this event.  I look
forward to seeing you at the grand opening and to working with you in the months to
come.  ↓2

Typist's
initials
xx ↓2

Copy
notation
c  Fred Perez

Left tab 0.15"

**University Business Incubator**

# Memo

**To:**   All Incubator Companies

**From:**  Nicole Cox

**CC:**   Fred Perez

**Date:**  Current date

**Re:**   Grand Opening

We are finally ready for our grand opening!  Everyone has worked so long and so hard to
complete everything on schedule.  I would like to take this opportunity to thank all of you for
everything that you have done to make this day a success.

We're expecting a large turnout, and none of this would be possible without your help.  Thank
you for providing information, staff, and other resources for this event.  I look forward to
seeing you at the grand opening and to working with you in the months to come.

xx

1

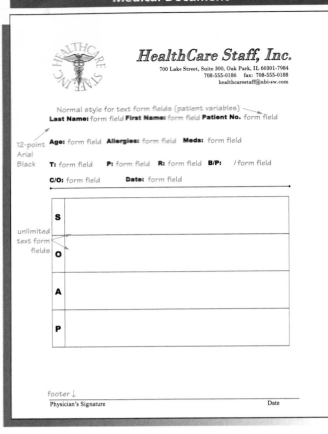

HealthCare Staff, Inc.

700 Lake Street, Suite 300, Oak Park, IL 60301-7984
708-555-0186    fax:  708-555-0188
healthcarestaff@ubi-sw.com

Normal style for text form fields (patient variables)

**Last Name:** form field **First Name:** form field **Patient No.** form field

12-point
Arial
Black

**Age:** form field  **Allergies:** form field  **Meds:** form field

**T:** form field   **P:** form field   **R:** form field  **B/P:**  / form field

**C/O:** form field   **Date:** form field

unlimited
text form
fields

| S |  |
|---|---|
| O |  |
| A |  |
| P |  |

footer ↓

Physician's Signature                              Date

---

↓ 8

# EXERCISE:

## IS MORE BETTER FOR YOUR HEART?

↓ 8

Prepared for

*P*acific *N*ewport *M*edical *G*roup

↓ 8

Prepared by
Student's Name

↓ 8

Current Date

---

Tap ENTER 6 times

↓

**Table of Contents**   Heading 1 style centered

Exercise:  Is More Better For Your Heart?...................................................1
What Happens When We Exercise ...........................................................1
How Much Should We Exercise? ..............................................................2
   Weight Training.......................................................................................2
   Normal Activities.....................................................................................2
   Time.........................................................................................................2
   More Is Better for You............................................................................3
Other Benefits ..........................................................................................3
   Heart Function........................................................................................3
   Osteoarthritis..........................................................................................3
References..................................................................................................4
Index..........................................................................................................5

ii

---

Tap ENTER 6 times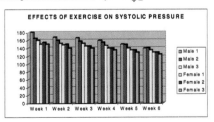

Heading 1 style centered
**Exercise:  Is More Better for Your Heart?**

Studies have shown that physical inactivity is a risk factor for heart disease.  Regular physical activity (even mild to moderate exercise) can help reduce your risk of heart disease.  More vigorous exercise can help improve fitness of the heart and lungs, and improve blood circulation throughout your body.

**What Happens When We Exercise**   Heading 1 style

As we exercise, the heart must provide more blood flow; it does this through increases in contractility and cardiac output.  There is increased blood flow to the tissues through vasodilation, and the heart rate is elevated through the activation of the sympathetic nervous system.[1]  During aerobic exercise (such as running, swimming, or bike riding), the blood pressure is not markedly elevated, but with anaerobic exercise (such as weight lifting), there may be significant rise in the arterial pressure.

Below is a chart of a study that was performed at the University of Southern Utah illustrating the effect of exercise on blood pressure.  ↓ 2

---

[1] Barbara L. Bullock, *Pathophysiology, Adaptations, and Alterations in Function*, 4th ed.  (Philadelphia:  Lippincott, 2006).

2

Exercise training over a period of weeks to months increases (1) the number and size of mitochondria in the muscle cells; (2) the capacity of muscle to oxidize fat, carbohydrates, and ketones; (3) the capacity to generate adenosine triphosphate (ATP), a high-energy molecule; (4) the level of mitochondrial enzyme activity; and (5) myoglobin levels. The net effect is to increase the capability of muscles to extract oxygen and to increase aerobic capability at any given workload. In addition, regular exercise seems to reduce the risk of myocardial infarction, perhaps by increasing HDL levels.[2]

### How Much Should We Exercise?

An article in *Harvard Men's Health Watch* suggests that you add physical activity to your daily life by climbing stairs, carrying your own parcels, and walking for transportation. The article suggests that you incorporate 30-45 minutes of moderate to vigorous exercise on an almost daily schedule (dancing, singles tennis, biking, swimming, brisk walking, jogging). To balance out your exercise program, add resistance (weight training) exercise and stretching exercises.

*Weight Training*   Heading 2 style

Speaking of weight training, many older individuals, while well aware of the need for regular aerobic exercise, tend to dismiss weight training as an activity predominantly for the young or the vain. However, weight training is the only type of exercise that can substantially slow, and even reverse, the declines in muscle mass, bone density, and strength that were once considered inevitable consequences of aging.

*Normal Activities*

Recent studies seem to indicate that moderate physical activity, such as yard work, heavy household chores, walking when possible, and taking the stairs, when done daily, is as effective as a structured exercise program in improving heart function. A 2006 preliminary report from the *Nurses' Health Study* found that women who walked briskly (3-4 mph) at least three hours a week had a 54 percent lower risk of heart attack and stroke than those who were inactive.

*Time*

Over the past few years, there has been a shift in emphasis away from recommending 20 minutes of vigorous activity on most days to accumulating 30 minutes of moderate intensity activity each day. For more than any other reason, physiologists have determined that any amount of physical activity is far better than no activity and have advocated this shift in an effort to eliminate a nation of "couch potatoes."

---

[2] Emanuel Rubin and John L. Farber, *Essential Pathology*, 2nd ed. (Philadelphia: Lippincott, 2006).

4

Tap ENTER 6 times

**References** ↓2   Heading 1 style centered

Bullock, Barbara L., *Pathophysiology, Adaptations, and Alterations in Function,* 4th ed. Philadelphia: Lippincott, 2006. ↓2

*Harvard Men's Health Watch*, "Back to Basics—Way Back," Vol. 4, No. 2, September 2005. ↓2

*Health News*, "Arthritis Guidelines Emphasize Exercise," November 2006.

*Health News*, "Exercise for Heart Failure?," August 2006.

Rubin, Emanuel and Farber, John L., *Essential Pathology*, 2nd ed.. Philadelphia: Lippincott, 2006.

Use a hanging indent format.

5

Tap ENTER 6 times

**Index** ↓2   Heading 1 style centered

anaerobic ............................................................................................1
blood flow
    aerobic ...........................................................................................1
HDL ..............................................................................................2, 3
heart attack........................................................................................2
ketones ..............................................................................................3
LDL ...................................................................................................3
mitochondria ......................................................................................2
myocardial infarction ...........................................................*See* HDL
osteoarthritis......................................................................................3
stroke .................................................................................................2
vasodilation........................................................................................1

14-point, bold, centered

12-point, bold

12 point, numbers right aligned or decimal aligned, 1.5 line spacing

| MONTHLY BENEFITS AT RETIREMENT | | | | |
|---|---|---|---|---|
| Present Annual Income | | | | |
| Age in 20-- | $20,000 | $30,000 | $45,000 | $60,000 | $76,200 |
| 65 | 742 | 973 | 1,246 | 1,354 | 1,433 |
| 64 | 761 | 999 | 1,283 | 1,398 | 1,484 |
| 63 | 794 | 1,041 | 1,340 | 1,465 | 1,560 |
| 62 | 813 | 1,067 | 1,377 | 1,509 | 1,612 |
| 61 | 814 | 1,068 | 1,380 | 1,518 | 1,626 |
| 55 | 820 | 1,077 | 1,393 | 1,564 | 1,713 |

The main heading (title) may be placed inside the table as shown here or outside the table.

Center tables vertically and horizontally on the page. Within a document, DS above and below the table.

A table AutoFormat may be applied.